Praise for the French edition of *The Bad Life*

"A courageous and moving account set down in beautiful, simple and lucid prose."
—*Le Monde*

"Frédéric Mitterrand took a gamble and won. He finds the perfect balance between modesty and immodesty. His writing reflects his persona: delicate, cultured, rich and spirited."
—*France Inter*

"In *The Bad Life*, Frédéric Mitterrand recounts his journey as a man crippled by loneliness. An exceptional book, surprising and honest in a way that such autobiographies rarely are."
—*Têtu*

"Astonishing, turbulent, almost Proustian lucidity . . . this book is magnificent."
—*Le Point*

"A moving and disturbing confession, far removed from the crafted image of the genteel chronicler of movie stars and royals."
—*Point de Vue*

"This book is admirable in its combination of confessional audacity and restraint of expression."
—*Le Nouvel Observateur*

"Frédéric Mitterrand has opted for the gravity of self-revelation and the power of distance. He takes every possible risk, including that of literature itself."
—*Le Journal du Dimanche*

FRÉDÉRIC MITTERRAND

the
bad
life

a memoir

Translated by Jesse Browner

Soft Skull Press
New York

First published in 2005 as *La Mauvaise Vie*
© Éditions Robert Laffont, Paris.

Translation © Jesse Browner, 2010

Ouvrage publié avec le soutien du Centre national du livre—ministère
français chargé de la culture.

Published with the support of the Centre National du Livre, an institution under the supervision of the French Ministry of Culture.

Library of Congress Cataloging-in-Publication Data is available.

ISBN: 978-1-59376-260-5

Cover design by Sarah Juckniess
Interior design by Elyse Strongin: Neuwirth & Associates, Inc.
Printed in the United States of America

Soft Skull Press
New York, NY

www.softskull.com

contents

the
bad
life

childhood

childhood

childhood

He stowed his bicycle in the little front courtyard of the house. He'd gone off for a final spin while he waited for me and had hurried back when he saw the car arrive. I'd bought the bike a few weeks earlier, choosing a model that was slightly too big because I wanted him to still be able to use it when he came home for the summer holidays. He'd managed very well on it, and I'd see him from time to time zipping around the backstreets of his neighborhood. The gift gave him even more pleasure than the soccer balls and cleats. Having set the bike aside, he stopped for a moment before the cage with the bird he'd caught early in the summer in the reeds down by the wadi. The children over there are very good at catching birds: they creep up slowly, very slowly, they hardly move, and then they grab them with a snap of their hands. They sell them to the village bird peddlers. This

one he'd kept, and he was no doubt thinking about letting it
go free, since he was leaving home, but then he changed his
mind and confided the bird to his mother. At least, that's what I
understood—they have their own way of talking to each other.
He went into the house, and I lingered at the entrance with his
mother, who was trying not to cry. I, too, looked at the bird in
its cage, and I thought of "Rosebud" from *Citizen Kane*, but
it was too late to back out now. Neighbors and children were
streaming in, watching me in silence. It was one of those mornings when the wind from the plains makes every shape stand
out sharply and the sea sparkle in the distance, a little like the
mistral in Provence when it blows through that very distinctive
silvery light. Any other day, he certainly would have gone to the
beach with the children who were now staring at me. I heard a
commotion through the windows, probably his sisters clinging
to him, one after the other. When he came out of the house with
his little suitcase, they all followed him shedding fat tears. His
father wasn't there; he'd wanted me to take the other brother,
the middle one, who was also nowhere to be seen. But we'd
come to an agreement; having taken the oldest son ten years
earlier, I'd opted for the youngest this time because he resembled
his brother and we had to act as soon as possible to give him the
best chance to adapt. That's what I told the consul, too, when I
went for the visa, with the forced exuberance of someone who
feels himself the object of suspicion. As for the middle brother,
I'd said we could look into that another time, and the father
hadn't insisted. We never have gotten round to doing anything
about him; he's still waiting, sad and listless, and his brothers
are constantly on my case to bring him over. I'll have to get to
it one of these days. The neighbors crowded around the car in
ever greater numbers. People had been making the usual kind of
comments—partly out of jealousy, partly out of humiliation—
ever since the news had spread through the quarter. They were

saying that I'd taken the parents under my protection when they sold me their children. The speculation about my intentions went no further, but it was at moments like these that I could feel the full weight of rumor that surrounds a shady deal.

Nine-year-old boys are very perceptive. He hugged his mother furtively, without a word, then climbed straight into the front seat of the car. He lowered the window to look at his mother; he ignored his sisters and playmates. He looked only at her with those wide eyes of his, dry and intense, only his mother. She couldn't hold back her tears any longer, but like him she said not a word. I wanted to make some gesture to comfort her, like putting my hand on her shoulder, but I sensed that it would be useless and totally inappropriate; anything coming from me would have been intolerable at that moment. I'd never before had such a strong sense of the symbiotic nature of their bond, witnessing this mute exchange in the midst of a throng of friends and relatives whose jostling only seemed to oppress mother and child further. All that remained for me to do was to stow his valise in the trunk, slide into the car beside him, acting as natural as I could, and ease calmly into my U-turn. I was anxious to get it over with; in cases like these, you never know what might happen unexpectedly to disrupt the whole thing. As I picked up speed down the hill, he turned around for one last look at her, and she splashed a bucket of water in our direction to ward off bad luck and ensure his promised return. It wasn't until later, much later, when we were already on the highway, that he glanced at me timidly and mistrustfully; it was the first time he'd looked at me since I'd pulled up at his house. He'd allowed himself to be led away without seeing me. All the same, at the airport he took my hand—the crowd and the clamor upset him, but he was also excited by the prospect of flying in a plane. Now he was just a little boy who was entirely dependent on me. That was no particular source of satisfaction to me; I knew that I'd need a lot of time to win his confidence, and I wasn't even sure that I was entirely up to it.

He'd been no more than two years old when I'd seen him for the first time. I had joined his teenage brother for one of those exhausting meetings in which, over a glass of warm Coca-Cola, I had somehow to explain to his parents using fanciful sign language that all was going well for him in France. The living room was modest to a fault but had been gradually upgraded with banquettes, upholstery, and a brand-new television blaring in the back; pale light fell from a single bulb hanging from the ceiling. A little breeze, children everywhere, a constant ebb and flow of neighbors come to see the two great hopes of the family—the older son whom they'd let go, and me, who'd taken him away and cared for him. The little one, in diapers, his feet and legs bare, spun like a top from one visitor to the next, clamorous and restless. He was a fine boy, snot-nosed and unruly, still free of the fretful passivity that comes with poverty, anxiety, and inescapable overcrowding. Feeling comfortable in my role as mellow godfather-protector, I tried to put him on my knee, but he'd pulled away furiously and everybody laughed, as was only right, I a little louder than the others. Clearly, I meant nothing to him.

The second time, he must have been four or five, and his big brother had brought him to me. He was intimidated by the unfamiliar house; he'd certainly heard whispers about me as of some creature from another planet, and he couldn't make heads or tails of my Franco-Arabic gibberish. He clung to his brother and stared at me anxiously. His mother had dressed him formally for the occasion, perhaps at the older boy's injunction, and he was a real-life postcard cherub, the kind with a smile and a bouquet of jasmine. Only he wasn't smiling, tense as he was from the effort and apprehension of the visit. My attempts to win him over failed that day, and he hesitated at length before accepting, with a kind of uneasy gravity, the ice-cream bar I offered him. Deep down, I was gratified by his mistrust, as I was by his wide-eyed shock and yearning when I opened the door of my well-stocked refrigerator. If one can say that a little boy has charm, then he had it to spare. He was in a more sociable mood by the time he left, but watching him scamper after his brother, I still had the impression that he was very happy to be leaving. Later on he grew a little more used to me. My picture stood on the new sideboard in the living room; he heard wonderful tales about his brother's life with me in France; he saw me in the street when I came to visit his parents during the holidays. But he had no reason to be drawn to me; I was just a grown-up and French into the bargain, some distant family relation.

Things really began to change when I gave him his first ball. He was seven at the time, and like every kid in every neighborhood in every country of the South, he played endless soccer games on the street outside his house with the neighborhood kids. But all he had were balls made of bundled rags, and it wasn't hard to imagine how much he'd love a real soccer ball like the kind he saw on televised games. I wasn't mistaken; he'd lit up when he saw the ball in the sports bag I presented to him, and he looked me joyfully in the eye when he thanked me in French before tearing away down the street with a treasure that would make him the provisional king of the world. There are a lot of rocks on the ground around his house, and he must have kicked too hard; the ball didn't last long. I bought another, many others; he could always count on me, and he grew bolder and bolder after each irreparable puncture in impressing upon me how his future as a champion was in my hands. One day as I was driving through the area, he ran up to the car at a red light like one of those street kids who sell jasmine to the tourists. With a look of desolation on his face, he held out a deflated ball to me. His mother told me later that he'd been watching for me for several days and asking if I would stop by again before returning to France.

I'd already visited them more often than usual, I had little time before leaving, and the prospect of another interminable family reunion held little attraction for me. Still, I didn't want to leave him behind with that sad little sack of useless rubber. So on my way to the airport I stopped by with an indestructible brand I'd managed to track down that cost me a small fortune. And for the first time, he stayed at my side until it was time for me to go; they all went inside when I got in the car, but he stood staring at me from the doorway, unmoving and mindful, his officially approved French Federation professional-quality ball under his arm. That gave me all sorts of ideas: he wanted to thank me in some way deeper than language; he'd only just realized that he wouldn't be seeing me for several months, and it made him sad; he was in shock from the sudden realization that this semi-stranger had never failed him on a critical issue in which the other grown-ups had shown no interest. Maybe none of those things occurred to him, but the fact is that I have retained the image of that little boy and his ball, lingering motionless on his doorstep on an empty street and following me with his eyes until I disappeared in swirls of ocher dust. The idea of taking him with me was surely born at that moment and from that image, which is as indelibly etched into my mind as a memory from my own childhood. I dismissed it hastily, however, since it was one of those crazy ideas that occurred to me every time I met a lost child in the course of my travels. Not to mention that he was not a lost child but a child with a family and a deeply rooted, happy, and protected life. Nevertheless, the image stayed with me.

I can't remember exactly when or how the decision was taken. I'd be lying, of course, if I were to deny that the final decision was mine or if I were to refuse to acknowledge that I made it with joy and hope. I'd be equally dishonest if I were to dispute the fact that I firmly preferred the youngest over the middle son when it became a near certainty that one of them would come to

France and live with me and his older brother who was already there. And yet, despite appearances, I didn't have to stoop to any special scheming to achieve this outcome. I was perfectly happy knowing that I had gained the affection of a little boy to whom I was becoming increasingly attached, and that I would be extending my assistance to him from afar until he achieved adulthood. No doubt, some will be troubled by the avowal of such a strange weakness, but he was far away, I saw little of him, and I could not seriously imagine how the situation might change. I didn't want him to run the risk of suffering in any way from my excess of personal investment. To be sure, I had not entirely dismissed the fantasy of having him more fully to myself, but it was just that—a fantasy, the vanity and dangers of which I had real-life experience with his older brother. I seem to recall in any case that it was he who first brought it up with his parents, and it's more than likely that they had spoken among themselves of the eventuality of entrusting me with one son after the other. For them, it was the precise opposite of abandonment; it was the opportunity to provide a better future for each boy and for the entire family as a whole. The prospect was most painful to the mother, but it was she who was also the most resolute. The hardness of her own life encouraged her to reenact a transaction that made her neighbors seethe with jealousy, because in her own eyes she had saved her oldest from the sorry fate of the other neighborhood boys. She also trusted me, and her sons were an extension of her.

Granted, I resisted for a long time. Despite all my affection for him, her oldest son had not made my life easy, and I'd been thrown headlong into the chaos of his adolescence. The prospect of another, similar experience had little attraction for me, and I could foresee the approaching nightmare of paperwork and visas, the pressures of organization, the vast expenditures of time and money that would constrain my freedom even further.

I had no fear of responsibility, however; I'd enjoyed raising my own son, and I'd been happy to take on the older boy. I'd had my share of colds and teachers, sorrows big and small, and I was quite convinced that I would make fewer mistakes. I sometimes asked myself if I'd have gone to so much trouble for a little girl. Boys clearly touched something more intimate and more ambiguous in me—although . . .

The summer he turned eight, he got into the habit of dropping by my house on a regular basis. I took him swimming, I showered him with presents, I bought him clothes and shoes. The machinery of corruption had been set in motion without my being fully aware of it. Even so, he took everything I gave him without excessive gratitude, and he asked for very little. When he really wanted something, he told me so, distinctly and without flattery. Switching between worlds made him neither more reserved nor more modest. I had no way of knowing what he thought of me, and if he occasionally gave me a kiss, it was only a kind of formalized gesture. In his world, children kiss adults, guests, and each other as a customary pledge of allegiance that ensures a little breathing space; it had nothing in common with the way he curled up with his mother or with the openness and tenderness he exhibited with his brother. He'd explored every nook and cranny of the house, whose overabundance of books, etchings, and knickknacks struck him as extraordinary, and he was capable of amusing himself for ages if I was busy, although the truth is I rarely was when he came to see me. He enchanted me with his curiosity, his energy, his oddly husky voice; I never tired of watching him pacing the terrace, his feet bare and his slender body topped with a straw hat that was too big for him, deep into his discoveries and secret thoughts. Language wasn't a problem: we'd each made some progress, and we understood each other very well in that environment of games and holidays. The fact is, I was happy to be drawn into the childhood of a lively

THE BAD LIFE {9}

and charming little boy. It was a strange situation: the house was full of friends, as it was every year; I led an active social life and did not always sleep alone, but all I ever really looked forward to were the unpredictable visits of the little local kid with the raspy voice and mysterious dreams. When I brought him home in the evening after each of his visits, he did not hide his pleasure at driving through the village in a car while I wondered fretfully if he'd come back—an anxiety that I was careful to conceal.

Back home, I questioned my own symptoms, the increasingly central place that he, all unawares, had come to occupy in my life. When he wasn't around, I couldn't get him out of my mind. One evening, when we were sitting in traffic, a woman of a certain age approached the car and harangued me viciously. She asked me with biting sarcasm if I was happy to have such a cute little boy sitting beside me and if we foreigners, we tourists, weren't ashamed to corrupt the defenseless children of her country. Under the violence of her assault, I stuttered that she was mistaken—I cared for the boy as if he were my own son, and I was bringing him home to his family. My explanation did nothing to disarm her hostility; that was hardly surprising, since the situation was pretty much inexplicable. So she turned to the boy, speaking in their own language, and he replied very calmly. I couldn't understand what they were saying, but I inferred that she was ordering him to get out of the car and that he repeatedly refused in that unruffled tone of voice. Ultimately she calmed down a little, glaring at me mistrustfully all the while, and I was happy to move on without becoming embroiled in another series of abashed explanations. The incident had shaken me much more, apparently, than it had the child, who began to hum to himself and play with the electric windows as if nothing had happened. He came back two or three days later, and when I was driving him home I noticed that he looked for the spot where the woman had accosted me and seemed relieved that she wasn't there.

When he was at my house, he often called his mother on the phone. He kept her photo in a little wallet along with a calling card he'd swiped from me, the only theft I ever knew him to make, although he could have made many others. Whenever I took his picture, he insisted that I make an extra print for her. I saw no trace of his father in him, however. Since our verbal exchanges were still somewhat limited, I was able to draw no clear conclusions about that. Maybe he was afraid of him; I'd noticed that he hated it when adults raised their voices or made abrupt movements, even though he argued lustily and even fought with the kids he went swimming with at the rocks. His older brother seemed more or less to occupy the paternal place, but we hadn't seen much of him that summer—he'd passed his driving test and was leading the typical nomadic, nocturnal life of young people his age.

I avoided speaking to the little one about France, but his brother and family certainly talked to him on my behalf, up there in that dim living room where they crowded in on each other with no means of escape. Then too, he'd never have come to see me so often without his mother's consent. He'd told his brother that he'd follow him to the end of the world if he asked him to; he must have heard the phrase in a song, or else his brother had thought it up to test its effect on me. He'd also dumbfounded the cook by telling him that he was soon to go to school in Paris. By his own account, I'd promised to take good care of him and make sure he grew up educated and rich; when he was big, he'd buy a big car and build a fine house for his mother where she could rest and watch television. In a word, it was a childish variant on the usual line of patter adopted by the little neighborhood louts whenever they buttonholed foreign tourists of all ages and sexes. At eight, the future and distant lands are vague concepts; I was mostly concerned with protecting our current arrangement, and my house on the outskirts of the village was a perfectly adequate stand-in for the ends of the world. Loyal to his own folk and naturally secretive, he remained cautious in the midst of all these baffling intrigues, from which he certainly drew a sense of personal importance that had already begun to set him apart from his soccer buddies. He told me nothing about the plans being brewed up for him because I was the primary party concerned, and it wouldn't do to hustle this foreigner whom he had not yet learned to love. Still, I had the feeling that the moment of truth would soon be upon us. At the end of the summer, I promised to think about taking him home with me, and said goodbye with a heavy heart. But it was already set; all I had to do was come back to seal the deal.

He was very unhappy in Paris in the early days. How could I have imagined it would be otherwise? He was completely lost. It wasn't only the language; practically nothing was like anything he'd known before—the apartment was too small, the street unfriendly and dangerous, his schedule too exacting, the climate gloomy and harsh, my family unknown and noisy, the other kids indifferent and inaccessible. A compassionate headmistress had agreed to take him into her institution, where benevolent teachers led special classes for young immigrants, but he was unable to follow because he'd basically never gone to school before. Torn from his familiar setting, he missed his usual haunts, his friends, and his mother terribly. I'd shown him how to use the phone to call her, which he did constantly, but she was no comfort since she blubbered at the other end of the line. I reluctantly put a stop to the calls, but he continued to phone her secretly whenever my back was turned. I'd hired a Moroccan lady to take care of him in the afternoons and when I was away. She was a fine person, intelligent and gentle, who'd had children of her own and could talk to him in his own tongue. She loved him from the very first, with that inexhaustible fund of kindness and self-effacement that Arab women reserve for little boys, but he supposed she was trying to replace his mother and was cruelly hostile toward her from the start, refusing to walk beside her when she took him to school and speaking to her as if she were the enemy. She was on the verge of tears when she went home at night, but she forgave him and never complained of his attitude. Her embracing indulgence reminded him of his mother, but far from appeasing him, the resemblance increased his animosity and made him even more suspicious and disagreeable. He cried all the time, wet his bed at night, and refused to eat what was set before him. Having gotten a crew-cut from his mother before his departure, he had the grim, morose look of a little Palestinian stone-thrower, and I was on the constant lookout for fits of rebellion and rage that never materialized. His distress had pushed him far beyond anger, and all he had left were tears, withdrawal, and silence. I found it difficult to recognize, in that frightened and defenseless child who almost never spoke to me, the proud and independent little boy who had been so clever at communicating his needs. It hurt me to see him suffer; I was wracked by guilt and increasingly worried. His brother tried to avert catastrophe by visiting him at home. In the older boy's presence, he recovered a little of his old spirit and launched into long diatribes about his unhappiness. I could hear that husky little voice retailing his grievances, but I was careful not to interfere; in any case, at such moments I ceased to exist for him. His brother was reluctant to translate the particulars of his complaints, but it wasn't really necessary. I had gauged the gravity of the situation and was mortified enough as it was. He himself could do little; he tried to console the little one by listening to him, but he went no further. I had solved many a problem for him, and he thought I would find a way to heal this wound as I had healed the others. At twenty and with little real-life experience, he was still leading the chaotic life of many boys his age— girls, nightlife, adventures—and he was sometimes gone for days before I saw him again. I couldn't count on his help. I was even concerned that the boy would be sucked into all that disorder and find himself more confused than ever. I had no excuses, as his entire family was counting on me. The fact is, this is what I'd asked for, really. There was no getting away from it, and I would just have to figure it out for myself.

I'd completely altered my lifestyle to accommodate the boy. I'd stopped going out and cut back on my leisure activities, rearranged my schedule and work habits so that I could be with him as much as possible and also to keep a lid on my considerable expenses, for I wanted him to lack for nothing. I'd resigned myself to it all with a relatively light heart; in the end, the hardest part for me was waking up as early as a schoolboy. I'd set him up in his own bedroom, bought him clothes and all sorts of things he would like: a transistor radio, a Game Boy, another bicycle to be ridden only on the sidewalk. I'd signed him up with a soccer club and arranged for his sitter to take him to the park or the movies every Wednesday. I'd jumped through all sorts of hoops and signed mountains of paperwork, saw to medical exams, insurance, various documents. I'd run up against administrative regulations, supercilious attitudes, suspicion. Given the shock of being torn from his home and the risks I had taken for him, I wanted to give him the very best opportunity to adjust by seeing to every last detail. But neither the sense of guilt at playing with an innocent life that was not my own, nor the fear of harming a helpless little being, nor yet the unbearable waves of anxiety that tore me from my sleep were enough to make me throw in the towel and send him back home. It seems to me now that I have never taken care of anyone the way I took care of him.

Yet he persisted in rejecting me. He'd double-lock the bathroom door when bathing as if in considered response to the woman who had accosted me, which was deeply mortifying. He insisted that I buy gifts for his mother that I had no way of sending to her, and if

I happened to refuse he'd sneer and gesticulate scornfully, grumbling in his own language. Despite all my efforts to fix him breakfast to his liking, he'd stare at his bowl without eating. There were complaints about him at school: he disrupted the class, fought at recess, or undressed in front of some little goody-goody who ran off to tell her parents. I was called in and informed that he was to be expelled; I pleaded at length and to such good effect that he was reprieved, but it had been a close call.

The gentle Moroccan nanny was showing signs of despondency and treated me with pity. Even so, he was making speedy progress in French and generally obeyed me without resistance. I'd found that he enjoyed being taken to school on my moped, riding horses in the country, and making trips to the department stores, where he scampered from one section to the next like the little thief he was not. His calls to his mother grew less frequent, and when my family or friends saw us together they were surprised by my concerns—the child who behaved so coolly toward them stuck to me like glue and anticipated my every movement as if afraid that I would abandon him. I sensed that he was torn: on the one hand, he'd latched on to me because there was no one else to cling to; on the other, he withdrew into his own world where I was not welcome, impatient for the coming vacation when he could get away. The conflict was eating him up, and I could not imagine how he would resolve it.

One evening when I was especially anxious and exhausted, I lost my temper. I shouted and slammed my fist on the table. I couldn't take it any more; all the built-up tension came pouring out, I accused him of malice and reminded him of everything I'd done for him. It wasn't very fair of me, since he'd never personally asked for anything; if anyone deserved the scolding, it was me. At least I resisted the temptation to threaten to send him home, which would have been an even more dishonest kind of blackmail. He was terrified, and in his eyes I read the expectation of a beating. Instead, full of remorse for my loss of control, I sought refuge in my bedroom and cried for the first time since I was his age. Shortly afterward, as I was sitting at my desk still horror-struck by the violence of my reaction, I heard him come up behind me. His fear was gone, and he watched me in silence with an air of serenity that I had not seen in him since his arrival in France. I asked him to leave me to myself, and he went to bed without saying a word. The next day I was still not ready to talk to him, but he ate his breakfast normally and asked if he could fire up the moped himself. When we got to school, he did something he'd never done before—he gave me a quick kiss and slipped away giggling. Some girls called out to him, and I realized that he was actually far more popular than I'd understood. Arriving home that evening, I heard Arab music and laughter. The Moroccan sitter had put on a record and he was dancing with her, looking like a miniature Ottoman bailiff in the Moroccan fez and djellaba she'd given him as gifts, although he'd never so much as sniffed at them before. He explained eagerly that he was practicing for a forthcoming festival at school, then he told me a Pokemon story and asked if he could invite over the little Korean boy who'd become his best friend. He was tireless, and I'd never seen him so cheerful, neither over there nor, of course, over here. His only moment of anxiety came at bedtime, when he asked if I was going out again. I reassured him that I wasn't, but he wanted me to leave his bedroom door open, both for the light and to make sure that I wasn't going anywhere. He had finally come home and begun to unpack. What happened after that was a whole other story, one that he may tell one day.

ALL THESE years later, his bedroom door still stays open to let the light in, and he can't sleep unless he knows I'm there. Only rarely do I go out once he's asleep, and even then I worry the whole time I'm away. I sometimes find him wide awake in the semi-darkness, waiting for me after having woken up alone. Before going to bed, I look in on him, watch him sleep, listen to his steady breathing. He's growing up fast. I imagine he'll soon get used to sleeping in the dark with the door closed. When my grandmother died six years ago, I felt as if I'd never get over it. She was very old, and I'd had a lot more time with her than one often does. The boy had come shortly after her death. He knows nothing about her; still, I'd like to be for him what my grandmother was for me.

litany
litany

litany

There are people I've met and never forgotten. Sometimes it only lasted a moment or a few days at most, but they've been with me ever since without knowing it. Some never even noticed I was there, others exchanged a few words with me without knowing the effect they'd had on me, and some had a vague feeling and went on their way with a shrug. They all left me with an undying ember, a violent feeling of loss and nostalgia, a dreamlike desire that continues to blaze. Nothing openly sensual ever occurred, and none of them ever became my best friend either; there was no gesture or movement toward a lasting friendship, however tepid or merely banal. Just these indelible flashes. Occasionally I forget one, but the memory is never very far away, and even the most suppressed pop up again unexpectedly every so often. All it takes is one of those brief encounters, wordless and hopeless, to awaken them, blowing like a breeze over the inner sea of regret and loss; every desirable stranger reminds me of someone else, of several others. The first few times it happened, I was very young. These experiences were very confusing, filling me with fervor, enthusiasm, and anxiety, but I didn't understand the cause of my emotion or where its extraordinary strength might lead. The truth only came to me slowly, very slowly, a little more each time, and in little glimpses—it was impossible to get a full picture of the unfathomable and mysterious fate awaiting me. In those days I had no one to confide in and no way to get my bearings; the future appeared to me now and then in frightful caricatures. From the very beginning I chose secrecy, the hidden life pursued by fear, exaltation followed by shame. There's no escaping such a prison. Some strangers will haunt me my entire life; they're my unwitting accomplices. Sometimes they feel closer to me than my own family, and the precision with which I can picture them comes as no surprise to me.

Childhood. I'm six or seven years old. A friend of my older brother is taking off his riding breeches in the bathroom. I confess to him that I lied to my father about my notebook. He smiles at me in partial understanding and some embarrassment at my secret, which I've revealed to no one else. He tells on me later, setting off a whole cascade of disasters. He's blond, with some hair on his legs already. Some time ago I asked my brother about him; he couldn't recall him, and I've never seen him since. A short while after that, in third grade at the Janson school, I invite a Vietnamese classmate to come to my house on Thursday. When school lets out I show him the way to make sure he won't get lost, everything's set, it's all quite straightforward. I wait for him all afternoon, heart pounding; he never shows. Yellowish skin, slanting eyes, very shiny black hair. He tells me his parents wouldn't let him; my feelings are hurt, and I let it drop. Afterward it's a blur, I don't know what became of him. Around the same time, a little blond boy, dressed English style in a round cap and flannel shorts, very chipper and smiling. After class, under the chestnut trees on the Avenue Henri-Martin, he asks if we can be friends. His mother is very nice, and I say yes, of course. They both die a few days later in a car crash that will be the subject of idle gossip for the rest of the school year. In fourth grade, there's the class cut-up, a kid who pesters the girls and scores the best goals at soccer. He never speaks to me until the day I take the blame for an infraction of which he's been falsely accused. The teacher, who takes sadistic pleasure in browbeating him, is aggressively skeptical. It's the beginning of an ardent friendship; he takes me under his wing, and I become his faithful lieutenant. I scoff at the brownnosers in the first row, I'm still pathetic at soccer, my grades are in free-fall—no matter, we're inseparable, and he takes it upon himself to show me pictures of starlets in bikinis in back issues of *Paris-Hollywood*. He has the look of a street urchin, his hair a mop of curls, dark eyes and tanned skin, always raggedy as if his skinny, limber body were trying to escape his clothes. Address unknown, he never talks about his parents, though sometimes he gets picked up after school by a chauffeur driving a black limo with consular plates. The little hobo must be the son of a diplomat, an enigma that excites me even more. But it doesn't take long for the teacher to avenge himself by having him expelled. It makes me doubly miserable to see him go and that he doesn't give a damn. At least he promises to write, and he sends me a postcard of wolves in the snow, packed with spelling mistakes, in which he describes his new Swiss boarding school where he skis and there are lots of girls. I answer with a vow of eternal friendship, and that's the last I hear from him.

A little later that same year, a rich kid whose father works in the oil business takes a dislike to me and punches me whenever the mood is on him. Officially I despise him, but secretly

I dream more or less of being his slave. Fine-featured, pale of skin, impeccably dressed from Manby's, they say his father beats him with a belt whenever he brings home poor grades. I make the mistake of complaining about him to my other brother, who finds him after school and threatens to break his face. Now he's just a frightened little kid, and I feel for him in his humiliation. We become friends on a new footing, and he invites me over to his vast apartment, gray and gloomy. His mother is a tall, gray-haired woman, distant and dry, and I think that his life can't be all that great despite his large-gauge electric train set and collection of tennis rackets. But the school year comes to an end, and I already know that the school's blind and heartless administration will see to it that we're in different classrooms the following term. And that's just what happens—it's hard to overstate the pain that such separations, imposed by faceless bureaucrats, entail for powerless and sensitive children.

I saw him in the street not long ago. I recognized him right away—very stylish, very handsome, an elegant woman on his arm—and I didn't have the nerve to reintroduce myself fifty years after the fact. I also happened across his mother at a restaurant recently. She'd grown very old but had changed very little. This time, I mustered my courage, greeted her, and asked after her son. She fixed her steel-blue gaze somewhere over my shoulder and replied that he was very well, thank you, the way one swats a fly away with a fan. She seemed furious, some quarrel over inheritance, no doubt, or some earlier grievance. I read somewhere that he's taken over his father's oil business. I'll bet he plays golf and takes his children to La Baule or Corsica on vacation.

A different type, still in fourth grade—the chaplain's little pet, a cherub who always takes first prize and who basks in the added glory of being the grandson of the headmaster, a sweet old gentleman in a wing collar and black felt hat. Our teacher is no dummy: she dotes on him, always holding him up as an example. I'm fascinated by his dimples, his slightly protruding ears, his skinned knees. He has no interest in me at all; his entire focus is on his twin sister, a shy little crybaby who has trouble keeping up with the class. When they're handing out prizes and he's staggering under a pile of red-and-gold-bound books, I suddenly panic at the thought of losing him—another bout of the separation anxiety that seems to be my unique burden. I dream of a fire, a hurricane, an atom bomb dropped on the awards ceremony for the honors students so I can show him what I'm really made of by saving him in heroic fashion. I was sure he'd be eternally grateful. But nothing happens. He remains stone-faced and as he's passing thanks me very politely for having consoled his sister when she failed to win anything. I'd only done it to get closer to him, but this sort of ploy doesn't work very often. When I look at the class photo now, he seems awfully dull, but when I close my eyes I see someone else entirely.

There are others. I'd like to get them all down on paper, people I'd rubbed shoulders with for months without noticing and who revealed themselves to me suddenly with a look, a smile, a chance exchange of words, and others who left such a light impression that I thought I'd forgotten them. There may be some who remember me the way I remember them but they never told me so; I write them down on my list the way you might throw a bottle into the ocean. Jean, for instance. We listen to the *Blonde in a White Car* soundtrack for hours, he talks about Marina Vlady and how beautiful she is while I stare at Robert Hossein's picture on the sleeve. Jean's a little older than me, very clever and funny: he tells me that it won't be long until, like him, I'll be leaving night stains on the bedsheets—it's perfectly normal, it happens to every boy, parents understand, it's nothing to be ashamed of. I don't dare ask him to show me his. We go home together on the subway, become good pals but it's not the same thing; despite our growing trust in one another I continue to protect my secrets. I can't remember how we fell out of touch. Practically every time I pass through Auteuil I make a detour to his street and lift my eyes to that second-story window where we sat whistling *The Bridge on the River Kwai* and made fun of the passersby.

Guillaume de T., slender and cheery, a lock of hair always hanging over his face; so ingenuous that by comparison I seem to have it all figured out, so devoted to me that I never want to let him out of my sight. With my power over him we live in a kind of ether, make plans to join the Cub Scouts together: we'll go to the forest, we'll make campfires, we'll sleep in a tent, I'll take care of him if he gets hurt. Another cruel class transfer breaks us up forever. I just recently learned that he's running an important newspaper in the provinces. I jotted down the phone number, I really wanted to call him, and then I didn't. I have a feeling we'll run into each other again one day.

Patrick, whose mother is dead and whose father forces him to sit down to dinner with sordid women who are always impatient for him to make himself scarce. He wishes I could come with him on holiday to Catalonia, where they dance the *sardana* with their hands around each other's necks. He's such a lost soul that he sometimes comes to sleep at our house. I think he's very good-looking, and we get undressed in the dark. Once at the gym he shows me how he's beginning to get hair down there; he's no happier for all that, and I turn beet red. His father sends him off to boarding school at the end of the year. His buddy, François—we don't get along but he's got a lively little body, lithe and lean. He dies suddenly late in the school year, of what, no one knows.

Georges, who bullies me sadistically and corners me in the bathroom to show me his dick, interrupted by the arrival of a hall monitor. He became a realtor, and I happened upon him when I was looking for an apartment—very pleasant, very polite, he recalled the good old days without going into detail. I had no desire to pick up where we'd left off. Gérard, the best soccer player in our grade: blond, quiet, a little stoop-shouldered, with long legs always covered in mud and scratches, part martyr, part athlete. He thinks I'm useless, but he always chooses me for his team. We don't talk much: I work hard to improve my game, and he's not the kind of guy who makes empty compliments. One day he tells me, looking the other way, that he has a cousin who's a fag; the cousin had tried to kiss him, and he thought it was gross. I act all dismayed on his behalf and try to picture the dreadful cousin. But then he suddenly turns to me, puts his hand on my shoulder, and says that he wouldn't mind kissing me, it wouldn't be the same thing, it would be almost like kissing a girl. It's true that I'm the youngest in the class and that some of the boys are already on their way to becoming young men. I'm sure it was just idle talk, unless he was trying to test me. He never takes it any further and then he gives up on me, telling everyone that I'd never amount to anything on the playing field. I'm hurt and humiliated but decide not to get even, although deep down I'm convinced he let his cousin kiss him. And then there was François, playing the fool by stroking my hair in the dark while the teacher runs slides of the Egyptian pyramids. Jacques, whose eyes water at the swimming pool, and to whom I bring scented handkerchiefs swiped from my mother. Raoul, the blond loner from New Caledonia whose sharp, muscled body resembles that of the main character in *Alix l'Intrepide*. I ran into him a few years later with an older man who was certainly more than his "godfather." Bernard, another blond with a melancholy smile, always shadowed by a greasy school prefect who gave him private lessons. Luc, little Luc, to whom I describe the plot of Vadim films I've never seen. Hervé the clown, who would cross over long before me. The brooding David, as attractive as the olive-skinned villains in the racist drawings from *Tintin in Land of Black Gold*. And there were others still . . .

I'm about twelve now. There's a young Tahitian, brought over
to France by a guy in our building whom we've known for years
from running into each other in the elevator. People find him
cute; I think he's a savage. He throws chestnuts at cars from the
sixth floor and has bad table manners. But I've had a narrow
escape from the Hungarian orphans my mother talked about
adopting after the tragedy in Budapest, and being this island
boy's Parisian buddy seems like a reasonable compromise. We
watch TV, which has only recently been introduced, and go bik-
ing together in the park. He's a very funny kid, with a supple
body and an unpredictable streak, and he tells me about Tahiti in
a singsong accent that I find delightful. He tells me you shouldn't
trust girls: they're all like his mother; they abandon their children to foreigners who take them far away from home. There's
some mystery between him and his fake dad, but he likes him
very much and doesn't seem to be scared of him. The grown-
ups say he's very lucky; he'll never be poor again and will have
a good education. But my brothers snicker when they pass his
benefactor, a big handsome man who looks like Jean Marais in
his waisted camel-hair coat, blond highlights, and Chevy convertible. I grow fond of Mowgli, and I can tell he feels the same.
One day he says he won't go back to the sixth floor and wants
to stay with me for the rest of his life. Sounds all right to me, but
then Jean Marais storms in furiously and marches him home.
Some time later he returns to his family in Tahiti without having
had the time to turn mean like Zamor. I ran into his benefactor
by chance in Thailand not long ago. He no longer resembled
Jean Marais, but he still had style. I asked him about the little
Tahitian, and he told me that he'd just died of cancer. He had
tears in his eyes, and I understood that he'd never stopped car-
ing for him and had surely loved him like a son. He showed me
pictures of a man in his fifties with a wife and kids in a tropical
setting. I didn't recognize him at all.

There's even an awful kid, all fat and ugly, who follows me around the schoolyard. He uses gold fountain pens, he goes skiing in Austria, his parents are very rich, but no one has any interest in him. He invites me over a few times; the elevator opens directly onto the apartment, and his mother gives me an art history lesson by showing me the Old Masters on the walls. I'm surprised at her beauty; how could she have brought such a squinty-eyed, sweaty monster into the world? He tells her I'm his best friend with a beatific smile that reveals his braces. I must admit I'm a little flattered and also a little sorry for him. I could easily make him my plaything; he'd do anything to keep our friendship going. The fact is, he's no dummy; he reads all sorts of books and knows a lot of things. His parents move to America and take him with them. I miss his kindness and affection much more than I would have thought, and I'm dismayed to learn that he won't be coming back. I came across him a few years ago in an American interiors magazine devoted to the finer apartments of New York City. There was no doubt about it—it was definitely the same name. Standing before a picture window overlooking Central Park was a magnificent fellow, slim, tanned, sporting a neat beard and elegant glasses—the kind of corporate lawyer you see in made-for-TV movies. All the horrible stuff must have been there still, but refined, restructured by time, unrecognizable. The article talked about celebrity affairs, the reputation of a playboy whom no woman could resist. I considered writing to him but thought better of it. He probably did not have especially happy memories of his childhood, and I felt a little guilty for not having been nice enough to him. You can never be too careful; nothing ever unfolds the way you expect it to.

On summer vacation in Évian, things are different; families reassert control over their children. On the beach, on strolls, in the villas, there are always mothers hanging around who need to be placated, all sorts of invasive relatives and cousins you have nothing to say to and probably won't ever see again. The weather report and complete strangers control the agenda of invitations and outings; a miscellany of modest adventures replaces the initiatory routine of the classroom and the liberating throngs of school, where we live among our own. Everything is unpredictable, uncertain, disappointing. I'm even more guarded than usual, and I don't often venture beyond the territory of home and garden; the family nest has reclaimed me, too. Even so, men do stop in. One of my uncles is a well-known sportswriter in the motor racing world, and he knows all the famous drivers, who often drop in at the house. Young, handsome, friendly, they speak English for the most part, and I can barely understand what they say. And they've got this aura of romance about them because they risk their lives at the wheels of their hellfire machines; you never know if they'll come back alive.

Apparently they're very successful with women for the same reason; at least, that's what my uncle tells me. Phil Hill is in his late twenties, with the dazzling smile of a movie pirate, and his blond hair cropped short. He's of medium height but incredibly built, and his muscular arms bulge out like hams from his red T-shirt. In my grandmother's parlor, surrounded by her antique furniture and trinkets, he reminds me of Godzilla in the shabby streets of Tokyo. A very sweet Godzilla, shy and gentle as champions often are, as I would come to see much later when I was no longer a boy paralyzed by ignorance and mute admiration before the virility of sporting types. I don't know what ever became of Phil Hill; I'm afraid he may have been killed in a race in the early 1960s. Or else, like a lot of former champions, he took some dull job with a car manufacturer. The only Hill people talk about nowadays is Graham, a mustachioed Brit who never smiled at little boys.

Stirling Moss is another man of the world, bald and naturally reserved, with the muted brutality and guarded manners ascribed

to the English in histories of the Hundred Years' War. But he has
an aura of command and strength that soon has me captivated.
He likes children and is very friendly toward me; he corrects my
bumbling English and takes me to the beach in his Ferrari. He
drives very slowly, steering with his fingertips; I sense the preda-
tor ready to pounce. On the mat on the great waterslide, which
no longer exists but which used to make me horribly dizzy, he
sits me between his knees and squeezes me in his arms on the
descent; I hear a kind of husky bellow in my ear as we hit the
water. We do it several times until he decides that I'm ready to
go it alone. On the way home, he buys me an ice cream and taps
me affectionately on the head as if I'd just won the 24 Hours
of Le Mans. I sometimes see him on television documentaries
about the drivers of yesteryear, an aging gentleman standing on
a lawn before a brick manor house. Jim Clark, Jean Behra, the
young Jackie Stewart—at home, no one could ever have guessed
the real reason I was so interested in motor racing.

Every so often I meet up with a little gang staying at a chalet on the lakefront. After lunch, by orders of the parents, the
sacrosanct ritual of digestion confines us to a sort of boathouse
that serves as a game room. I'm in the middle in terms of age,
and there's a sentimental little redhead who, like me, is equally
indifferent to the salty sex jokes traded by the big kids and to
the mini-golf enjoyed by the little ones. It's a little late in the day
when we go for a swim, and the lake water is cold. I swim better than he does and he tires quickly; the two of us hang out on
the raft after the others have gone back to the boathouse. He's
from Lyon and he's in the same grade as me; happy-go-lucky
and sardonic, he's the kind of kid about whom his parents say a
little apprehensively that he's mature for his age. As it happens,
his are divorced, and he adds in a whisper that his mother is
getting remarried. Confidences like this are the weighty seals of
young friendship. Our teeth are chattering when we leave the

water, we have goose bumps, our bathing suits cling, we laugh as we rub ourselves vigorously with the towels, we change without looking at each other. The light goes on in the boathouse. My mother doesn't like Évian, she says there's not enough sun here on the north-facing shore of Lake Geneva, the Swiss side is warmer, prettier, and even the mountain views are nicer there. It's true that the lakeside chalets are damp and get dark quickly. We take advantage of this by exploring in the park, where the plane trees are already beginning to lose their leaves. We rehash plots from the Bob Morane adventure series and make up others. On the shore of a lake like this, as big as the sea and with an international border in the middle, it's easy to come up with scenarios: storms, shipwrecks, smugglers, mysterious villas. It's as much fun with him as it is with the books themselves; there's always someone coming to the rescue. We also both love the book jackets: Bob Morane is very handsome, like Prince Eric, only more up-to-date. His mother doesn't like it that we're our own twosome. She always shows up too early to tell me it's time to go home, that they must be worrying about me over there. He waves his arms dramatically as I recede down the road on my bike. There are only two or three visits like that this summer, no more, sadly. I'd be willing to bet that the redhead asks for me by name, which must irritate his mother. The tradition of reciprocating invitations works in my favor, however. One afternoon, the little group tracks me down in my grandmother's garden. The others dive into the pool, but the two of us climb into a fir to build a tree house; we've found some crates, some planks, some sackcloth, and it's quite a job hoisting them up, but it's also a joy to be together again and to work on our house in the treetop. He's a lot more nimble than he was in the water, and he laughs at my awkwardness, my fear of falling. The situation is reversed now; he's the stronger one. It's a tie, we're equals, we should have been brothers. I'll go visit him in Lyon, he'll come

to Paris, we'll see each again next summer, we'll be together forever. We know very well that it never turns out that way, but at
that moment, in our fir tree, we're the kings of the world.

It had rained the day before, some of the branches are slip-
pery, he takes a false step and ends up motionless on the soggy
ground. I cry out his name, I scramble down as best I can, he
still hasn't moved; when I finally reach him, my heart pounding,
fit to burst, he gets up laughing. He's not hurt, there's nothing
wrong with him, he just wanted to see my face. My face is bright
red, distraught, he'd really got me going and suddenly he's sorry
for his nasty trick. We stand face to face without speaking. The
tension has spiked abruptly and may even lead to a fight. He can
see that I'm furious at him and that I might burst into tears at
the same time; this makes him sadder and sadder, and he tells
me again how sorry he is. And he'd been scared too, it was a
hell of a fall, after all. So much for the unfinished tree house,
we'll never go up there again. His pants are totally ruined, he's
covered in mud, and I must say it kind of makes me want to
laugh. Affection must need an occasional dust-up—it comes out
stronger afterward. The damage has to be repaired. I lend him
pants and clean clothes.

Berthe worked for us in those days. She was a young Corsican
girl, very beautiful and really nice. A few days earlier we'd taken
a trip to the mountains, and a friend of my mother's who'd
arranged to take us there by car had come on to her pretty
strong. She'd laughed it off politely but I could see that she was
embarrassed on my behalf and that she could care less about
that old letch. One of my brother's friends was crazy about her
too; he used to clamber over the roof to surprise her in her room.
She's a pure soul, she loves Marino Marini and confesses to me
that she's been seeing an Algerian who wants to marry her, to
her parents' fury. Berthe takes charge when she finds us in the
laundry room. "That child is filthy, we can't send him back to

his mother in that condition." She runs a bath and forces him into the tub. I can hear them through the bathroom door, and I'm a little jealous, I can't resist the temptation to go in. She's washing his hair, he's got his head between her big boobs under her blouse, his eyes are closed against the stinging lather and he's purring with pleasure. I creep in silently, they pay no attention to me, it's the first time I've ever seen him really naked. I look at his lovely, pale redhead's body and I want to get in that tub with him and have her lather us both up with her fine strong arms and her bright, happy laughter. It only takes a moment for them to notice me standing there, but it's a moment of intense happiness that I can still recall. We let him towel off and get dressed by himself. We'd forgotten about the others, they're done with the pool and ready to head home, their mother has come for them. The little redhead is wearing my shorts and one of my sweaters; Berthe has put the torn pants and dirty things in a plastic bag. His mother says she could have washed them, at least. We say a quick, sad goodbye, weighed down by this other world where children are scolded and maids rebuked. This will be our last time together; the summer holidays are almost over. I write him once or twice during the year, and he answers with postcards that he signs "Carrot-top." The following summer, we don't get to Évian until late July. I bike straight down to the lakeside chalet. It's all shut up. All I can see through the gate is fallen branches and weeds covering the lawn. A lady in the house across the street sees me and beckons me over; she seems eager to tell me something. There was a terrible tragedy on the third day of vacation, a little boy was drowned, you never can be too careful, a very sweet kid, maybe you knew him, yes that's right, a red-headed boy, forgive me, I'm sorry, I didn't know, they're all gone, my little redhead, go ahead and cry, it will do you good, should I call your house for you, the raft, the tree house, Berthe, poor children, my little redheaded love.

Berthe doesn't work for us any more. The Algerian left her, her parents refuse to see her, she found a job at a store in Albertville, then another. She doesn't answer my letters; I've lost track of her. I've got to face this dark summer all alone with my little redhead sequestered in my heart, swollen with grief. He's there still, cheerful and sardonic, smiling as if it were the first day we met, but it's amazing, try as I might I can't remember his name.

Beginning with that school year, my life is no longer bound by the schoolyard. My movements are subject to a tight schedule and circumscribed by the gilded boundaries of the sixteenth arrondissement and the area around Janson, but there are a few nascent opportunities for escape on Thursdays and Sundays: play dates with classmates, the Bois de Boulogne, the Molitor skating rink, the movie houses on the Champs-Élysées. This tidy little realm, these innocuous arrangements don't leave much space for social experimentation or amorous adventure, yet I sense that they go hand in hand, I've always been sensitive to the vagaries of street life. There is, for instance, an atmosphere of intrigue surrounding the apparently serene Avenue Montespan, a kind of private street lined with little townhouses that I take on my way home from school. They say at school that one of the detached homes, the one where the shutters are always closed, is a brothel. Such establishments no longer exist, and it's more likely a house of assignation, but I'm not old enough to know the difference and the fantasy is rich fuel for speculation among us. Women in makeup, men with averted eyes are seen coming and going; we regularly ring the doorbell and run away at top speed. It is in that very lane, which is already enticing enough, that I happen across a disheveled laborer, his open shirt revealing a chest damp with sweat, singing a lewd ditty about Gina Lollobrigida at the top of his lungs for a group of smirking associates. Gina is very famous—they dragged me to see *Fanfan la Tulipe*, in which I found Gérard Philipe bland and irritating, but the beautiful Italian

slew me. And everybody's seen her on TV, on Henri Spade's show
La Joie de Vivre, sighing "Bonjour Paris" in her plumed aigrette,
her bottomless cleavage, and that delicious accent. And then
there's that unlikely name that somehow highlights her natural
charms and makes everyone in class break up in ribald laughter.
"Eeny meeny miny mola, get a load of Gina's lolas." I've never
heard the song again, maybe he'd made it up, but there's no mis-
taking the appalling sexual energy with which he belts it out. He
bangs out the rhythm on the hood of a car, his buddies crack up
riotously, I don't know where he's taking them but I've got this
wild itch to go along for the ride. I pass by with my head down
and then I find a spot where I can listen and watch without being
seen. It's totally new for me, very vulgar and very exciting, this
man who's face I haven't really had the nerve to look at, who
may be drunk, but whose taut body and syncopated voice draw
me in like a feverish lover. A southern type for sure, very passionate, carried away by a violent, mysterious vision.

Another day, at the end of the same little avenue—there's really
nothing special about the place, yet I find myself more fascinated
with it by the day—under a poster for *The Ten Commandments*,
totally dominated, like me, by Pharaoh Yul Brynner, all bronzed
muscle and smoldering gaze, three workers are drinking beer in
a builder's hut and have left the door open. I feel that same hot,
tormenting wind begin to blow from the dark interior of the hut,
where I can make out men's clothes hanging on the walls and
hear bursts of laughter, muted conversation. They're North Afri-
cans, half naked, their muscles gleaming in the streaky light. All
anybody talks about these days is Arabs cutting the throats of
little French kids in Algeria, but it's something far stronger than
fear that's urging me on toward the black hole of the hut. The
workday is almost over, I'm sure they're perfectly nice, and why
wouldn't they welcome a visit from me? One of them sticks his
head outside and catches me watching him: young, olive-skinned,

dark tousled hair, worn features. "They've all got that same nasty look," the newspaper vendor outside my building would say. He smiles at me, he's got dark eyes and a gold front tooth, and his look isn't at all nasty to me. Still, there's something odd to him about the little boy standing stock-still on the sidewalk and staring at him while ineptly pretending to look at something else. He pulls on a shirt, buttons it slowly, and smiles at me again, but it's not the same smile this time, it goes right through me, and when he winks at me I'm suddenly scared. The thing is, I don't know what he's trying to tell me or what I'm supposed to do. His friends call him, he disappears inside, obviously I don't follow, I'm not old enough for that kind of rebellion. The next day the hut is no longer visible, the worksite has been hemmed in by palings, but Yul Brynner is still hovering above it all. Even if it's all a little confused in my mind, it's like a prophecy: the Arab proclivity has been set in motion. A few days later, I go to the movies to see *The Ten Commandments*. I only have eyes for the Pharaoh, whose face I see superimposed on that of the laborer at the door of his hut, and I talk about him so much on the bus ride home that my brothers are quite nonplussed. I understand that there are some things you keep to yourself.

It's just around this time, funnily enough, that my mother moves to Morocco with my stepfather. I sense that their marriage is hanging by a thread, which makes me sad. So the exotic transplant is not destined to last long, just enough for my brothers and me to spend the Easter vacation with them. And there, of course, it starts all over again, though not at all the way it happened in Paris. Morocco has just won its independence, and the French, now more than ever, live among themselves in a kind of aquarium from which no Arabs—other than their servants or those who look just like them, the wealthy elite surrounding the King—are visible. With the spring weather, we put on our shorts, we go from tennis court to swimming pool, we pass the time at high-security beach clubs where we avoid getting too much sun so as not to look like *them*, the others. The atmosphere is favorable to growing bodies, and just as distracting. But the absence of Arabs is untenable; the more we avoid them, the more present they become. They occupy our every conversation, fuel anxieties along the intangible borderline that we continue to patrol. There's definitely less ill will at our house than in most families who have always lived immersed in colonial arrogance and resent the erosion of their privileges. Even so, we do as all the French do—that's the normal state of things in a strictly cloistered world. As for me, I'm from somewhere else, and I'm certainly not staying long. The diffuse sensuality of the Arab street, the outdoor coffeehouses patronized solely by men, the kids playing soccer in dusty open lots, the shoe-shine boys and tradesmen who glom on to foreigners, even the music calling from the radio—I find it all irresistibly attractive. All the more so because it's forbidden, even if no one says so explicitly. I'm also too young to ask questions, I continue as ever to drift through the fog, my soul shrouded, my nose stuck to the car window as we drive past young people lingering on the sidewalks or heading down to the port and the shore.

Even so, I manage some fleeting contact. In Mazagan, a little street urchin who serves as our guide; about twelve like me, but a lot sharper thanks to the poverty that keeps children out of school. Cute as can be, cheeky without overdoing it. My mother's girlfriends want to buy him clothes and play dress-up with him; they don't dare say that it's a shame he has to grow up, but you don't have to be a genius to guess that's what they're thinking. The kid knows the rules of the game, he knows his days are numbered, we'll eventually bore of Portuguese battlements, and in any case in two or three years he'll be too old. He piles on the charm, and his tour-guide patter melts their hearts. I am both jealous and smitten; he's the king of the hill and I wish he'd focus exclusively on me, but he's sized me up and gone back to the ladies. He really works them; who knows how much they've given him. I'm on to the ragged, worm-ridden, half-blind, tooth-less kids who swarm us asking for money to buy notebooks and pencils—white lies I've been told to ignore. But he, the golden boy, chasing them off furiously with dark threats, has made a lot more than that without stooping to transparent excuses. Maza-gan was restored to its original name, El Jadida, long ago, and he must be an old man by now, all that charm long fled—it happens faster there than it does here—unless he's dead. Like those boys in tattered boxers on the sea wall in the port of Casablanca, diving among the rusting hulks and climbing like snakes up the chains, their muscles dancing as they hop from one foot to the other and laugh and whoop like savages, apparently indifferent to the young French kid whom they have surely noticed and who has asked to stop for ice cream at the top of the quay. Stu-pefied by the glaring sun, the fear of staining his white shorts with the dripping ice cream, the anxiety of his laughable pretext, and many other things besides.

Back at the house, a different kind of encounter helps open my eyes and nudges me down the path toward awareness. The cook, who makes delicious *tajines* and treats madame with such deep respect, is constantly kissing me whenever I venture into the kitchen. Greasy, greedy, and sticky, he harasses me with wet-lipped effusiveness that disgusts and interests me at the same time. I know that no good will come of it if I follow him into the garden as he's always urging me to do, but I continue to loiter in the kitchen. I've learned that I have an unusual power over this fellow with his rotten teeth, who coos and sweats whenever I'm within reach, and I take cruel pleasure in having him at my mercy every time he touches me with his wandering hands. Plus, he must be afraid that I'll tell on him, since he pretends not to notice me whenever I'm with my brothers. It would be so easy, my stepfather would cream him, and I'd get to play the lovely role of innocent victim. I no longer remember why I ended up dropping him; maybe it was his increasingly desperate expression, or finally I just began to feel sorry for him; in any case, I'd seen enough. So I say nothing, just to avoid trouble, and I stop playing with fire by staying out of the kitchen.

Just then, my mother falls gravely ill, my grandmother hastens from France to take care of her, my stepfather is beside himself with anxiety, my brothers forget all about me, the entire household is on the brink; like all children whose mothers fall ill and who find themselves sequestered by the adult world, I feel guilty yet independent for the first time in my life. A different servant befriends me, an old man who exudes kindness. He never makes a mistake when he serves us at the table, as if mother were still among us, and between servings he withdraws to the side of the room, his deeply wrinkled face, with its tattooed chin, alert and calm. I try to be as polite as possible whenever I ask him for anything. He takes me for rides on the back of his bike; it's exhausting for him, and I'm grateful. He doesn't speak much French, but his kindness envelops me and I have complete trust in him, a sense of protected safety that I owe to him and that I still feel whenever I'm with his people. We go into little groceries where he buys rolling tobacco and offers me candy; a hovel where he introduces me to his wife, a toothless old Bedouin who wraps me in her arms in a gale of laughter; a café where he spends forever greeting the old men like him and playing dominoes. Sometimes we push on to the souk, where everyone haggles in Arabic and every stall sports a photo of Nasser. The French are quite comfortable equating the Egyptian president with Hitler, but my companion doesn't seem to find him in any way repulsive, and I think he's quite handsome with his eagle eyes and his dazzling, wolfish smile. When we get home from our travels, the old man looks down at me gently, with melancholy affection, before he goes off to stow the bike. I think he gets it about the cook, and in his own way he's trying to convey his regret for the whole affair, but it's at the risk of losing his job, because an Arab who takes a young French child to the *medina* without telling anyone is automatically suspect in the current climate, when Europeans are undoubtedly being abducted and murdered by fanatical hordes. I tell no one about our escapades, and he trusts me, too. I'm not sure I can explain my silences, but I'm quite certain that if I didn't denounce the reprobate, I cannot betray my friend. I go home to France a few days later in a big propeller plane; the stewardess points out Port Lyautey through the porthole; in Paris, the chestnut trees are already leafed out and lilies-of-the-valley are on sale for May Day. My stepfather has stayed in Morocco, and my mother has recovered; they've separated, just as I feared. A new life is beginning. I learn that the cook has been fired for stealing, and the old servant was sent away as well; a single man doesn't need a large staff. Pointless looking for Port Lyautey on the map, it's called Kenitra now. I often think of my friend; he was a beautiful soul, he taught me that men could be tender, too.

My memory of Sheikh Ben Toukouk falls somewhere between the two—I believe he had the cook's tendencies moderated by the old servant's affectionate generosity. I'm a little older now, and my mother has married a new stepfather who treats us as well as the previous one did. One of her many qualities is that she only marries men who are willing to take the kids as well. It's not for nothing that my brothers and I compare her to Liz Taylor. My new stepfather has business in Algeria, where he met the sheikh, a prominent pro-French Muslim who fled to Paris after an entire wing of his family was massacred by the FLN. He is of proud bearing, always in immaculate traditional attire as if he were commanding a detachment of indigenous cavalry, his black beard and mustache neatly trimmed, but he's

also a little ridiculous with his ceremonious way of opening every
phone call with "Hello, Trocadéro 2612" to assure himself he's
dialed the right number, or how he rolls his r's when speaking his
grade-school French, or how he always gets lost in the Metro.
No one knows where he lives, some little room in the fifteenth
arrondissement where he spends all day listening to Koranic
surahs, my mother says; she has taken pity on him and kindly
invites him to dinner on a regular basis. One gets the sense that
he has no other friends, that he's very lonely and certainly very
unhappy, even if he never complains. He seems like an old man to
me, although he's probably no more than forty, and I'm very fond
of him without quite knowing why—no doubt that romantic aura
of tragedy and mute sadness that hovers about him. When I sit
beside him on the sofa in the little red parlor, he takes advantage of moments of general distraction to press me to himself and
breathe me in like a flower or to stroke my arm and my hair. I can
tell there's something sensual in it for the sheikh when he fusses
over me, but it's very gentle, very sweet, neither frightening nor
repulsive. No one knows if he was married, and perhaps I remind
him of someone from his past. It never goes further than that,
and he is surely anxious not to betray my mother's solicitude. His
visits grow less frequent as time goes by; he must feel embarrassed
at being unable to reciprocate. I saw him in the street three or
four years later, his white burnoose floating in the breeze amid an
indifferent throng; he had a lost look in his eyes, gray in his beard,
and an uncertain stride. A bout of juvenile self-regard prevented
me from going to greet him, for which I reproach myself to this
day. Watching him walk away, I thought of that wonderful story
in Alphonse Daudet's *Contes du lundi* in which an Algerian emir
staggers miserably from one ministry to another in search of the
Légion d'honneur medal he's been promised. A while later, my
mother caught a final glimpse of him in a brief newspaper article:
He had been assassinated by an FLN cell in Paris.

BY NOW I'm beginning to understand what I'm up against. It's an obscure, incomprehensible attraction that never lets up; a kind of game, too, with the capacity to make me happy or sad. I feel that there must surely be other boys like me, but I've been unlucky because I haven't met any. I know more or less where it will lead, but I still can't quite imagine the details. It's funny; my brothers don't talk about it in front of me. Well, sometimes they do, but always in a light, jokey tone that makes me feel less alone. But I latch onto everything their friends say, the oldest ones usually, whenever the subject comes up; their voices drip with scorn, insult, and mockery. In any case, I'm careful to toe the party line whenever they come for me. I know I'll have to keep my secret, tell no one—positively no one—until the day I can share it with someone who has been keeping his own. The descent into secretiveness, a permanent state of alert, has begun without my really being aware of it. A brief moment in the eye of the storm when I do not yet feel any particular shame or fear; that will come soon enough, my hundredfold reward. Deep down, I don't think it's irreversible. At the Janson school there are girls, too, and I enjoy their company. We have play dates, pass each other notes; I dream up little infatuations and persuade myself it will all work out. It's true, however, that I'm a little less sure of myself when they introduce me to their brothers. Everything's mutable, I tell myself, nothing stays the same; maybe I'll change the way my child's body is growing and transforming itself—a little too slowly, to my mind. Come on, it'll all turn out for the best; my biggest concern in life is not to get an F in math from Madame Martin, another one of those delicate-featured witches.

Back in the South for another summer vacation. My father has remarried too; my stepmother is young and nice, they've rented a great house on the beach in Formentor, on the island of Majorca, for the month of July. My brothers have brought friends with them, guests come and go, no one pays much attention to me. Franco's Spain is still an exotic destination, vaguely reprehensible, and at our house there's practically no one besides us, except a few families who come from the village of Pollensa on Sundays to picnic on the sand. The weather is magnificent. I spend hours in the water; I am a happy and serene child no longer bothered by the troubles of winter. Social life on the cape is concentrated a ways down the beach on a grand hotel that we reach from the house by a path through the pine woods. We occasionally spend an evening there. It's like a dream with its millionaires sipping cocktails and its orchestra playing paso dobles. Everyone's in an uproar because George Hamilton, the young American movie star, is there. He's dancing in a Balinese sarong, a garland of flowers across his bare, tanned chest, with a bejeweled woman who could be his mother. Many besides me find him magnificent, and he signs an autograph for me with a little flower next to his name. My oldest brother, who reads *Cinémonde* every week and is probably a little jealous of this extraterrestrial creature, lets out a little snicker. George Hamilton may have made some big movies in Hollywood, but he's also a high-class gigolo. You only have to look at him: a pretty boy available to anyone who pays him—yes, *anyone*, provided the price is right. That's news to me, I didn't know that such things as gigolos even existed. It's a new, unanticipated hope; I dream about becoming rich one day, far richer than the bejeweled woman, since it's bound to be more expensive for men. I'm impatient to become that very lucky man who will whisk George Hamilton off to palaces where they dance the paso doble on the terrace. There's another handsome boy at the hotel, the guy who pilots the Chris Craft for waterskiing; he has broad shoulders, a stomach ridged like a chocolate bar, and a tight-fitting bathing suit that drips water onto his muscular legs when he climbs into the boat, and he smiles all the time. He takes me

with him when my brothers go out onto the water. He speaks no
French, clearly he's a little more rustic than George Hamilton,
but I tell myself that if he were a gigolo, too, he'd surely be less
expensive. That's how far I've got in my calculations when I find
out that the American star, taking advantage of free time from
the lady protector guarding his room, has discovered in himself
a passion for waterskiing and has permanently requisitioned the
young Spaniard for his personal use. They disappear together in
the dinghy for hours at a stretch. The situation is so complex,
it's beyond me; I'll never be anything but a poor little penniless
French boy, landlocked with his ridiculous yearnings. We get
the Chris Craft and its skipper back a few days later—George
Hamilton has left the hotel with his lady in jewels, the young
Spaniard smiles as much as ever, but I no longer dare sit next to
him when he takes my brothers out skiing. I stay at the rear of
the boat and watch his back, his profile when he turns; when I
notice that he's looking at me out of the corner of his eye in the
rearview mirror, I pretend to admire the skiers and sulk a little
harder; he can't understand my attitude, and neither can I, for
that matter. It takes a fire to drag me from my sullen mope. The
pine forest is on fire and the flames are closing in on the hotel, the
guests are shepherded down to the beach, where they anxiously
follow developments. Firemen are summoned from throughout
the island and the hotel staff try to hold back the calamity, but
the trees go up one after the other, in sudden bursts, igniting
like matchbooks. I fear for my pilot, who is on the front line
of the struggle; in all this chaos, it's probably not the right time
to show him that I'm over my snit. That's when I notice a boy
who must be about my age standing among the guests, somewhat apart from his family, grown-ups and little girls who look
just like him. The inferno holds no interest for him—it's me he's
looking at, unsmiling, fixedly. He's in shorts and white moc-
casins, no shirt; he's blond and tanned, everything about him is

beautiful, but what strikes me most are his eyes drilling into me, and another odd detail I find fascinating—he's got tufts of hair under his arms. I'm not there yet. If he has hair under his arms that means he's already crossed one hurdle I've been desperate to reach, and yet this difference between us doesn't seem to bother him since he continues to train his gaze on me, immature as I am. He says not a word to me. He must be German or something like that, a different language, but that's irrelevant since I am in no doubt about what his eyes are telling me. I dream up some fantasy of escape—the two of us could "borrow" the dinghy from the pilot and motor away, run off together through the hotel, eluding the scrutiny of a staff overwhelmed by the blaze. I'm still not exactly sure what two boys of the same age can do together, but with his tufts under his arms he surely knows; all I need do is follow him. At that moment, a flame higher than the others disperses the besieged, the hotel guests are led further down the beach, and evacuations begin by boat. At the same time, we're sent back to our villa at the far end. As he boards, he sends me a little hand signal in farewell, and perhaps to say what a pity. I'm always dreaming up some disaster conducive to heroic escapes and adventures, and yet here I find myself instead in one of those war movies in which love-struck refugees are separated, never to meet again. I try to follow him with my eyes as long as possible, but the confusion is extreme, the wind beats clouds of smoke onto the beach, and the boat speeds off to evade the flaming trees toppling off the cliff into the sea. The hotel remains shuttered after the fire; the guests never return. Then the holiday is over. My brothers and their friends go to Tito's in Palma, said to be the best nightclub in the world; we go to bullfights and listen to radio updates about the fighting in Bizerte. We also celebrate my thirteenth birthday a little early, but it means nothing to me. Ever since the fire, it's as if it hasn't stopped raining.

I passed through Formentor again about twenty years ago on

a cruise with some friends. The pine forest had recovered, and there was no trace of the fire. The hotel was intact, once again filled with bare-chested young Americans and women in jewels dancing the paso doble on the terrace. Despite a few new villas strung out luxuriously the length of the beach, the place was still isolated and magnificent. Only the boat pilot had changed. He was corpulent and bald now, and little prone to smiling. If you spend enough time hauling around rich people who use you for their own amusement and then drop you, you age fast and end up embittered. Even so, I recognized him right away and talked to him about George Hamilton and the great fire that had threatened the hotel and scattered its guests. He remembered it all very well and was a little surprised that a stranger should bring up all that ancient history. I didn't press it, I didn't want him to have to lie and say that he remembered me, too. The fact is, I'd asked my friends to call in at Formentor so I could recall the boy from the fire at my leisure—the boy who had chosen me in the midst of catastrophe, the rest of it be damned—but I didn't really have the time. When you're on a cruise, somebody's always in a hurry to get to the next place.

A classified ad in *France-Soir* says they're seeking a boy my age for a movie starring Michèle Morgan and Bourvil. It's a substantial role—a son of the featured family—but acting experience is not required. Shooting is scheduled around the summer vacation. I've already been in a TV game show with Jean Nohain, and the ad gets me dreaming. My mother has no problem with my giving it a shot. The following Thursday finds me in the waiting room of Corona Films on the Champs-Élysées. There's already a good dozen hopefuls with their parents; each has a portfolio of headshots, a resume of prior movie roles, sometimes even press clippings with his name in it. They're dressed to the nines, some are wearing bow ties to give them an air of good breeding. Real professionals. The parents chat spiritedly among themselves, their gossip focused exclusively on the biggest child stars like Georges Poujouly and Joël Flateau. The mothers are especially scary; they eyeball their little treasures with the look of she-wolves, and smile at the receptionist as if they were in a police station. I'm by myself, I'm sweating because I ran all the way from the metro, I feel lost in this atmosphere heavy with dog-eat-dog voracity. It is precisely my awkwardness that catches the assistant's eye. The solitary kid hiding in the corner, empty-handed and speaking to no one, must strike him as unusual. He ushers me into an office where several gentlemen eye me curiously and question me cheerfully. They ask me to come back the following Thursday. On my way out, the mothers glower at me; they must have guessed that I've taken the first round. Back at home, I say nothing, and my mother forgets all about it. On a series of Thursdays they keep asking me to come back; I think I'm making progress. They take my picture, they have me read lines from the screenplay, they try me in 1940s-style clothes. There are no more kids my age in the waiting room. When they ask me where my parents are, I say they're on vacation but that they're okay with me being in the movie. My lies must be convincing because no one questions my answers; they must like my dogged determination to manage on my own, too. Finally, the director, a big, friendly kind of guy, calls me in for a screen test. At home, I'm still guarding my secret; I find it so incredible that I don't say a word about it at school, either. They drive me from the Champs-Élysées to the studio in Saint-Maurice; I don't want to give myself away by having the chauffeur pick me up at home. At the studio, I find that I have a rival of whom I had known nothing, the director's nephew, very charming and relaxed. The situation is complicated: I should ignore and despise him, but he's the kind of boy who interests me, and the attraction is mutual. With that impulsive generosity of sudden childhood friendships, we each insist that the other will get the job. There's another little boy, much younger, who would be playing the youngest son. Brown-haired, blue-eyed, cute and sprightly, he looks a lot like my unexpected competitor. The fact is my hopes are sinking fast, they're going to get to be in the movie and I had been quite right to hold my tongue. Anyway, they're called in first, and I'm left by myself on a bench outside the soundstage door. What I really want to do is go home to nurse my disappointment, but I don't even know where Saint-Maurice is and there's certainly no metro back to Paris. I'm sunk in these gloomy thoughts when a car pulls up—a Cadillac, the conveyance of stars. A magnificent blond woman is at the wheel, she glides by slowly like a golden cloud. It's Michèle Morgan; I should run after her, make her see that it's me they should take, but by the time I muster my courage she's already gone. And yet this vision has bucked me up; now I'm ready to stick it out to the end, and I'm ready to storm the lines when they finally call me. I'm not at all scared during the screen test, I see only the camera's eye, hear only the director's voice; everything else is dark and silent. I play the good boy keen to make the best impression, eager to please and happy to be there. The voice asks me school-essay-type questions—my best friend, the best vacation day—and I also describe what I remember of the film's plot even though I never really had the time to read the screenplay. It takes place during the war: Michèle Morgan has had to flee the Germans with her two sons; she's a member of the swanky set, a real high-society Paris lady. The older son has already become a little snobbish, but the younger is still very sweet. A resistance cell led by Gaby Morlay assigns Bourvil the mission of protecting the fugitive and her children. Bourvil's character's name is Fortunat, he's a good country boy, very funny but with no education and a little rough around the edges. Things start out badly between them, but as they're obliged to go into hiding and the war drags on, they fall in love with each other. The little brother, who adores Bourvil, has no inkling of what's going on, but the elder is furious; Michèle Morgan chews him out, he sees the folly of his ways while playing Chopin on the piano, Bourvil forgives him, and everyone makes up. It's a very sad ending, though, because Michèle Morgan's husband returns from a concentration camp and Bourvil, who's changed so much that the folk from his village don't recognize him, steps aside, broken-hearted. There are also plenty of dramatic sequences: an American paratrooper finding shelter in a safe house, or the nice Jewish neighbors being led away by the Gestapo. My summary must be pretty accurate, since the voice behind the camera says I'm very good. Obviously, I don't have the nerve to tell him I don't much care for my character's name, Maurice, or that I might have trouble crowing "Neato!" after almost every single exchange, as the voice asks me to do because, it seems, that was a choice expression of enthusiasm among boys at that time. As I'm leaving, an assistant tells me quietly that they'll call my parents with the final decision, and I can just imagine the look on their faces when they hear about all this. My rival has already left; it's better that way. I'm feeling in top form but a little ashamed with respect to him. It's true, then, that you can betray the one you love. I calm myself with such thoughts in the car ride back home. In the days that follow, I behave as if nothing had happened, but I can't shake the image of the friend I've already lost. I wonder if he's thinking the same thing.

I've never seen that screen test. I imagine now that it must have been a shameless display of ham, and yet it got me the part. When the producers call my house a few days later to negotiate the contract, my parents are obviously dumbstruck; the prospect of my acting in the movies, even during the summer vacation, is not a component of the bourgeois educational agenda they've been pushing with even greater devotion since their divorce. Mostly, though, they're appalled by the idea that

I've been able to pull off this whole scheme without their knowing; their obedient little boy is a dissembler leading a double life. My mother feels guilty for not being sensitive enough to my feelings; my father is concerned for the future of a child who creates his own hidden realities. Neither of them reproaches me, but it's a painful shock to them. They have no better idea than I do, however, of the true reasons behind my ability to conceal myself, my capacity to lie by omission, this nascent tendency to live apart. The movie project is my first escape fantasy to have overcome the obstacles of security and family trust. Any other child would have told his parents. *What are you trying to get away from, darling, why such secrecy?* I don't have an answer, and if I did I'd be even less inclined to give it. They're also quite tickled, and start to make inquiries. The producer has a very good reputation, my father reads the screenplay and finds nothing objectionable in it, and my mother meets with the director, who assures her that he'll care for me as if I were his own son. At the end of the day, it'll be a good apprenticeship, these movie people work as hard as anyone else, there's no reason to deny the child such an interesting experience. They sign the contract. Just before principal photography begins, I hear that they've changed my little brother: the sweet little boy who was so cute and well-mannered has been replaced by a budding professional who's already done some movie work and is accompanied everywhere by his mother. I mostly like sad children, but this one's unruly and entitled; we'll never be very close. From the very first takes he's vibrant with natural talent, and I'm no doubt a little jealous. There must be some soft spot beneath the little prodigy persona, but it's not obvious to me in these circumstances, and I don't make much effort to try to understand him or to forge a bond between us. I'll eventually come to regret that with great sorrow, but by then it will be too late to do anything about it. In any case, for now even that disappointment can't dampen my delight in discovering the joys of moviemaking: the team spirit, the very particular smell of the set and its props, that magic moment when action is called, and even the little perks of being chauffeured around, dressing rooms, the studio commissary. I'm on call every day, and when I'm not needed I hang out with the crew in a dark corner, listening to their jokes and watching them at work. There are some fantastic people, like Micheline, Michèle Morgan's enormous dresser-cum-watchdog who also works for Jean Gabin and spends all day long regaling us with anecdotes from her career, a corn-paper Boyard cigarette glued to her lips; Raoul the mustachioed communist props man who's constantly moaning about something or other and befriends me because I take an interest in the lives of miners and chimney sweeps; Liliane, the affectionate and lyrical stills photographer whose Leica I borrow to play at paparazzi whenever Jean Marais or Brigitte Bardot stop by the set unexpectedly from the studio next door where they're shooting. More than anything, there's the delicious sense of being completely swept up in the moviemaking; of being liberated from it all, without the time or need to think about anything else; of living in the world created by the movie, now suddenly more real than the real world. It's the kind of feeling that leaves its mark on a childhood, and which still seems to me to have been one of the most wonderful experiences I have ever been given.

And yet, things go badly for me from the very start. When I had finally got a chance to read the screenplay, I'd found some scenes in which I had the best role and which I thought were deeply moving—crying in Michèle Morgan's arms, noble manly exchanges with Bourvil. I was going to be able to show myself off to best advantage. But the movie would have turned out too long, so those scenes were cut before the first day of principal photography. On the other hand, I'm haunted by all those appalling "neatos" that I have to chirp with the conviction of a cheerful young idiot, and I begin to lose confidence. The director clearly senses that something's up and takes a sudden dislike to me; the kindly, reassuring daddy turns out to be quick-tempered, unpleasant, and singularly unjust; perpetually displeased with everyone, he obviously doesn't dare to gripe about the stars or openly attack the technical crew. The mother of the kid playing my little brother wouldn't allow her cherub to be bullied without putting up a fuss, so I'm the only one left for him to sink his teeth into. I certainly started out a ham, ill at ease, unnatural; but without clear direction, frightened and disoriented, I only get worse from there. Already hung up by my shrill voice and my body in full-blown awkward phase, I sense that my intonation is off and that I move all wrong. As assiduously as I learn my lines and follow my blocking, I'm well aware of the difference between me and my little brother, to whom acting comes as naturally as breathing. I know that some directors act like tyrants on the set; the crew speaks often of Henri-Georges Clouzot and Claude Autant-Lara with a kind of infuriated resentment tinged with admiration, but they are tormented artists whose despotism can be forgiven. My director just chips away at those weaker than himself. He mutters during my appearances in the rushes and makes me do take after take with an air of exasperation. His vexation is so blatant that the crew take me gently in hand. They tell me it's the way he works: he picks a scapegoat on every set. And then, one especially volatile day, he asks me in front of everyone if I might not have a twin brother, the one who sat for the screen test on the Champs-Élysées, and whom I have replaced with my own incompetent self without letting him on in it. All the accumulated tensions suddenly ignite. I burst into tears, I howl out that I hate him and flee to my dressing room, devastated with humiliation and distress. I can still see his look of stupefaction in the face of this unanticipated revolt. I lock myself in my dressing room and refuse to open for the assistants

who come after me; I can feel their anxiety radiating through
the door. Then Bourvil himself comes knocking. I haven't had
many scenes with him yet, and I haven't had the nerve to talk
to him between takes; he and Michèle Morgan make appearances on the set only when they're needed; their stand-ins are
used when the lighting needs to be adjusted. They're always very
friendly but a little distant and very intimidating, especially for
an inexperienced and overly proud child like me. That's how the
movies worked in those days. The situation must be serious if
they've sent Bourvil. I guess I've gone too far; there's no excuse
for rebelling against the director and interrupting a day's work.
I'm feeling a little stronger now and prepare myself for another
earful when I let him in. But he smiles at me in the nicest way,
plunks himself down, and begins to tell me about all the diffi-
culties of the profession I've been learning. I start crying again,
but they're no longer tears of anger and spite, just the grief of a
child seeking to be consoled. On the screen Bourvil was a comic
genius who had me rolling in the aisles, but sitting here before
me he's curiously solid and solemn, exuding experience and
kindness. He makes me sit beside him and dry my tears; he goes
on talking about the disappointments of his early years, and
gradually, imperceptibly, he cheers me up. No, I'm not bad, my
role's not an easy one, once the editing's done the final cut will
really be very good. He does more than comfort me; he winds
me up like a watch. Any more problems and I should come find
him in his dressing room, his door will always be open to me,
I mustn't forget that. I feel like hugging him in gratitude, but
I sense that Bourvil is an emotional man and I think it might
embarrass him. In any case, we've come to an understanding
that forms the beginning of a friendship. Now he accompanies
me back to the set, the director acts as if nothing has occurred
but he's no longer disagreeable, and shooting resumes. There
are no further incidents of this kind; someone tells me later that

Bourvil had taken the director aside after my meltdown, and afterward he'd emerged whistling a happy tune while the director seemed gloomy and disgruntled. I go visit him in his dressing room often in the following weeks, not to vent but just to listen to him; he's taken a real shine to me and tells me about his children, his family, even about women, whose complicated workings he attempts to explain to me. He can be very funny, but his feeling for comedy is not cinematic; his sense of humor tends to the disenchanted and melancholy. Although he seems to take little interest in politics, he doesn't care much for de Gaulle and, despite all his kindliness he is openly suspicious of honors, disdainful of official compliments and awards. There is something solitary and decent about him that touches me deeply; the fact is, I have never before met anyone as free as him.

Michèle Morgan, too, takes me under her wing. The assistants had told me that she was very different from her image as the great lady of French cinema, the one she usually reflected in her dramatic roles, but I'd never imagined just how very different. Far from being cold and distant, she proves to be cheery and warm, as ardent as a romantic young girl. There's been a lot in the press about her fight to get her son Mike back from her former husband, an American who took the boy to the States and is holding him there. I'm completely bowled over by the pictures of Mike that I've seen in the papers: a teenager on a California beach, as beautiful as his mother, smiling as only the boys from over there can smile—boys who can drive a car at fourteen, wear Bermuda-style bathing suits, and take their sweethearts to the movies. I don't look like Mike, but I get the impression that his mother finds something of him in me, almost the same age and a bit of a lost soul. She's very considerate, she brings me stamps from all over the world because she knows I'm a collector, and she compliments me frequently in front of the director. On the nights when I sleep at my grandmother's house in Saint-Mandé, she takes me there herself in her sumptuous Cadillac, gives me a quick, light kiss, and says "See you tomorrow, bunny." Yes, I'm Michèle Morgan's bunny; not many boys my age can say that about themselves, but I'm also practically her fiancé. The fact is, some English reporters are doing a big spread about her, and she insists that her movie children be photographed alongside her. But for some reason I don't recall, my little brother isn't there that day and the English, casting around for an original concept, suggest that we pose in bed. Michèle Morgan is tickled by the outlandish notion of cuddling with the young imposter posing as her son, and I find myself under the sheets, right next to her, my head propped on her shoulder or in her arms, depending on the pose called for by the reporters, who are pretty liquored up. She's in a nightgown, I'm in pajamas. It's not exactly intimate, since we're in the props room; we can hear the stagehands setting up a shot next door as Michèle provides running commentary, comparing me to some of her co-stars from earlier films; she doesn't bring up Gabin or Henri Vidal, but she does put me up against a few Italian names, which I find flattering. Above all, I can smell the perfume, the firm and supple body, the cool skin of Michèle Morgan pressed against me. I can't quite remember if she's my movie mother or the first woman to take me into her bed. She seems to intuit the game's ambiguity and my confusion; she teases me gently: "My little bunny will remember his lover-girl." Yes, he still remembers her with a shiver of delight, all the more so as he hasn't known many others.

And then there's Erica, the stand-in for Michèle Morgan, whom she resembles enough to have secured this odd and somewhat frustrating job. In a cruel irony of fate, a full-time stand-in is the star's pale reflection; she lives in her shadow and anxiously follows the ups and downs of her career because her own depends on it. Her personal dreams of stardom having faded long since, the regular stand-in obsessively cultivates a likeness

that remains tenuous despite all her efforts; she inhabits the attitudes and habits of her role model, and if possible she changes
and ages at the same time, then disappears like an outdated
counterfeit when the star is no longer in demand. It's the perfect
sad story for a child fascinated by the double life, the perilous yen to be someone else. But that's not the case with Erica.
Just for this one film, she's standing in for the regular stand-
in, who ran away with a stagehand during the last shoot and
hasn't been heard from since. Erica is a young Swiss actress for
whom it's just a job that she doesn't make a big fuss about; she
bubbles with life and imagination, extremely pretty and alluring and apparently not unsociable, judging from the bantering
boasts of the assistants, each of whom claims in my presence
to have slept with her; she's the kind of girl whose tits spring
up when she pulls off her sweater, they say. Even I still picture
those perfect tits as if I had actually seen them. Everybody on
the shoot loves Erica, and I enjoy the particular advantage of
spending a lot of time with her; I'm too young to have a regular
stand-in when we're blocking my scenes with Michèle Morgan.
At other times, we take walks in the studio grounds, go to the
commissary or her dressing room. I learn a lot about her life in
Geneva, her sisters, her parents, who let her go reluctantly and
are ready to come to her assistance at a moment's notice if she
gets into trouble. They're complacent folk, sheltered from want,
whereas she's a bit of the grasshopper who never worries about
tomorrow. I know Geneva, its pervasive atmosphere of placid
prosperity, and it's easy for me to picture the pleasant, orderly
family welcoming its prodigal daughter with open arms every
time she comes home from her Parisian adventures. When she
sees me growing irritated with my younger brother, she takes
his side and reminds me that he's not old enough to understand
everything yet, and when the director reverts to his threatening
ways she stays close by and reassures me. She's intuitive and

fundamentally compassionate. We sometimes talk about politics. The war in Algeria is dragging on forever, and I have an
opinion on the topic, that of my parents, naturally: we have to
grant the independence demanded of us and get it over and done
with as soon as possible, but she assures me that I understand
nothing about it and simply smiles and looks away when I get
all tangled up in my argument. I tell myself that she has a good
excuse; Switzerland has never had colonies, and they've been
neutral for ages. We also plan out her life after the movie—she's
decided to take her chances one last time by knocking on the
door of every producer, but deep down she doesn't really believe
in it anymore and thinks that she'll need to return to Geneva
in the very near future. She has friends in the theater there, it's
right near Évian, I could come see her on my next vacation. I
find it hard today to recall every detail of our conversations, but
the main thing I remember is that she's always available to me,
a friend and confidante. Oddly, she never discusses her love life.
I don't know if she has a boyfriend and she never comments on
the assistants who, for their part, are so garrulous about her. I
can see quite clearly that there's something electric about her
when she passes among the men on the crew and that it amuses
her, but with me she's a big sister who only wants to have fun
and a girl with her romantic secrets. I'm only half convinced,
but that suits me fine; it feels like I have her all to myself in that
blessed childhood fairyland that goes on forever and ever.

And yet, there's one incident that bothers me and hints at the
possibility that I'm mistaken. One evening my father comes to
the studio to take me home, and we bring Erica, who doesn't live
far from our house. As always with her, the ride home is very
jolly, but even so I'm exhausted and my father drops me off first.
I watch that good-looking man of fifty and the young sweater
girl drive off. When I ask dad about Erica the next day, he acts
oddly evasive and changes the subject. I plug on a little, but he

falls silent, and I sense an indefinable discomfort in his attitude. For her part, Erica finds him charming, absolutely charming, and she goes on to talk of her own father, the good fortune of having a father who's still young, Geneva, and so on; we move off the subject at hand so fast it leaves my head spinning. Yet I am convinced that something happened between them, something I'm not supposed to know about but that I have no trouble imagining; where, how, how far I prefer not to think about. It sinks into the depths alongside the assistants' gossip.

Toward the end of the shoot Erica suddenly disappears. She was with us the evening before, in a joyful mood as usual; now she's gone, the driver can't find her, and she's not answering the telephone. They spend the whole day looking for her, the director is furious, I'm sad and worried; without knowing why, I'm also quite certain she won't be coming back. Before we leave the studio with the final scene of the day in the can, the day's issue of *France-Soir* is passed around. Her picture is on the front page, she's handcuffed, surrounded by cops, a haunted look in her eyes. The headline blares: "Swiss Acting Student Worked for the FLN; Police Find Cache of Weapons, Money, and Pamphlets at Home; Terrorist Network Broken." The three-page article tells the whole story in detail, describing Erica as the new Mata Hari; the couriers, the attacks, the lengthy police surveillance; the violent arrest; the Algerian lover who ran the network and escaped at the last minute, leaving Erica in the trap. In the context of the times, even for an anti-colonialist smarty-pants like me, the whole affair is frightening. I think of her parents living their placid lives in Geneva, loving their daughter so much; they must be consumed with anguish and maybe with shame, and then I think that maybe there are no parents in Geneva, no warm and indulgent family, but just a series of quarrels, furtive love affairs, with Arabs naturally, handsome dangerous Arabs who caress her upward-springing breasts and teach her to handle weapons. The assistants stop talking about her; I resist the temptation to tell them that I had the best of her. They wouldn't understand. Erica's disappearance plunges me back into my little boyhood of secrets and silence; at the same time, I'm glad the end came so abruptly; Erica might have fleeced me, but I'm sure she loved me a little bit too, in the midst of all that peril and chaos she hid so well. I admire her lies and her courage; she left my life through the front door of defiance and rebellion. I hope she still remembers me after all these years, and whenever I happen to be in Geneva I carefully scan the streets for women in their early seventies. Maybe I'll be lucky enough to run into her one of these days.

While all this is going on, the American paratrooper falls from the sky. He has only one scene but it's a very important one, the pivotal moment in the movie. The Resistance has assigned Bourvil the mission of spiriting him away to Spain, but during the course of the evening he spends hiding in our refuge, his charms go to work on Michèle Morgan, who's still playing the grand lady in distress. She dances and flirts with him in front of her son, who is equally smitten with the newcomer. Bourvil, tormented by jealousy, gets drunk, abruptly interrupts the little party; his rival has no choice but to go with him when he says it's time to leave. Initially outraged, Michèle Morgan soon regrets having let herself go and comes to see that it's Bourvil she loves. Mission accomplished, he returns sheepishly, and she gives herself to him. Although this key scene occurs in the middle of the movie, we shoot it only in the final days; the right actor was hard to find, and the shooting schedule had to be changed several times. When he finally arrives on set, the atmosphere is charged with jangled nerves and anticipation, and I tell myself that the wait was worth it because I think he's sensational.

He's in the Tab Hunter/Troy Donahue mold, blond Hollywood Adonises whose photos I pore over in my oldest brother's *Cinémonde*. Long-forgotten now, these actors had their heyday in the early 1960s in teenage beach movies and overblown melo-dramas of fatal passion in the arms of starlets attempting their comebacks. In Cinemascope. I don't think I've ever seen such a gorgeous boy, with all the grace of those young American heroes, always smiling, resolutely optimistic, and apparently quite inno-cent. I have only one or two lines with him, but during the course of his three days at the studio I make sure I'm by his side every minute. He is in fact Australian, his golden hair has been bleached for the movie, and he's been living in Paris for several months, which explains his excellent French, enlivened with an accent that I try to copy by parroting his speech in front of the mirror of his dressing room while he's changing, and I have to pretend not to notice that the mirror also happens to allow me to watch him. His skin is very pale, he wears print underwear like the kind my brothers buy at the Shape surplus stores, and he brushes his teeth with a mentholated paste that strikes me as the acme of sophistication. My presence doesn't seem to bother him. He takes an interest in me and asks me questions about my life. I sense that his has been more eventful than he lets on: he left home very young and has no contact with his family, he's done a lot of traveling with friends and fell into the movies by chance in Rome, where he was discovered by a producer while bartending; since then, he's played minor roles alongside Danielle Darrieux, Pascale Petit, and Françoise Arnoul—he prefers French starlets above all others. He doesn't know how long he'll stay in France, he's been called back to Cinecittà, where boys with the Ameri-can look are in great demand. All of this seems very romantic and a little disturbing to me. I've always lived such a sheltered life, almost never away from home, and I'm quietly astonished that one so young can lead an international existence with noth-ing to tie him down. He answers with an angelic smile that you need to learn to make it on your own and that I'll surely figure it out for myself one day; I suddenly see that he is fundamentally unknowable, secretive, and hard. For that matter, if it weren't for my being constantly at his side, he'd be pretty much alone on the set; when he's not on camera, no one pays any attention to him, and the crew's indifference strikes me as strange. If Erica were still here I'd ask her what she made of it all. But then one of the assistants, who has certainly been put up to it, slips me a casual warning with a disagreeable undertone of hostility: according to him, the guy is just a fag who hangs out with older men, one of whom picks him up at the end of the day's shooting; he parks his English car at some distance from the studio so as not to call attention to himself, but everyone has figured out their little arrangement. I express my disdain just for show, but the truth is this revelation suits me very nicely, and I continue to shadow my disreputable hero as if no has said a word to me. Alas, it's his last day and we'll soon be saying our goodbyes. I picture him in the English car with the old guy, who smokes a cigarette while he waits. He tells him all about his three days of shooting: Michèle Morgan is even better than Danielle Darrieux, you can't expect anything good from a French crew where arrogant and unpleasant assistants make the law, the little boy who's in love with him insisted on taking down his phone number and it makes him laugh. The old guy shrugs and takes him to the Côte d'Azur.

The end of a shoot is always heartrending, like the breakup of a Resistance cell in the stories; we were so close and suddenly we don't know if we'll ever see each again. Every time I come across the movie on television, a wave of memories washes over me with each new scene, and I can see the members of the crew behind the images. The director died a few years ago; we'd been getting together of late; despite his early successes, no one would help him relaunch his career and he ran himself ragged trying to get a new movie going. He was happy to talk about the good old days with me, and I had no interest in upsetting him with ancient grievances; after all, he'd given me an extraordinary opportunity that has served me my entire life. He wasn't really a bad guy, with all his heart he loved a profession that he was pretty good at; I'm glad we met up again toward the end. The American paratrooper didn't disappear like Erica. Through a series of circumstances I've never quite understood, he ended up marrying a friend of my brothers, and I saw him once with her in a trendy restaurant: his whole iniquitous past was behind him, and before me was an Anglo-Saxon businessman in his thirties, brown-haired, likable, and easygoing, saying "my dear" to an elegant young woman who was clearly in love; he was barely able to recall his career in the movies and had no desire to speak of it. They spent many years in New Zealand where they were in gemstones, and after their divorce I was reminded of him again while reading a book in which he featured prominently. A lovely portrait, in truth, in which the author made no effort to conceal the feelings he had had for him and how dearly he continued to miss him. I don't know how he feels about his own life; from the scraps of hearsay I've been able to pick up over the years I have hope that he is not too harsh on himself. Not every boy who decides to make it on his own with nothing to tie him down is clever enough to make himself beloved for three days, years, or even longer. It seems he lives near Paris; I sometimes think I'd like to look him up, but I'm afraid he may have turned into one of those old guys who used to wait for him at the studio gates.

In the end, though, the one I miss the most is my little brother. Erica was right to reproach me: I never did manage to understand him. He never got over the success of the film, in which he was delightful, and the musician's career he chose to pursue as an adult no doubt brought him meager satisfactions compared to those he'd known as a child. Child prodigies have a hard time forgetting, but they are rarely remembered after they've grown. I bumped into him once on the set of some dismal television variety show. He made the first move because I hadn't recognized him; he was friendly and a perhaps a little too humble; I didn't feel blue until later, when I got home to the solitude that always brings other people to mind. I suddenly saw him as one of those people who are insatiably hungry for affection. We'd promised to get together and he called me for dinner, but I was busy, didn't have the time. When I thought to contact him some time later, I couldn't find his number and then I forgot all about it. I can't remember who it was that told me he'd killed himself, citing motives that I'm all too familiar with. I still regret not having been on his journey at the right time, and I doubt very much that his mother survived her grief.

summer 1947

summer 1947

summer 1947

It was so hot that summer that mother couldn't take it anymore. At day's end, father would take her to catch her breath on the western highway; he lowered the convertible's roof and drove at top speed all the way to Orgeval and back. There was practically no traffic because of the gas rationing, only two lanes in either direction, and in any case the highway stopped there. Finally, once past the Boussac stud farms, one entered the Marly forest and the cool shade of mature trees.

I don't remember the make of the car. Certainly, mother once drove a superb Alfa Romeo, but that was for a fashion show and the organizers had only lent it to her for the occasion; they must have been pleased when she won the grand prize and let her hold on to the magnificent vehicle for a few days, but no longer than that. On the other hand, Madame Carven let her keep the dress, an outfit of her own making in green stripes, "for the *piquante Parisienne*," even if mother was more Danielle Darrieux than Dany Robin. It was good publicity for the new house of Carven, and for that matter neither of them ever forgot it; they ran into each other at a restaurant the other day and they talked about that show, that dress with green stripes, and of those beautiful but brutally hot summers over fifty years earlier. It was moving to see the two of them together, dusting off such memories—the little things that can make life more pleasant. Madame Carven has changed astonishingly little, as has mother; I find her as beautiful as ever. True, Danielle Darrieux is no slouch either, as we all saw at the Molière Awards. But how sad for Dany Robin, burned alive in her apartment, lost to the cinema and practically forgotten.

So it wasn't an Alfa Romeo. Father definitely had an American convertible with an electric roof, but that was after the divorce—partly to console himself, and partly to try to impress mother, because he still hoped she would return to him. We children—the three witnesses to his loneliness and sorrow—could tell, just from how hard it was for him to talk to us about anything but our schoolwork, that he continued to pine for her. It all worked out eventually; these things always have a way of working out one way or another in the end. Still, I imagine it must have been a fine car; high-speed convertibles were not exactly a common sight on the roads in those days.

Plus it's impossible to ask them about it; father is dead and mother recalls only the heat, the highway, and the grueling trial of being pregnant and overdue with me. They had counted the days, I was late, it seemed to drag on forever in that heat wave. Mother often told me the story when I was little, no doubt so I would know that they'd had good times together, times of attentiveness, consideration, and mutual trust that a young couple have all to themselves; and so I would know, too, that she always held him in great affection, despite a separation that remains somewhat inexplicable to me to this day. It was no one's fault: the very difficult years of the war, the youth they thought they had lost; after the war, that powerful resurgence of youthful vigor opened a gulf between them—for her more than him, I think, as women tend to endure suffering better than men and emerge from it more resolute. There are exceptions, but this case wasn't one of them. As I grew, mother spoke to me less and less frequently of the heat and the highway; I think she feared that I would feel guilty because I was the one who was late, I was that other heat burning in her belly and stealing her breath. She avoids any subject that might make me feel that I was a bother or a source of pain to her. That's understandable; I certainly had no qualms about being either when I was no longer her little angel, her little prince. As for father, when he remarried he forgot just about everything from those days, which also strikes me as quite natural. He would rather recall another summer I spent with him in Paris, just the two of us. He took me to see the fireworks on July 14th, and the heat was so intense the asphalt melted under our feet; he let me sleep naked and got up in the night to make sure I wasn't thirsty. The two of us went to see the Tintin movie *The Shooting Star*.

It was on one of those evenings, coming back from Orgeval, that mother finally went into labor. It had all been arranged to take place at home, but the doctor was nowhere to be found; he'd gone off to take the air in the country and father had to manage all by himself; he had the bright idea of calling the fire department, since firemen know how to handle any situation. Even so, it was a pretty grim scene in that oven of a room where father and the firemen were bathed in sweat and mother thrashed in pain upon the bed. She almost died that night, and I did not exactly get off to the best of starts in life; I was strangled by the cord, and for several minutes father and the firemen took turns reviving me, holding me by the feet, head dangling, and slapping me vigorously about the body. I have always wondered if it didn't take too long, a shortage of oxygen creates irreversible lesions on the brain, and that would explain a great many things in the end. Father and mother never believed that; they would simply tell me: "We had a hot time of it with you that night, darling." I never learned more than that; the next day brought thunderstorms, and with the rain everything returned to normal.

the cruel and the kind

the cruel and the kind

the criel and the kind

there were the cruel lady and the kind lady, and I've managed to track them both down. When I was little, the cruel lady beat me every day. That's what I say, mostly out of resentment but also to bother my mother, who is deeply pained by the resurrection of these stories. By dint of repetition, it's become an official family truth. The fact is, I'm not so sure that the cruel lady beat me every day, mother or someone else in our circle would have been aware of it; I couldn't have held out, I'd have gone mad, although I now believe that there were days and even years when all that suffocating terror and secretiveness were not unjustified. What is certain, however, is that blows often rained down on me with great violence at the least infraction, or even at random, for no reason at all. The blows were mostly slaps but sometimes punches or kicks when I walked too slowly in front of her during our brisk hikes through the Bois de Boulogne. One punishment was having my head immersed in cold water in the bathtub because, according to her, I was not alert enough during my reading lessons; having cotton swabs jammed up my ears to the eardrums to get them good and clean; suffocating steam inhalations, standing over the radiator, to clear out my bronchial tubes; the series of revolting potions, the burning-hot porridge that had to be eaten the moment it was served. There was the unqualified prohibition of coughing when I was sick, leaving any of my things untidied, or getting my clothes the least little bit dirty; the obsessive monitoring and immediate punishment of the least infraction of the code of good conduct at the table or when the little parrot was in the presence of adults; the continual denigration of anything I might do among other children of my age, who, however ill-mannered, were held up as role models; the infernal procession of absurd duties and humiliations. Ultimately, the blows created an atmosphere, the terrifying feeling that she was always right behind me, even when she wasn't there, a life led in perpetual expectation of punishment. It lasted ten years, from my earliest childhood memories until our trip to Morocco and my mother's separation from my first stepfather; she stayed with him, then fell into the job of head nurse at a clinic whose Arab patients were lucky enough to get a private preview of Nurse Ratched. My brothers got their share: I remember the eldest, beaten ferociously, crying in pain and defenselessness beneath the wailing of that raging witch, as I looked on paralyzed with horror and fear. The other got off easier; she was afraid of him in some indefinable way. But they were older and soon went to live with our father; it was nearby yet beyond her reach, safe from her power. She and I remained together, face-to-face.

I loved the cruel lady far less than my natural mother, but I loved her nonetheless. She took up all the room, she was a shield between me and the rest of the world, and she had broken me from the very start. She was young, almost beautiful, with big round breasts that clung to her bodice when she was in a sweat. She was often in a sweat because she was almost always angry with me. I sometimes saw her naked in the bathroom; she undressed in front of me, without shame and without looking at me; I didn't count for her, or perhaps I counted for a great deal; she had the firm body of an athlete. I didn't have the choice to turn away: it was either her, stark naked at her ablutions at the sink, or the lurking bathtub in which I would inevitably find myself being dunked. Sometimes there were these kinds of blood-stained rags on the tiled floor; I didn't know what they were, but I understood that they were not for my eyes, or perhaps, again, they were. Otherwise she was the gray-skirt-white blouse type, mackintosh and flat heels, never any makeup. My mother gave her dresses, but I never saw her wear them. She was a fervent equestrian; it was her only leisure activity. She rode on Friday nights at the Stirrup Club, always for instruction and the obstacle course; promenading was for amateurs and sissies, she said. Among other things, she particularly hated sissies, and she never passed up the opportunity to drum it into me, rolling her eyes whenever she saw me on the verge of tears; thankfully, I'd learned to control myself and very rarely cried. I'm still haunted by the boundless stupidity of it all, and it probably caused me more anxiety than the chronic threat of a beating. When she left for her riding lessons in her equestrian gear and her silver-pommeled whip, I was already in pajamas, well pumiced and well combed, ready to say my prayers and go to bed. I would never have dreamed of exploiting the freedom evoked by her absence or of infringing the strict lights-out curfew; the aggressive scent of her eau de cologne hovered in the air.

Occasionally she could be affectionate—brusque, but affectionate all the same. It never reached the point of cuddling or emotional confidences; it was more in the line of a sort of virile camaraderie, embodied in moments when, for instance, she'd tell me how she used to have to crack the ice when she washed herself at her girl's boarding school during the war, or that she was quite satisfied to be eating meat once a week when everyone in France was dying of hunger. There was always a lesson on the benefits of discipline and the dinner plate to be finished lurking in there somewhere. One day she bought me a little Dinky Toy car as the result of an unexpected promise she had made me in a moment of weakness if I made the honors list. I hung on to that little car for a long time, it was my favorite toy, I carried it in my school bag like a talisman to protect me, and then one day I burned it on the balcony with some 90% alcohol I'd filched from a pharmacy. It took a long time to burn; those Dinky Toys are well made. I was really scared that she would catch me, but she never suspected a thing, she never asked me about that little car, I guess she'd forgotten all about it. One night she cried; she'd received a telegram saying that her brother, an Army lieutenant, had just been killed in Indochina; I saw her sobbing in her room, pictures of a soldier spread across her bed. My mother said it was terribly sad and went in to her, asking me to go play and not make any noise. I was sorry for her and wanted to comfort her, but she never called for me; we never talked about it afterward; the truth is, she had no need of me.

In any case, I knew very little about her family. A tall woman, dressed in black and looking like a crow, came to see her now and then. It was her mother. I never saw them embrace; their relationship seemed very cold and prim to me, and she'd soon call me curtly to order—I had better things to do than moon around the front hall with the grown-ups. I never knew her to have any friends; the servants were afraid of her and watched their step around her. I can't quite imagine what she thought of my mother, despite the affable formality of their relationship:

captivated like everyone else, no doubt, and envious in a poor-cousin kind of way. She had a charming nickname redolent of a happy childhood and harmonious family life, but her real name was as aristocratic and resonant as a lesson from my history book; she had a coat of arms on her signet ring, for she was from the impoverished branch of a dynasty of provincial nobility, and I think she hated having to work as a governess in a social milieu to which she didn't belong: the sixteenth arrondissement, upper-middle-class businessmen who drove fancy cars, went out for dinner, and vacationed in the South. Worse yet, perfectly smug and left-leaning. She must have been secretly disgusted on top of feeling that she'd come down in the world. And this brat with whom misfortune had stuck her, so submissive and eager to please, an exasperating burden, a duty, a regret perhaps . . .

Some of my schoolmates also had governesses, young Scandinavian au pairs or English-style nannies, who were readily replaced upon complaint to the parents; some were also very nice and had raised generation after generation. I envied them, but I wasn't in their position; I had been totally broken and was incapable of raising my head; protest was entirely beyond the realm of possibility. The cruel lady and I were bound together like addicts, we had no need to account for ourselves; our drug—violence—had pulled us down too soon, too deep, and there was no escape. It's the old familiar story of the child who says nothing because he's come to believe that he deserves whatever the tormentor inflicts on him, while the tormentor takes that belief as the ideal justification for persevering. A life in perfect balance, as it were. Apparently she was the ideal governess, a little strict perhaps, but able to deal with any situation, from colds and poor grades to dental appointments and packing for the holidays.

She didn't loosen her grip on me even over the vacations; she was gone for barely two weeks, staying with mysterious cousins in the southwest, whence she peppered me with harsh proscriptions in a steady, elegant hand in blue ink, and whence she returned fully recharged. And, apparently, I was some kind of little wonder of a boy, a bit of a dreamer maybe, but marvelously equipped to meet the future, positive and cheerful, polite to everyone and mature in conversation. I knew just how to pull off the deception, even with my mother when she was stricken by doubt. However, one night, alerted by a friend who was able to see what was normally hidden in plain sight, my mother came home suddenly from a dinner she had pretended to attend, and caught us red-handed in a scene of casual brutality. My face was still red from the slapping I'd received, while that of the cruel lady was twisted in rage. Appalled, mother gave her notice on the spot. I could have seized the moment, but a complicity like ours was not easily broken. I burst into tears, claiming that nothing had happened, it was just a little love tap. My mother, troubled by my obvious distress, called for the wicked one, who had gone to her rooms to pack her bags and now shuffled in, humble and distraught, pleading that her hand had slipped, it had never happened before and never would again. We were just one falsehood apart in our clandestine undertaking. She had recovered her full serenity and composure; how could she hurt a child she loved so dearly? To plead on her behalf, I sobbed ever more desperately even as I watched my freedom evaporate. My mother wanted to think it over, but the deal was done, the star-crossed couple was reunited. We celebrated our victory later with a vigorous thrashing; it was our way of reminding ourselves that the terms of the contract hadn't changed. I'd signed on for another two years, up to my liberation in Morocco. But was I truly liberated?

She never expressed any desire to see me again. I remember one or two courtesy visits to my mother, at the very most, in which I made a brief appearance in the parlor. Hello, good evening, how he's grown—a little bit of make-believe and very little effort. The whole sorry mess was ancient history; I hadn't memorized the dialogue from the farce about happy childhood memories, and she had never had much imagination and was no longer up to prompting me with my lines. I had worked painstakingly to put the pieces back together, and the truth was beginning to dawn on me, little by little. She must have sensed it. After that, no word for more than forty years. My resentment rose slowly, very slowly, inexorably, one degree for each hurt, each failure. I hadn't yet learned that there is no guilty party and that it takes two to commit a crime. It wasn't linear; there were detours and dead-ends. Sometimes, in those moments of utter confusion that punctuate every life, I found myself wishing she'd come back to comfort me for all the harm she'd caused me. Go figure. In any case, I was perfectly convinced that I would see her again. I even looked up her address in the phone book. I had a very romantic picture of our reunion. It would be like in a Bergman film; one day I'd ring at her door with a bouquet of flowers or some chocolates. She would be surprised, a little flustered, but I would be charming, and she would soon mask her discomfiture. She would offer me an orangeade or, correcting herself, a coffee—more age-appropriate—and I would look about her little spinster's apartment and ask if she still rode. We'd exchange niceties, family news, and the silences would grow increasingly drawn out and fraught. We would hear cars, buses passing down the narrow, dusty streets of her modest neighborhood, the flowers or the chocolates, still in their wrappers, would lie in a corner like the bloody rags of yesteryear. And then, out of the blue, and in the same affable tone of voice, I'd ask her the questions that she'd been waiting for from the start. That's where it gets a little foggy for me; she'd saddle up her high horse and deny everything, voices would inevitably be raised, I'd trot out some of her foulest deeds, she'd order me to leave but I'd dig in, it would be long and painful and I'd manage to undermine her confidence just a little before slamming the door shut. She would throw the flowers or the chocolates out the window, they'd splatter on the sidewalk at my feet. In another more melodramatic version, she'd hesitate a moment and claim to have forgotten before coming clean and answering my reproaches with claims of youth, thoughtlessness, the hardships and injustice of her subordinate condition. She'd tender me her remorse and apologies, perhaps she'd cry, we'd stumble toward some vaguely satisfactory compromise; it would be vintage Bergman, minus the Swedish. Standing at the threshold, she'd wrap her arms around herself, and we'd make false promises to see each other again. After I'd left, she'd keep the flowers or the chocolates just so she could throw them in the garbage or give them to the concierge. The American detective novel version was pretty exciting too. I'd tail her from her building's front door, memorizing her routine, and pick the perfect moment to confront her among acquaintances—a shopkeeper, for instance—and cause a scene by denouncing her in public. The plot twist in which the former transported convict finally catches up, decades later, with the sadistic camp guard, now a peaceable housewife well liked by her neighbors. Too grandiose and unrealistic, impractical for a guy like me who tries to live inconspicuously and within the law; but I've considered it all the same. I should have preferred instead to reenact the repentance of Madame Fichini in La Comtesse de Ségur's Les Vacances; that would give me the best part and satisfy my bent for maudlin endings. Sophie, a beautiful young woman, meets once more the dreadful shrew who mistreated her throughout her childhood. The wicked woman has asked to see her: she's grown very ugly and very poor, she's at death's door and prostrate with remorse. Madame Fichini bitterly regrets everything she put poor Sophie through; the latter hears her confession with deep emotion. As usual, the underhanded Countess pulls no punches in her summary of all the cruelties one can inflict on a defenseless child,

not one unfair punishment or painful caning is left out. Madame
Fichini has forgotten none of her own abuses, while Sophie, now
living a new, busy life of dress-up, pleasantries, and pious resolutions, has barely thought of them at all. And Sophie forgives,
anointed by a torrent of grateful tears from the dying woman,
for whom her noble outlook has opened the path to redemption
as she awaits her imminent eternal judgment. A little forced, I
know, but overall that's the way I saw things going for me, too.
Funnily enough, I never pictured her as being old in any of these
scenarios; it's true that I am still a child whenever I think of her.

In any case, she didn't seem that old when I saw her last winter, shuffling into church for my stepfather's funeral service. I recognized her immediately. She seemed smaller to me, a gray veil
pinned to her hair; I couldn't help thinking of those fine breasts
of her youth, long gone, but she was brisk, her gait steady, her
body slim; she had certainly continued to ride horses. There was
no mackintosh, and I was too far away to see if she was wearing flats. In that crowd where she knew no one, her expression
was neutral, but it could have been the face she wore routinely
in sorrowful circumstances, or perhaps she was genuinely sad-
dened by my stepfather's death, as were all of us to whom he
had never been anything but kind. He had helped her to rise
above her status as a domestic servant and to find a respectable
place among the few remaining nabobs of colonial society. I had
forgotten that episode and was not expecting to see her there.
As often happens when one has waited so long for something
and rehearsed so many scenarios in one's mind, it had practically no effect on me; I found the situation banal, practically
absurd; I experienced none of the sometimes incredibly violent
emotions that had disturbed me over the years; no bitterness
or rejection, just curiosity and the desire to observe her quietly
before she noticed and recognized me in turn. Being in church
called to mind all those endless low masses in the Spanish chapel

to which, draped in her black mantilla, she had dragged me; her lessons in church history had been illustrated with a morbid assortment of mortal sins and divine punishments. Now she was clearly less invested in ritual; her head was bare and she had no missal in hand. Perhaps she had broken from the church when she was no longer obliged to act as a director of conscience, or had she reviewed her principles in the light of foreign shores? No, the singular gesture, the solemn gaze, the unimpeachable correctness associated with that indefinable aura of severity and solitude made me feel that she hadn't really changed. The fact that her physical appearance was so little altered was another discouraging omen. As the observance proceeded, we were inevitably brought side by side. I greeted her soberly, in keeping with the circumstances, but in a purposefully casual, even light-hearted manner; her response was spectral, without warmth; for her this was clearly neither the time nor the place for displays of affection. It felt for me as if we had been instantly transported back to the old days when she was the inflexible guardian of the code of manners; we stayed that way for a moment, two effigies of constrained discretion, and then the moving crowd delivered us from one another. I began to feel that old malaise. My mother was watching her discreetly from a little farther off; she passed by her without a glance. I very much doubt that she had not noticed her. It was obvious that she wanted nothing to do with us or the past that we embodied. I should have been satisfied with this briefest of surprise encounters, which had bru-tally laid bare the futility of all my ambitious fantasies, but the opportunity, however dismal, was unique and I was desperate to milk it for at least one modicum of truth. As she prepared to leave the church ahead of the crowd, I waited on the portico to see her one last time; she began moving away across the square, but having grasped my intentions and hesitated a moment, she abruptly turned toward me. We were on neutral ground, people were gathering to talk in groups around us, and we were free to speak. But we didn't have much to say to each other in the end. While explicitly stating that she did not watch television, she offered me a few standard compliments; I asked her how she had organized her life, and she spoke of a little house near Toulouse to which she had retired and where she led a pleasant and uneventful existence. So I had been mistaken—the address in the telephone book was not hers—but I did not bring that up, it would have taken us in too deep. On the other hand, the funny thing was that she claimed to know where I lived; funnier still, I suggested that she write me, and I would be sure to write back. She seemed not to understand me; her reaction was perfectly normal, since my suggestion had made no sense at all. And that was it; the cathedral square was filled with people I had to greet, and I lost sight of her. In the car, my mother asked why I had been so friendly, and I didn't know what to say. Ultimately, what had struck me most was that, throughout our brief conversation, she had addressed me with the formal *vous*. She'd used *vous* with me all through my childhood, and I'd forgotten all about it.

The kind one came to our house two or three years after the cruel one left. It was late June, and my mother had hired her as a vacation helper. The nanny agency had called about a woman who had just left her alcoholic husband and had never been in service but had made a good impression at her interview. I was alert to that kind of detail, since after all we would be spending more than two months together at my grandmother's house in Évian. My mother was concerned about her competence; she had no references for cleaning, cooking, or ironing, while a fearsome dragon lady had been ruling the roost of servants at the villa for the past twenty years now. There was the added risk of the kind of melodramatic conflict that can ruin the vacation for an entire household. But there was no choice; the season was already too far along to find anyone else.

I was the one who opened the front door when she arrived. She looked like one of those women of the people that I'd seen in tragic movies or on the Metro. Ageless, heavy-set, thick chestnut hair parted in the middle, a plastic comb on either side, one eye that pointed slightly toward the other, and at least one gold tooth. She was lugging an enormous wicker trunk in which I immediately grasped she had crammed all her worldly possessions when she fled the drunkard's clutches. Children of wealth can smell tragedy and poverty, and it scares them, but she, contrarily, emitted a reassuring aura of strength and steadiness. She seemed not in the least intimidated and introduced herself merrily with a big smile that went straight to my heart. I knew from that very instant that she would be my friend. My mother arrived just then and they disappeared into the little parlor for a lengthy confab; I hoped she would stay. When the interview was over, she emerged with the same warm smile that gave her such a youthful turn, and mother said to me: "This is Simone. She'll be with us this summer. She will help around the house and look after you." I said nothing, but I must have looked pleased, which mother noticed. In those days, my grandmother spent only part of her holidays at the villa, my brothers spent the summer in England, and my mother shuttled between Paris and Évian with her new husband. At the far end of the property there was the house where my uncle and little cousins lived, but she and I would be alone together much of the time. We took the train down together the next day; she didn't need my help carrying the trunk, but in our compartment she opened it to show me her prize possession: a Singer sewing machine with which she made her own clothes. I had always thought that you found clothes ready-made in the stores and only had to buy them. The journey was quite a long one in those days, and we spent it telling each other a bit about ourselves. I was a child of around thirteen, timid and secretive, but well-defended and given to boasting; I described my school for her, portraying myself as the good student that I really wasn't, and made some tentative propositions concerning my desired vacation pursuits and schedule, just to see if she'd leave me alone. She had her orders, but I could tell that we would work it out. She said "riding," "tennis," "swimming pool" as if she were reciting a new lesson learned by heart, and I could tell that they were as alien to her as China. I negotiated movies into the roster of activities approved by my mother, which would require a much later bedtime than the official one; she had no problem with that so long as the film was appropriate. She would check it out in *Bonnes Soirées*, which she read every week, rather than consult the Catholic rating at the parish hall, because she was not a churchgoer. She wasn't against it, but she didn't go. This news was rather shocking, but it suggested the possibility of skipping mass. The Singer had whetted my appetite: I wanted to know more about her life before we met. She was reluctant to talk about it; she felt that such stories were not for children like me. Even so, I learned that she'd lost her mother when she was little; she couldn't describe her because she had no picture of her. Her father had remarried, to a woman who turned out to be very harsh and had made her suffer; she had raised her half-brothers and went to work in a factory at fourteen. All her pay went into the household; there wasn't a lot to eat, but they lived in the outer suburbs, so she was able to grow vegetables in a neighbor's garden. At seventeen, she married a boy from the factory; he was handsome and took her dancing, but he gradually let himself be led astray by his buddies and began to play around, drink, and beat her. She dearly loved a little sister from the same mother, but unfortunately the girl lacked all common sense and had to be watched. Her answers opened up a new world for me; although I was singularly lacking in reference points, her frankness and sense of modesty provided them for me. And so we got to know each other in that roasting, smoke-filled train—still pulled by a steam engine in those days—and we liked what we found in each other. I was afraid of how the dragon lady would react when we got there, but Simone knew how to deal with bitter, aging domestics; they got along very well and I found myself safe from the dark moods of someone who had made my life miserable the summer before.

I have always liked domestics. In the class warfare that used to rage in bourgeois apartments, I instinctively sided with the kitchen. The rogue tyranny of the cruel one, who had set herself up as a sort of foreman, had made me one of the victims and forged unhoped-for alliances. It was a painful inner dilemma, because I didn't want to disavow mother either, but in the end I knew that I would have her forever, whereas maids come and go. The household ran very smoothly, and with the influx of Spanish workers the Rue de La Pompe Metro station was beginning to look like La Rambla, but even so the old ways were over and done with. Servants had learned to rebel, negotiating their hours with fierce tenacity, and no longer thought twice about handing in their apron for a better position or even a better trade. Supply and demand were gradually changing places, and the days of a humble and submissive staff that blended into the furniture were fast running out. I happily adjusted to the new direction in household history; to this day I am obdurately uncomfortable with being waited upon. But I was almost overwhelmed by a feeling close to despair every time a maid left. I remember Suzanne coming to my bed in tears to give me a goodbye kiss on her last night; Magali who smelled of sweat and confided with a sigh how difficult it was to stay fresh with such work; Christiane the orphan, who had worked for a movie star and dreamed of becoming an artist; Héléna the saint, who refused to wash my hair in the bath because she was disturbed by my altogether childish body and all she wanted to do was

retire to a convent in Salamanca; Esther who wrote poems on
the lost children of the war in Spain and recited them to me
with tears in her eyes; Lucienne, impregnated by a man from
Martinique with whom she was madly in love; and Milagros,
gone off to try her luck in America with a debauched pianist. I
also remember the men very well, but it's not the same feeling—
that complicit affection that made me linger in the larder for my
afternoon snack and save my allowance to spend on little birthday
presents. And to my dying day I will never forgive myself for
failing to visit Berthe the laundry woman when she retired to
Sarreguemines toward the end of her life, even though I still
patch up the outfit she made for my stuffed elephant, and I can
still see her before me as an old lady in the Luxembourg Gardens, a look of exhaustion on her face and a crust of bread in her
hands, telling me as she walked away: "Well, at least you have
always been very kind, I must say." Women from the industrial
provinces with a whole lifetime of labor behind them, women
who smelled of the mine and servitude and had never known
any but men who'd been killed in the war or run off with bad
girls. They were far better educated than one might have imagined but had learned at such cost never to talk of themselves
and to stay in the background that they were rather alarmed
by the over-casual little master who disrupted their routine of
silence and solitude. Accents, manners, and faces from all over
the map. Women from Brittany, ancient sea-wives, belles of the
communist suburbs, girl-mothers who'd left their babies with
wet nurses in the countryside; from Berry, who still thought of
Paris as paved with gold and studied Madame's style with envy
and resentment. The Spanish women were a breed apart; coming from a backward country, they were ahead of their time;
often young and fun-loving, running in fierce packs, they felt
no constraint whatsoever in the presence of the rich and made
no secret of their plans to redistribute the wealth or of their

own personal ambitions; for them, a middle-class apartment was just the first skirmish on the battlefield. I knew a great deal about my comrades on the sixth floor because I also did some investigating when invited home by my classmates. Sometimes my enthusiasm betrayed me: some of them drank, stole, lied when they told me they loved me, but I knew all about it, it made no difference to me, one little betrayal meant nothing to a parlor renegade like me.

That year, thanks to Simone, Évian seemed less sad. Children don't appreciate a beautiful garden or the charm of a quiet family home. The little thermal city was blissfully hostile to youth, drowsy with vague memories of its golden years, echoing with a Savoyard drawl and remonstrations of decrepit vacationers in peaked caps and floral-print dresses, lousy with gloomy hotels that could be mistaken for sanatoriums, its streets and promenades lined with flowers ad nauseam, and yet as empty as a set for a post-apocalyptic science fiction movie the moment the shopkeepers lowered their metal gates. Even the sports I sought to engage in lacked appeal. The riding master was a bullying, foul-mouthed jockey, the tennis teacher an irascible and grasping old fogey, and the swimming pool a bolt-hole of heart-breaking temptations. Once in a while I'd strike up dreary, hopeless friendships with children of the provincial bourgeoisie, essentially blind and deaf and totally useless as companions in adventure. Their parents in their silvery Peugeots looked at me askance; they never asked me over; there were usually several families sharing a single rental villa, and there were already enough kids at home. The beautiful lake, Switzerland across the water, the towering mountains were all ignored.

Simone had never traveled, and found Évian to be quite lovely. She broadened our field of action by organizing excursions: we rode paddleboats on the lake; made the crossing to Lausanne with stops at the Innovation department store, a house of wonders, and ice-cream blow-outs on the dock at Ouchy; ascended to the top of the Mémises in a cable car, walking back down along a goat path where she accused me of trying to lose her; and visited the local chateaux, of which I'd never suspected there were so many. Chateaux were not so fun, and I'd yawn with boredom just to get her mad; my behavior dismayed her, and she'd grouse that it was shameful conduct in a young boy who always had his hand raised in class. But it was all a game; she knew very well that I preferred these excursions to hauling myself out to the riding school. I would complain about the distance and having to go everywhere by bike, but she was the queen of public transport and connecting routes, she knew by heart the timetables posted at the jetty. For someone who had but a smattering of geography and was afraid of Africa, where gorillas abduct white women into the jungle, as she'd read in one of her favorite magazines, she proved to have the soul of an intrepid explorer, voraciously curious and eager to learn. I went to the movies just about every night, I guess. She would not come with me; for her, the movies were not the truth; she would rather wait for me and dream of reality. No matter how I described it and tried to get her interested, she never took the bait—even an artistic lie is still a lie. She preferred to fish for stories in real life, which had served her up a few whoppers; those projected on the screen seemed perfectly dull by comparison.

In any case, I had never met someone so open. Her honesty was like a second skin, and if a situation was not to her liking, she chose not to speak of it. Nor did she care much for politics, the apostles of social vengeance, blowhards of any stripe; historical figures left her cold, and my sketchy lessons in that domain did nothing for her; she pleaded to being half deaf, which was true, because her stepmother had bashed in her ear with a poker. Oddly, despite her dislike of the movies and her visceral suspicion of storytelling, she had a poetic spirit; she pooh-poohed the sentimental songs on the radio, including those of Édith Piaf, whom I adored, but she loved listening to highbrow music and looking at art books in the library, and she admired all scientists and creative types as a class. She knew she had no reference points, she had no illusions about her own ignorance and inexperience, and she was the first to make fun of her own failings, without shame or swagger; but her original cast of mind could not be reduced to stereotypes about the wisdom of the common people or conform to my simplistic prejudices, educated little monkey that I was. She spoke what I thought to be the language of the working man, with the kind of colorful expressions featured in our primary school dictation exercises, but I cannot recall ever hearing her say a crude word or using vulgarity of any sort; she loathed swearing and did not think twice of reprimanding me, because it was hardly worth my parents' "bleeding themselves dry for my education" if I went around using "gutter language that would scare them silly." Moreover, did I really need my hair "to be declared a disaster area" or to "dress like a scarecrow" or to stuff myself as if "the table had been rented out"? I was too eager to please her to behave like "an escaped convict" in her presence. She had intuited the key—my years under the wicked one—without our having spoken of it; she made me understand that it was no reason to get everything mixed up. She cooked everything I loved to eat, adding a few mystery recipes that she claimed to be fortifying. Not too much dairy, which weighs on the liver, but French toast, veal heart with turnips, stuff for poor people that I found delicious.

One evening—surprise, surprise—she decided to come to the movies with me. She was very fond of Brigitte Bardot, whom she called "the Cutie," even though she'd never seen any of her films. At the time, the prevailing hypocrisy was to criticize her as a bad actress and a shameless dissolute hussy who made millions by behaving scandalously, but Simone was having none of

it. The Cutie was beautiful and free and practiced her profession
with passion, and that was why people were jealous of her. I
think they were running *Love Is my Profession* at Cinémonde,
a drama in which she raises her skirt for Jean Gabin and which
even *Bonne Soirée* had described as an abomination. You had
to have a really good reason to go see it; I had some trouble
following her reasoning, but I was no longer surprised by anything she did and approved her decision. But this time the cen-
sor, who had left me plenty of wiggle room in the past, was
intractable: the movie was forbidden to anyone under sixteen.
We arranged for me to stay at home; it would be my turn to wait
for the end of the show to hear the latest critique. The dragon
lady, who never missed a chance to heap venomous censure on
the Cutie, was delighted at the godsend and signed on without
being asked twice; they dolled themselves up and set off for their
encounter with the trollop. I had been asleep for ages when I
was rudely awakened by the racket of Simone and the dragon
lady's return, dead drunk. They stood swaying at the foot of
the stairs, having removed their shoes like philandering slapstick
husbands. One of them had fallen over and the other had picked
her up, but there had been no harm done; propping each other
up and clinging to the banister, they cast a wistful gaze at the
stairs still to climb, puffing and panting. Alarmed by the spectacle, I retreated to my room; they'd been too drunk to notice
me; there was more noise, some staggering footfalls, hollering,
and laughing, and then they went off to sleep, each to her own
place. I spent a bad night of nervous anticipation; children who
make enough stupid mistakes of their own fear the weaknesses
of adults, and that sudden eruption of chaos filled me with anxiety. Above all, I took it as a betrayal. It turned out that Simone,
whom I had thought to be as solid as a rock, was capable of
sinking abruptly into drunkenness and bedlam; I went over the
stories she'd confided in me and saw a different life, darker and

shabbier, in which women tippled and loitered in cafés with the men. Obviously, I had a hard time imagining that there could be seedy dives and fellows with feverish eyes in the dead zone that was Évian at night, but she had definitely damaged her case by dragging down the dragon lady, who never drank more than a thimbleful of white wine; worst of all, that night I was forced to acknowledge that Simone had forgotten me.

The next morning, tottering toward the kitchen for my breakfast, I ran into her as she was vacuuming; she looked a little haggard still, ashen, bags under her eyes as if she'd been crying. I had no wish to kiss her, and my air of false detachment alerted her immediately to the fact that I'd witnessed the awful scene. She turned off the machine and watched me pass by, her arms dangling, silent, her face the picture of pure anguish and more squinty than usual. In the kitchen, the dragon lady was sniffling over her pots and pans with her back to me; she was a guarded person who had also had her share of unhappiness in life. Broadly speaking, a childhood on welfare, the shame of being a teenage mother whose kid was taken to be raised by the nuns and grew up to be a lowlife, the bitterness of a life drowned in the kitchen sink—all such stories tend to resemble one another. She brooded in solitude, the kind of person who won't ever admit when her head's on the block. The morning passed in a gloomy torpor. I played in the garden with my little cousins, but my heart wasn't in it, and Simone bustled in and out of the house casting furtive glances my way. Then she came to see me; we sat on the edge of a low wall by the hydrangeas; I had to listen to her, she needed to speak to me. She asked if I wanted her to leave; there was a train leaving for Paris that night, my mother would be arriving in two days, it was a short enough time, the dragon lady could chip in, all I had to do was say so and she would go. She stared at the ground, there was a tremor in her voice, it was sad. I saw the summer split open like a rotten piece of fruit; I was panic-stricken but tried not to show it; I was totally opposed to the idea that she might leave me. As I said nothing, she began to talk about the crazy time she'd had the night before; she spoke slowly, choosing each word carefully; I think her biggest fear was exacerbating my confusion; she was intent on explaining as clearly as possible just how her old "bitch of a life" had caught up with her—the expression struck me because it was so unexpected coming from her. The film had been really good, she had to admit; they'd both been taken up by the story and the Cutie had been perfect, so moving, you could tell that playing the role of a poor girl who does wrong to get out of trouble came naturally to her. Even the dragon lady had cried at the end. They were so depressed when it was over that they had stopped at the only bistro open to recover their composure. They didn't know what they were going to tell me because it wasn't really a film for children, and by the time they'd talked through how they couldn't tell me, they'd shared the stories of their respective lives, one fortifying glass following another. *Voilà*, that was it, she'd told me everything there was to tell and hoped that I would understand. She added that yes, it was true that she used to drink now and then in the old days, back when her husband beat her, back when she still loved him and thought she could hold on to him by following his lead. And now she was waiting; it was my turn. But I said nothing, I was too afraid of saying the wrong thing and losing her, and my heart bled for her pain, too. I just hugged her with all my strength and asked if she'd forgotten that we were supposed to have a picnic in the mountains the next day; and then I went off to make bows and arrows for my little cousins behind the hydrangeas. She stayed a while, thoughtful, still staring at the ground, and then went in to prepare lunch. She did not leave, we had our picnic, and we waited for mother. Soon after she arrived, my mother said to me: "That girl is perfect, everything is shipshape, and it's just amazing how well you two get along." We shared a new secret and I knew that I wouldn't have to hide the wine bottles. She'd never touch them again, that much I was certain of.

We argued a lot; Mr. Know-It-All got on her nerves the way he was always treating her like an ignoramus, he'd end up driving her around the bend with his questions. That was the primordial conflict. But she also accused me of being evasive, whiny, and a big spendthrift, a real rich kid with a silver spoon in his mouth who thought he could get away with anything, put on airs, and didn't know the value of money; he'd have been less stuck up if his father had sent him off to the factory at fourteen, as hers had done. She'd suddenly refuse to take any more lip, I'd answer back, voices would be raised, I'd say something regrettable, and we'd end up muttering in our separate corners. It's true that I must have been irritating with my need to always have an opinion on everything, but in my defense I had not had many moments in the sun in the days of the cruel one. We didn't sulk long, we'd make up just as soon as we'd fallen out, very quickly, without fuss, as if nothing had happened, until the next time. I became her own Bébé Cadum once again, the one in the ads with milk coming out of his nose; I was not entirely taken with the compliment, but this was no time to fall back on my dignity. She had no children, or rather she had almost had several and had lost them before birth; she didn't like to talk about it, but I sensed a connection with her husband's brutality; I could understand about the Bébé Cadum thing. Indeed, in everyday life I was her friend, her companion, almost her man. These arguments were a wonderful experience for me, my first with a grown-up without fear of a backlash; my mother was different; I suppose she was the next logical candidate in line, but even though I knew she would never lift a hand to me I still dared not approach her pedestal. But with Simone we could fight tooth and nail, since she didn't hold it against me. I trusted her, we were not allowed to go to bed angry at each other. She could have tamed an entire gang of young hoodlums on parole. When vacation was over, my mother asked her to stay with us. I held my breath, I tried to be clever by saying I didn't mind if she did, but I really needed her when the school year got off to a bad start.

My schoolwork had deteriorated in recent months; one of the youngest in the grade, I had barely scraped through and understood nothing about math and was disgusted by Latin. The awkwardness inspired in me by contact with my classmates, some of them now full-fledged teenagers, only got worse and was a source of continual anxiety. My mother was busy with my charming new stepfather, to whom I was only slowly warming, having been so fond of his predecessor. My father and brothers lived next door, yet that was another world from which I thought myself excluded. I gradually began to withdraw into myself once again. It was Simone who saved me from a scholastic shipwreck and averted any major crisis. I was somewhat independent now; she was not the only one working at the apartment—there were guests, commotion, the distractions of Paris, and yet I always felt closest to her. We could no longer talk to each other as we had in Évian, we'd lost our taste for arguing, but we understood each other tacitly; our connection was as strong as ever. It was expressed in tiny gestures—her smile when I entered the kitchen, my attentiveness when she sighed with worry over her flighty sister, the same way of riding the rhythm of the days, our shared habits, and the occasional laugh riot arising from our common derisive sense of humor. Plus, I had no sense of having betrayed my mother, despite the social abyss between them; they had a genuine affection for each other. Simone suffered from no sense of inferiority and admired her unreservedly, the way she loved the Cutie; mother held to a certain idea of the people's wisdom and was delighted by Simone's intelligence and dignity; relations between them were easy and natural.

As for the movies, I had won my case. Worn down, but still

continually protesting that it was a big waste of time, she agreed to accompany me to a show now and then, but with conditions— not to the Champs-Élysées, where rich people watched foreign movies in the original language with subtitles that hurt her eyes, and not to police movies, and no violence; she read enough crime stories in the papers. On the other hand, she'd found a nice little theater with cheap seats on the Boulevards; you needed to get there on the Metro, change trains, a whole adventure; they showed what she called lovely movies, like those of Fernandel, which were really dumb but made you laugh, she said, or the exploits of Joselito, another Bébé Cadum, though somewhat swarthier, but above all the melodramas of Sarita Montiel, who brought a tear to her eyes despite her ongoing aversion to sentimental songs. "Cleaning-ladies' movies," sniggered my school friends, who were into Eddie Constantine; and here I had been thinking that she sacrificed her days off to come with me. Even now it bothers me when people make fun of those old movies, which really ought to be revived every so often. She knew I was struggling in class, and the truth of the matter was obvious to her: the teachers were unfair, which was not altogether false, given class sizes of forty kids or more, where overwhelmed educators ground out their lessons by rote and openly played favorites. She couldn't help me with my homework, but she stopped by regularly anyway to lean over my shoulder, to see how I was coming along, and whenever I was plunged into despair she became my sports coach, distracting me from suffering with a hot chocolate to give me strength and set off again on a solid footing. Out of loyalty to my mother she was reluctant to write excuse notes, but she was willing to sign my workbook in my mother's absence, seeing only the least bad grades, initialing it in the same furious manner that she settled accounts with cheeky tradesmen.

One evening I was supposed to construct a cone out of Bristol board for the next day's math class, where the teacher was a real piece of work, and I was on the verge of a humiliating defeat. No matter how I drew outlines on the board, cut them out, glued my little heart out, tried over and over, that blasted cone would not stand up straight; I couldn't close the bottom and it leaned irremediably. It was getting late, I was beginning to panic, and the threatening shadow of the piece of work darkened the room. Simone found me in full-blown meltdown, blubbering at the center of a pile of shredded cardboard and crushed glue-tubes, being cruelly taunted by a mob of wobbly cones. She had never seen me in such a state; she ordered me to bed and promised that she would find a way to finish the cone. I can still see her as I saw her as I drifted off to sleep, in the light of my little desk lamp, her hair tousled and eyes agog, completely absorbed by the effort of solving the puzzle. She inspected my army of lame rejects, pored over my drawings, examined the casualties, sought the key hidden in the pages of my geometry textbook. Sleep overtook me to the sound of scissors snipping and the smell of fresh glue. The next morning, there were a good half-dozen cones as wobbly as mine; she hadn't been able to do it; one was in even worse shape than all the rest, all twisted, crumpled and sickly. We agreed that it was the best representative of our efforts and the absurdity of the undertaking, and I took the monster to class, where it caused a sensation; never has an F been received with such a light heart.

At the end of the school year, having miraculously escaped being held back, it was my turn to go to England. I was unafraid and quite excited at the prospect. I can't remember our goodbyes at all. She wasn't there when I got back; my mother said that she was with her ailing sister in the country and would return soon. I had brought her back a pudding, which I was sure she would like; I moped about the apartment with my pudding like a dog seeking its master. Then my mother took me to the South for August and Évian was no longer uppermost in my thoughts. At vacation's end, the pudding was still in the refrigerator and she still had not returned. My mother had hired someone new, and people said I had changed a lot, the standard allusion to the influence of English girls. I finally received a very affectionate letter in which she explained that she had met a really nice man who was ready to settle down with her. They would be living far from Paris; I mustn't hold it against her; she would always remember me. Under my interrogation, my mother confessed that Simone had known this man for several months; she'd been very worried about how I would react and ultimately hadn't had the heart to tell me; it seems that he was an Algerian who had gone over to the French, mother didn't know much more, she'd met him once in the hallway on the top floor, where he rented a service room in the garret; in any case, not at all the servant type, more a fellow with a little style who stood out in the servants' quarters. Simone loved him a great deal and would not have gone with any old person just to change her life. I should be happy that she had drawn the lucky number; indeed, I should not be selfish. I did not answer her letter; I ate the pudding, which had gone dry and bitter. I never talked about Simone again. My mother told her friends that she was relieved that I'd been able to put her out of my mind so easily; they responded that it's childhood's gift to be able to recover from disappointment so quickly. Children never recover quickly from the feeling of having been abandoned by a kind woman; it is their first step toward death, and it frightens them.

Later on, I did forget her for years. There was so much going on. But then it came back, as it had with the cruel one, in moments of panic, a little worse each time. Obviously, I'd forgiven her for having left me without warning, but I needed her, and in the tenacity of my childhood love I still believed that she would help me, come to my rescue; I knew it wouldn't be the same thing, of course, but if I could only bask once more in her affection and share our memories it would prove that I was not mistaken about the past and might help to soothe my anxieties. Intuitively, I was sure she'd had many good years with her man, but I also wanted her to know what she had been to me; I was afraid the day would come when it would be too late to tell her. No doubt she remembered me too, she must have seen me on television, but did she wonder if I still thought of her? Ultimately, all the usual reasons why we fixate on reuniting with those we have loved dearly and of whom we have long had no news. I had no clue how to find her—her trail had gone cold. I didn't even know what name she had taken after she'd moved on. She was clearly a master at vanishing.

It was pure chance that finally put me on to her: a cousin of my mother's was looking for a new apartment and asking around among the nannies in her neighborhood; she ran into Simone, who introduced herself after hearing her name. She asked what had become of us, my name came up several times in the course of the conversation, and she said that didn't want to call us because it would make her cry and cry. The cousin mentioned it to my mother, who had heard me bring up Simone's name recently for the first time in years; I got her address. It dragged on for months; there was never anybody in the concierge's lodge; one tenant explained to me that she'd only been there a few weeks to fill in for a sick concierge; then the insurance company that owned the building had decided to hire a security firm; mailboxes had been installed and the lodge was shut. It wasn't as nice, the tenant asserted, but there wasn't much you could do about it, young people are no longer interested in a job like that, with all its responsibilities, the lodges are too small, and the owners are reluctant to be saddled with old concierges who entrench themselves and then claim their retirement benefits. She was barely able to recall Simone, a rather forward and very friendly woman whose husband washed the tenants'

cars in the garage, the most obliging folk but they hadn't stayed
very long; in any case she didn't know where they had gone. My
mother became involved in my inquiry and wrote to the insurance company several times before she got a response; it went
on forever, I grew worried, I had never known her age and my
calculations had no factual basis; I tried to picture a fat lady
with hair like a string mop, but the picture was murky, features
soon fade when you have no photographs, despite having rum-
maged through all of mother's shoeboxes; alas, she throws out
a great deal when she tidies. We finally received a letter from
the insurance company: Simone lived in Sainte-Geneviève-des-
Bois, and they sent her address and phone number. I was not
in Paris at the time and my mother called her without waiting
for my return; she was afraid that something sad might have
happened and wanted to spare me further disappointment; she
was acting as she had done that first time, more than forty years
earlier, when I was a child; that made sense. Simone answered
the phone. She sounded barely surprised and very pleased. Her
voice was strong, but she had been through some bad times of
late; her man had died and she herself was recovering slowly
from a serious operation, she was alone and almost never left
the house. My mother told her that we wanted to come see her,
and Simone said that she would be really delighted; she would
make us lunch, and we should give her some advance warning
so should could prepare veal heart; she knew I liked that. This
one time, however, I wanted to go alone, and I chose the following Sunday to do so.

It's April. I ride my moped through the southern suburbs. It's a
fine, sunny morning. I know Sainte-Geneviève-des-Bois well: the
Russian retirement home and cemetery; the portraits of the impe-
rial family in the abandoned central building; the tombs beneath
the birches, those of Yusupov, Tarkovsky, and many others; the
lovely chapel designed by Benois; and the surrounding streets

which a Communist town council had scrupled to name after
Lenin or Maurice Thorez, without pity for the poor defeated
Whites. I had been there often; if only I'd known that Simone
lived just nearby. After the Parc de Sceaux, I get a little lost in the
maze of avenues lined with large affluent villas, and then I find my
way again at Longjumeau, the first orchards and fields. Sainte-
Geneviève-des-Bois is far; it's almost the countryside. There's not
much traffic, the spring air is delicious, I want to take my time, I
feel that lump around my heart that comes from wanting something very much. I haven't told Simone I'm coming; I want it to
be a surprise. I have no trouble finding her street.

It's a pleasant neighborhood of modest, well-kept houses with
little gardens in full bloom, sheet metal lean-tos for the cars and
building supplies. There's no poverty around here. Simone's
house looks taller than the others because its roof slopes upward
toward the back; even in the 1960s, suburban architects tried for
some modern effect. I try to see her through the windows, but
I'm at the foot of the house and can make out nothing through
the lace curtains. I ring the gate bell, then the one at the front
door; she was already a little deaf back then, it must have gotten worse; finally I try to open the door, but it's locked. And yet
she'd said that she spent most of her time at home; had I come at
a bad time? It's always an ordeal whenever you take old people
on a Sunday outing—you visit family, lunch goes on forever, it
takes hours and hours; this obsession of mine for always showing up unannounced has led me astray once again; I tell myself
it's too bad but never mind; I'll sit and wait until nighttime if
I must. Perhaps I'll take a walk in the Russian cemetery in the
meantime. The family in the house across the street is getting
ready for a barbecue, and I ask them if they've seen Simone. The
father assures me that she may not hear the doorbell but that
she's certainly at home; he confirms that she doesn't go out, it
hurts too much to walk since her operation; her neighbors go

shopping for her—all her neighbors, since she's done so many favors for everyone that it's only normal to stick with her now, especially since the death of her "companion," a guy like her, always ready to lend a hand. He says "companion" with the same friendly inflection he uses when speaking of her. I surmise that she never did marry her man; she had left the first so suddenly, there's no time for divorce when you're running away. As a matter of fact, the neighbor himself doesn't know what name she goes by; sometimes it's her maiden name on her mail, sometimes that of her companion; the mailman's used to it. So he calls her Simone, as everyone does, it's easier that way. It makes him laugh, he must like the idea of her as a woman with a somewhat shady past; when he recognizes me from television it only confirms that impression. Listening to him, I get the distinct feeling that Simone is a kind of star in her neighborhood. She's housebound—that's old age for you, he adds with a smile—but he has a copy of the key and comes back with his key ring. We go in, it's spotless in there and smells of wax polish, he calls out loudly to her, we pass down the hallway, there she is before me, squinting to get a better view of the stranger who reminds her of someone. She's wearing a housecoat, she's not so fat, there's little gray in her hair, one eye still wanders, her complexion glows, it's not that of an old lady. She gasps when I tell her who I am but does not look astonished. We hug somewhat awkwardly, I'm a good two heads taller than she, but she declares: "It's really you, Mister Frédéric, I'd have recognized you anywhere!" I wasn't expecting that, it rings strange in my ear. Just as the cruel one addressed me with the formal *vous*, so too had I completely forgotten that "Mister Frédéric." The neighbor withdraws. I don't quite know what to say; although I'd rehearsed it all down pat; it now feels like it would fall flat here in this house into which I've stolen like a burglar. We exchange family news; she knows about my father and grandmother, she doesn't say how she

knows and I don't push for an explanation; it's possible that she
has kept up contacts of which I have never known. She shows
me her living room: everything's neat and orderly, small pieces
in imitation mahogany, antimacassars, a library with an ency-
clopedia and books on foreign countries. It's simple, but nothing
is pretentious or ugly. On the wall, cheap color prints of Italian landscapes that you might find in the flea market. Certain
details, such as the way she's arranged her knickknacks, remind
me of how she had admired my mother's taste and talent with
interiors. Her bed is made up on the sofa in front of the television, she no longer goes up to her room because of her legs, and
she watches TV late into the night. No movies, still no movies,
she points out with a smile, but documentaries that teach you
things, and also Ardisson and Fogiel because they're funny and
often have interesting guests on their shows; this is no time to
ham it up, I suppose she hasn't seen me on the box as often as I'd
thought. On the sideboard is a photo of a handsome man with
strongly defined features, olive skin, a bold gaze. She speaks of
him without pathos; she misses him but he's also still there for
her; after he died, she remembered that he had left a daughter
behind in his own country, a daughter he had never seen again
because he was a *political* refugee. She says "political refugee"
with a kind of pride. I understand that there is to be no talk
of *harkis* here; the *harkis* are the vanquished, history's suckers,
whereas he, the political refugee, was a man who had to start
from scratch, true, but he'd made a success of himself; you only
had to look at the photo on the sideboard to see that. She had
found the daughter's address in Algeria and brought her over
for the probating of the will. It all worked out well in the end,
but it was a little dodgy to start with, since Simone was not married and had no right to anything. The daughter must have been
dumbfounded by all this French propriety and accepted the split
that Simone had offered—the savings for the child of a different

life, the house for the wife who was not a wife. I think of all the work she put into it, the visa she wangled by harassing town hall for the paperwork, all the trouble she went to for the sake, yet again, of unimpeachable honesty. Even so, I express a certain awe, and she tries again—after everything he endured and all he gave her, the happiness of their reborn lives, the least he deserved was that she keep the faith and take the risk of losing everything. Suddenly I feel tired, not from the long moped ride, but from the weight of those forty-five years of life without me, which fall upon me like a world of sorrow.

She was about to have lunch. She'll make me a nice steak, and if I feel like having a bottle of wine, there are some excellent ones in the cellar; she can't get down there anymore, but they must still be there. And if I want to see the house while the food is cooking, I can just give myself the tour. I go down, I go up, everything is spic and span, and so curiously familiar; it's as if I were falling into old routines, visions of the Évian house superimpose themselves in my mind; she must have thought of it as she was furnishing the place. Back in the kitchen with her, I try to talk about the past, but she's reluctant to follow me down that path; if I dwell on a particular detail—our outings, the little movie house on the Boulevards—she becomes evasive; she doesn't remember the cone that wouldn't stand up, and she no longer likes Brigitte Bardot, who turned out badly; when I press a little more, she becomes almost aggressive. Has she forgotten the little professor in love with his own knowledge, all those lectures I inflicted on her? I see now that it had been a bad time for her, washed away by the happy years that followed, a rather gloomy entr'acte that, fortunately, did not last too long; with hindsight, after all, it was a maid's life, with me as little master, perfectly nice no doubt, but used to being served and fussed over. She doesn't put it that way, she has no intention of reproaching me or expressing resentment, and yet she has overthrown my entire picture of the past by choosing words that, while not too harsh, are nevertheless fair and sincere. She will not allow my story to eclipse her own. I see emerging a different child whose existence I had never suspected, that Mister Frédéric she continues to pin on me, while I dare not ask her to stop. At the same time, it's like the old days; me in the kitchen, sitting at my plate, and she bustling around the stove and asking if it's cooked enough. The lump that's weighed on my heart since my arrival suddenly bursts and floods through me, and I start to weep uncontrollably; she's so sorry, she didn't mean to hurt me, she's so happy to see me again; come now, I mustn't get into such a state, I'm not Bébé Cadum any more. The expression leapt from her mouth without warning, surprising and almost confounding her. She must be asking herself if this guy blubbering at her table is a little nuts, where's he planning to go with this? Yes, I am a little nuts for having thought about her all these years, for having tracked her down so relentlessly, for having plunged into this solitary visit, which has only sharpened my regrets. She sits down beside me, she takes my hand, she calls me Frédéric, I sense that she's moved, she too is looking to the past now, she had stowed it all away carefully and here it is, spread out again before her, and she doesn't know what to make of it. I calm down, we grow silent, she suggests we drink our coffee in the garden. If I could just fetch chairs from the shed, she'll join me but it takes her time to get down the back stairs, one step at a time. There are two bikes in the shed, she must have taken spins with her man to the Russian cemetery, where there are still some woods. The afternoon drifts along very gently; she tells me of her flowers and her fruit trees. She tends to them every day, at her own pace and despite the pain of getting about; people come to visit, she's lost touch with her little sister, who behaved badly toward her, but her half-brothers come to see her. Her drunken husband eventually died, the municipality where she worked pays her a small pension, it's not much but it's enough for her, at her age one's needs are few and she never gets bored. She feels much better since her operation, the doctor told her that she still has a long life ahead of her, and that delights her. Here in this garden, where we shift our chairs every so often to follow the sun, I finally find her as I knew her, with her good cheer and avid curiosity. I tell her about my work, my travels; she's not afraid of the gorillas in Africa anymore—she thought they looked so unhappy when she saw them for the first time at the zoo with her man.

When I get up to leave, she insists on accompanying me to my moped, and she seems to be walking a little better. I promise to send her postcards from my vacation and to come back with my mother in the fall, as planned. The neighbors have put away their barbecue, the street is deserted, everything is peaceful. She embraces me, tells me not to push myself too hard, to take better care of myself. I have a feeling that we may never see each other again. I strap on my helmet, pull away; at the corner I see her one last time as she enters the house, which still looks too tall.

It's strange: the cruel one, the kind one, with whom I have never ceased to live—I didn't count for much with either of them in the long run.

carmen

carmen

carmen

Carmen is hurried on the phone. Friendly, but hurried. I sense that my unexpected call bothers her; I understand all too well that there's nothing more irritating than people we've met in passing who suddenly show up in our lives after years of absence as if we had nothing else to do but drop all our commitments to see them. We speak in English, her voice is pleasant and warm, crisply inflected—the voice of a woman who has to make herself heard; I picture a large office, busy schedule, meetings; I make chitchat and congratulate her on her apparent success, I play the role of one who has called just to touch base; but the surprise and the irritation have passed. It took only a few moments on the line to revive that which will never be said; I see her now as if I were by her side; she forgets about the glowing computer screen, she motions to her assistant to sit down and wait, perhaps she looks out the window, away into the magnificent Madrid summer that work had all but wiped from her mind but now strikes her in all its glory. It would be too stupid not to see each other, even if I'm only here a short while, she'd be very pleased to see me again, she insists, really very pleased. She suggests I meet her at her place that evening; we'll have dinner nearby or stay at home if she's had time to whip something up; it will be just the two of us—he won't be there. She gives me the address and I take it down as if I didn't know it. I had gone by just after arriving and had lingered a moment, looking at the balcony and the closed shutters. It was the hour of siesta, and the weather was decidedly fine.

I had obtained her phone number from a secretary at the Ministry of Foreign Affairs when I had vague hopes of running into her again. The secretary told me that *el señor Embajador* had taken up his post in Copenhagen but that his wife divided her time between Denmark and Spain, where she ran the local branch of an international organization. That was news to me after all this time of keeping my own counsel and entertaining the occasional lucid thought that it would certainly be wiser to have done with it once and for all and to draw a line through the past. The secretary was very nice but a little suspicious. She asked me if I were a friend of the family and I said, "Yes, I am," in a light-hearted and reassuring tone that must have come out sounding very cute in my poor Spanish. I must be the friend from Paris, she added, from which I concluded that he had probably tried now and then, in vain, to track me down. To make things simple, I explained that I was an old friend, going back more than thirty-five years; convinced, she gave me Carmen's work number; not her home number, to be sure, she still had her doubts and was not willing to go quite that far.

Carmen must be between forty-five and fifty years old; she's a little younger than he is and he's a year or two younger than me,

I reckon as I observe her discreetly. She has changed very little: classically beautiful, well-balanced features, slim, gorgeous figure. Her youthful spirit is intact, and the traces of time are light, just perceptible enough to make Carmen even more moving to me. Women of earlier generations teetered into obscurity and old age the moment their children reached adulthood, but all that changed a long time ago. She has that combination of stylishness and lack of snobbery that characterizes the Spanish upper classes and has always made them attractive to me; at the same time, she's unmistakably a woman of breeding—something about her hairstyle, her sober and soigné bearing, the discreet gold chain. It's easy to peg her as an ambassador's wife, the branch manager of an international agency. It's always a rather odd experience for me to discover the acquaintances of my youth looking just like my parents used to look.

Her apartment is superb, without ostentation, exactly what I would have imagined for myself if I had to live in Madrid: large, sun-filled rooms overlooking the Plaza de Oriente and the Palacio Real, overstuffed sofas, books, family furnishings. Carmen tells me they used to live in a villa beyond Castellana, on the Meseta, when it was still half-wild, before entire neighborhoods popped up like mushrooms there in the final years of Franco. There was a garden; it was great for the kids. But he didn't care for the area, it was too residential and too new, and since he and Carmen would be alone together once the children had grown, they had found this apartment, which was more to their taste. It was Carmen who had handled the negotiations with the former owners because, in their twosome, it is always she who takes care of such things. The children are finishing up their studies: the boy is working with an NGO in Afghanistan for the summer months, the girl is still studying for exams and is asleep in her room because she has a test in the morning. I would have liked to see her, but she doesn't know me and thus there's no reason for her to want to meet me; they each have a girlfriend and boyfriend that they go out with as part of a larger gang; they get along very well with their father, the girl even a little better than the boy, Carmen thinks; it's funny but I can't manage to remember the children's names. We end up eating in; it's much more pleasant that way, an excellent cold supper fixed in the superbly equipped kitchen. As I push the rolling table I pass the sleeping girl's door; she's left the radio on, playing Eminem or something like that, which would make for strange sleep—come to think of it, if she gets along so well with her father she must know who I am. Through the wide-open window in the dining room, we watch the royal family's American limousines gliding by in the distance. There's an official visit tonight, and a gala dinner is being held in the palace for an African president. In Copenhagen, Carmen accompanies her husband to such receptions.

Carmen and I know precisely where we stand. We both love the same man, and he has devastated us both. For me, it's ancient thunder that continues to rumble; for her it's the story of her life. She has the advantage of having held on and built a family with him. I can intuit the pain, the tempests of intense grief, the repudiations, everything she must have gone through. Poor little Spanish girl, just barely done with her schooling and only slightly tainted by the peace-and-love ethos current among her peers at the grim Franco school of manners, a young girl in love, so eager to do the right thing, more innocent than was reasonable—how did she ever manage to acknowledge the impossible? She seems to have become much more solid than when I saw her in New York some ten years earlier, crushed by all the secrecy, the comings and goings, the betrayals he'd subjected her to, as well as his absolute need for her. Real love feeds on itself, it ceases to demand that which it is not offered, and obviously it takes a great deal of time; and perhaps she has had her revenge. In any case, I get the impression that she is proud to have held

on, not to have left him; it is she and she alone who has got from
him the most he is capable of giving, whereas I have never really
had the right to speak. I admire and envy her, she has succeeded
where I was doomed to fail; and I thank her from the bottom of
my heart because she treats me tenderly and with a compassion
that, though unspoken, feels good and consoles me a little.

And yet, while Carmen and I have no trouble speaking to each
other, we still go at it like two injured people who might get hurt
if they touched; we tacitly take certain fundamental precautions;
even though the wound is over there, in Copenhagen, it would
only take a little thing to reopen it here, in the beautiful nocturnal floodlighting of the royal palace, bleeding over the cold
salmon and vanilla ice cream, between us two who calmly share
the grandeurs and servitude of the ambassadorial condition; a
recollection that is too specific, a detail that betrays an impetuous
emotion could lead to catastrophe. We are engaged, all in all, in
a sort of subtle ritual; the important stuff must remain hidden.
It's in the fissures, the voids, the margins; it is in our silences that
we speak of him.

Carmen takes good care of her in-laws, stops by to see them
almost every day. They must be very old by now; she confirms
that they are indeed very frail but their minds are still clear. Her
father-in-law is annotating his memoirs, going back to the days
before the civil war when he crisscrossed Spain with Federico
García Lorca's wandering theater troupe; her mother-in-law
has returned to strict religious practice and never misses a Real
Madrid match on TV. In Paris, where his father was posted in
the late 1960s—it's a family in which the post of ambassador
seems to be handed down from father to son—I felt an indefinable sense of transgression every time I entered their house;
I was barely out of my teens and shared the ideas current in
my social circle and among students my age about the Franco
regime—the Caudillo's Spain was a plague-stricken country and

its diplomats were considered to be agents of dictatorship. But nothing about them was recognizable from such stereotypes: welcoming, cultivated, remarkably broadminded, they attracted me all the more in that my Parisian friends, who shunned them tenaciously, had a hard time accepting that such a flip side might even exist. Even as I spent more and more time at their house, I avoided being alone with the father—I was afraid he would see straight through me, and I modeled my diffidence on the barely concealed animosity his son bore toward him. It seems that he's a very nice old man, very gentle, indulgence itself; I was certainly wrong to fear him. Conversely, I sought out the mother, whom I thought as beautiful as Cyd Charisse, and our conversations on history, poetry, and the movies we saw on television were flattering to my ego. It was very unusual for me to converse with adults in those days, and I assimilated her into the increasingly impassioned love I felt for her son. She certainly must have suspected something, but she never made the least allusion to it; I think she sensed that I was lost and was touched by that. When he returned to Madrid because Paris had absolutely nothing to offer him, I continued to see them from time to time: they took me to the theater to hear Renée Faure in *The House of Bernarda Alba* and out to eat once or twice; my hangdog bearing must have told them everything they needed to know, but they were the very souls of discretion. My heart wasn't in it anymore, I was capable neither of confessing nor of lying. Fortunately, the diplomatic life is all departures. I followed the rest of his life in the papers.

Carmen suggests we call them, and I may never have another opportunity to hear their voices. Her mother-in-law answers the phone; they've been watching David Beckham's arrival in Madrid on the news and are delighted, it's good for Real. Carmen preps them a little for the surprise, speaking of a young friend from the old days in Paris; it was a difficult time, rather troubled, I can sense them struggling to recall on the other end of the line, they didn't really have many French friends back then. Almost thirty-five years later, I could easily understand if they've forgotten me entirely. She recognizes me immediately by my voice. Hers is untouched by age, and her rather singsong French is still impeccable. She sounds genuinely pleased to hear from me; I ask her jokingly if it's better than the advent of David Beckham; she laughs and tells me it's much better. I can hear him growing agitated at the other end of the room, she explains to him that it's me, she returns to me and adds that he's very pleased, too. She's sorry to hear that I'm leaving the next day and urges me to come see her the next time I'm in Madrid, but I'll have to do it soon, they're nearing the end of their lives. I protest a little out of politeness, but she gaily specifies further that yes indeed, *al fin del fin*. I'm afraid this is tiring for her, I tell her how much she has meant in my life, we aren't always sure how other people see us; she answers that she knows, she has always known, with utmost certainty, and then she asks if I've ever seen Dreyer's *The Passion of Joan of Arc* again, the two of us having watched it together on the television in the large sitting room on the Avenue Marceau. I have seen it again, as has she; isn't it *our* film? We exchange a few more words in very tender good-bye, to convince ourselves that it is not a final farewell. I really feel like crying after I hang up. It's nighttime now: Madrid is farther south than Paris, so the darkness falls faster in the summer; Carmen's eyes glisten in the half-light, she turns away and switches on the lamp.

Later, I ask to see the little parlor with the framed photographs. There aren't many; he's taken most of them with him to Copenhagen. I recognize the house in Mojacar, on the Alicante coast, where it was so hot in the summer that the women there wore veils under their straw hats to protect themselves from the sun, as they do in the Maghreb just across the water; he had been so happy summering in that house as a child that I can describe it without ever having seen it. It was sold or divided, I've stopped listening very closely to Carmen, I'm thinking of something else: he's in a tropical garden, he must be thirteen or fourteen, he's staring straight ahead, unsmiling and with an obstinate expression on his face—Guatemala, no doubt, he told me that living there was like being in an ersatz United States, driving around in air-conditioned Dodges with the radio blaring and the mind empty, and he added that it had been good for him, as he only liked withdrawn and silent children. More family pictures, which I examine as if they were of my own family, and then those of their wedding, which I had cut out from *Hola* when I stumbled across them by chance; in fact, traumatized by heartache, I regularly leafed through that relic of the 1970s "people's press," looking for something. He had worn the uniform of the diplomatic corps, dark with a few silver stripes corresponding to his subordinate rank at the time; she is wearing one of those white dresses that just melt the old-maid cousins. He's playing the good boy role, sober and reverential, surely sincere at that particular moment; she gazes at him in radiant joy, she is so lucky; and I am just like her, I'm well aware of it, he's Tyrone Power, the true son of Cyd Charisse. I do not dare ask if they were married by his older brother, a young priest who used to sleep with him when he was little. That is, before taking his vows of celibacy; we all deal with these things in our own way.

I'm not feeling very well, I claim exhaustion following my long journey, I think it might be best for me to leave. She'll call him later in Copenhagen, he'll be furious at not having spoken to me, but it's his own fault, one never knows what he's up to at night in that Nordic city when she's not there. She says this with a kind of apologetic detachment that makes me want to hug her.

Outside, the beautiful American cars are leaving the royal palace; I watch Carmen turn out the lights one by one, the outdoor cafés are crowded with happy Spanish families; I linger a while in the nightclub district of queers, Moroccan gigolos, and transvestites dolled up like Sarita Montiel; I walk back to my hotel on the Gran Via, some sweet little African whores try to buttonhole me. A casting error; we're not in the same movie.

IT'S HARD for me to look back at that distant time, when I was convinced that he was made for me and that he would be my first man and my only, since I could not imagine how there could be any other. I have more than enough late-night dreams, places, and photographs constantly and randomly calling him back to mind as he was in those days, and his voice, his body, and his charm cling still to my wandering thoughts. I do not miss being twenty years old and I have no nostalgia for 1968, both of which coincide precisely in my case and generally elicit deeply emotional retrospection in people of my generation. At that time I was living in a state of mindless elation in which my central concern was to please him; cut off from the rest of my existence and blind to what was occurring around me, I was wholly devoted to the secret to which he alone was privy. I no longer recall the happy or even merely tranquil moments, which were too elusive and unsatisfying to me. Try as I might, all I see is perpetual fear of making mistakes and adding blunder upon blunder in my excessive love, which fear I still relive as sharply and cruelly as ever: the endless fluctuation between chaotic fits of exuberance and panic, with him and without him; hope in the wings and despair front and center without ever knowing if I was to end up getting him or losing him. Ultimately, my agonizing desire to sleep with him, my failure to do so, and my consequent frustration were the undoubted catalysts of the whole sorry story, and if I took to this mysterious impetus of sublimation and suffering with such extraordinary zeal, it was also because he needed my passion to help him bear up under the disappointment of earlier affairs, the fear of a future life of secrecy, and his sad, doleful, and wasteful life in Paris. Were I to plunge back into our meetings at the university and my visits to the Avenue Marceau; relive our intimacy, our fits of laughter, our endless telephone conversations; round up the friends we hung out with—to some of whom he had ceded that which he had refused me; listen once more to Hazel Scott singing "Le piano de la plage" or see *Bonnie and Clyde* again; slip one more time into those English shirts he bought me for Christmas in London—it would all end up merely reviving old falsehoods and the pretenses of a screenplay that we wrote together but interpreted in different ways. I wrote it all down every day in notebooks that I never look at, I've saved letters in neatly ordered boxes that I never open, I await the evening when I shall be able to consider it without pain as the poignant and pathetic ashes of a former life; that evening has been long in coming. That may be because I continue to believe he was almost as innocent as I was, only more mature and more familiar with the rules. Sorrow has not helped me catch up; it's simply undermined me to the extent that I can't help feeling that I shall regret to the day I die that he did not love me. Despite all that, I do remember that the fall and winter that preceded the definitive puncturing of my illusions and the eruption of the notorious events of May were exceptionally fine and sunny—unless that, too, is another trick of the memory.

WE LEFT Paris in late June in Cyrille's Volkswagen. I had introduced them to each other a few weeks earlier and it was if they had always been together; the newly inseparable pair had completely botched the school year and thought only of amusing themselves while I slogged away at my exams. Pleasant to look at and blithe of soul, Cyrille is my bosom buddy, exuding the elegantly bohemian charm of a scion of White Russia;

he tells me salty tales of depravity that leave me pensive and parades me before his delightful parents as if I were the good example to alleviate their concerns; he asserts with conviction that I have nothing to worry about and lectures me gently if I happen to doubt his word; in a word, he's the ideal partner for the inexorable melodrama of betrayal. One cannot go to more trouble planning one's own misfortune than I did. When the exams are postponed and I try to climb back into the driver's seat, it is clearly too late, from here on out everything we do will be by threes. The paving stones of 1968 are still hot, and Greece is under the Colonels. In other words, we have a flexible anti-establishment streak. In any case, we had gone through the great happening in a dense fog—they had literally played among the smoke bombs every night, while I, more figuratively, had lost all touch with reality several months earlier. In the beginning, everything goes as well as can be expected; in atonement for whatever it is they've been doing behind my back, they name me supreme leader of our adventure. I've chosen the itinerary: Provence, Italy, the ferry from Brindisi to Patras, the Peloponnesus and the Cyclades—the same route I'd taken three years earlier with a rucksack on my back. I want to share with them all the beauty that had so excited me. We leave the revolution behind, we cross Tuscany, we head toward the sun and the sea, I'm with my friend, I'm with my love—a fine recipe for euphoria. I do most of the driving, it's hot on the Autostrada del Sole, we're in our bathing suits, Alfas pass us at top speed as if we were in *The Easy Life*, Adriano Celentano is singing "Preguero" on the radio, they flirt with each other and say it's only to tease me; they also think I drive too fast.

In Rome, there's a room problem. We're staying with his uncle, yet another ambassador, at the Palazzo di Spagna near the Holy See. I'm intoxicated by the *enfilade* of dazzling salons, the explosive collision of Castilian pomp, patrician majesty, and

Vatican purple. Some sort of priest wearing the Falangist insignia on the back of his habit shows us to our quarters. They go to one end and I to the other, but I don't have the nerve to argue about it; I wonder why they need to use the phone at the restaurant in the rest stop overlooking the highway near Florence. The uncle has asked us to dine with the black-clad Spanish nobility: papal chamberlains, graying, pearl-drenched ladies who question us benevolently about the young generation and its discontents. There are at least two ambassadors at the table: the master of the house, who clearly prefers cassocks to long-hairs; and me, whom my two shrewd companions delegate to respond on behalf of the insurgents. I recite the basic platitudes, which draw their interest; I invoke vague references, citing Pasolini, who is unknown to the ranks of their eminences; they shudder at the thought of what Palmiro Togliatti would do if he were a French communist; Italy still has a way to go before things go sour. I'm not entirely blinded by vanity—I'm a little tired of having been promoted to official good boy, and my status as learned monkey makes me uncomfortable. I suspect them of playing footsie under the table while I'm holding court and distracting attention from them. Even so, the atmosphere is conducive to illusions; I am consoled by convincing myself, like any idiot thrown by chance into a Roman palazzo, that I have become a young hero from a Luchino Visconti movie.

The embassy closes early and we're given the keys. New venue. In the Beetle we cruise the drives of the Villa Borghese, where there's a hustler under every bush. Having hoped to show off the ancient temples and churches, romantic sunsets over the ruins, and the Tiber, I could never have imagined such a spectacle. I have no relevant experience from my student days in Paris, and although I've got certain movie scenes floating around in my head, this is more like the original version of Bolognini's *La notte brava*, and I'm naïve enough to believe it's some sort of party, the promise of newfound freedom. Our headlights pick out handsome boys our age who resemble the adolescent martyrs of Renaissance paintings and who, in the heat of the night, carry their jackets over their shoulders, hooked by the collar on one finger; I have yet to learn about Caravaggio, but it seems like some ancient ritual being acted out for the benefit of us sniggering, ill-mannered rich kids. Lambrettas brush by us. Guys with transistor radios glued to their ears call out to us in Roman dialect. Plumed *bersaglieri* pace the shoulders of the road two by two and stare at us as if they were out shopping rather than policing; every time we slow down, swarms of *ragazzi* hop on the fenders and beat against the windshield with obscene gestures and gales of laughter. On our return, the high walls of the embassy, dark and severe, greet me like a reproach. In those days, Roman monuments were not floodlit. I barely sleep a wink that night under the distant gaze of heroic frescoes, crushed as I am by the breadth of my room and my loneliness; my crude struggle to convince myself that they're innocently asleep at the far end of the labyrinth keeps me awake like a caged mouse on a wheel. In the early morning, I hear the ambassador greeting his domestic staff as he crosses the courtyard to the chapel to attend daily mass. Passion is an insidious malady, it inspires us to heights of purity and angelic élan and to dark scenarios of revenge and treachery. I am having a dream in which I've escaped from the citadel and am running through the deserted streets of Rome, looking for the Villa Borghese boys, when the duo wakes me from the sleep into which I had finally fallen, sheets twisted and drenched in sweat. I am a drowned man, limp and leaden; they are fresh, joyous, and eager to get moving.

On a wild beach near Patras, they swim naked and leap about, splashing each other between waves that alternately conceal and reveal their bodies. I remain on shore, I say that the sea is cold and dangerous, someone has to watch our clothes piled on the sand, you never know who might show up. As they dry themselves, tanned already and zestily comparing their rapidly disappearing tan lines, they tell me I'm looking gloomy and there was no need to come all this way just to sulk. I buck up as we cross the Peloponnesus—Olympia and its olive trees among the ruins, the beautiful Balkan villages like those of Syldavia in the Tintin books, traces of the whitewash that went up for a visit by the royal couple before the coup, signs to decipher. All of Greek history has touched this place. I am the inspired teller of lovely legends in the hope that some of their radiance will rub off on me: Achilles and Hector, the soldier-lovers of Thebes, Byron's flashes of inspiration and Victor Hugo's Greek child asking for gunpowder and bullets, that sort of thing, carefully targeted; they could care less, they drowse, they've drunk too much retsina, and the winding road has nauseated them. The ferry that serves the Cyclades skirts the coast of Yaros, the exposed island where the Colonels imprison and torture people. The tourists who had been looking for dolphins crowd the rails to take pictures, while I squint in the sunlight trying to make out the watchtowers. I emerge in extremis from my stupor to assert loudly that no prison of the heart can justify gallivanting around the penal colony that Greece has become. I am clearly being sincere, and at the very least I am in a confrontational and impassioned frame of mind. They're a little disturbed by my speech and taken aback by its vehemence; they worry what will become of me; he, especially, is sorry to have taken me so lightly, he promises to put an end to their displays and to return to the two-plus-one formula in which I am again part of the two. I am immediately back on track, I forget all about the executioners and their victims, Yaros and its rocks vanish in the summer haze. Above the deck, crowded with backpackers and families traveling from island to island with their sleeping bags, enormous parcels tied up with string, snacks, and cheeky

goats, loudspeakers blare the hit of the summer. We all take up
the chorus at full throat, the passengers beat rhythm with their
hands, fat ladies dance with little children, *Oneiro Apatilo*, let
us dream . . .

At Mykonos, a young guy collars us on the dock, offering
to rent us a room. Black curly hair, deep blue eyes, chest hair
peeking through his vest, sponge-diver's shoulders, the whole
array designed to shake Cyrille up; seems like a good solution
to me, a promising start to this leg of the trip. The room is big,
with whitewashed walls, and it overlooks the sea from the kind
of balcony you see in postcards. With quiet irony the guy points
out that the three beds are well spaced from each other, I guess
he's used to threesomes of over-the-hill queers; our youth and
urbanity are a first; he continues to explain in the same bantering tone that we can bring girls up here but not the boys who
hang around the tavern patios, there are enough beaches for
that sort of thing. The good feeling lasts a few days, the island is
not yet on the tour group itinerary, and the locals haven't been
spoiled by tourism. Mostly we run into pseudo-artistic Nordic
types; American beach bums; stylish Dutch chicks, girlish and
maternal; the golden youth of Athens. Life is cheap and easy, we
get by on a few drachmas a day, we live on souvlaki; there's only
one club, where the entire little colony gets together to dance
the *sirtaki* and knock back glass after glass of ouzo and retsina. We are adopted at first sight, the Athenians are thrilled to
speak to me in French and find me very sweet though a little
shy; he makes the vacationing KLM stewardesses swoon with
his apparently abundant but ultimately empty promise; Cyrille
vanishes at the height of the evening and reappears with sand in
his hair. Zorba the Greek would have nothing to worry about
from him. We drink Turkish coffee at daybreak on the dock,
lashed by the *meltemi* winds; we count the yachts at anchor
and wait for Onassis to float in on his, but he never comes.

The beach after breakfast, plans for the evening: it doesn't take long since we always go to the same place. The life of a merry little gang, summer friendships that will of course last forever, a time without limits. It takes some getting used to, I feel like I'm discovering the pleasures of my age for the first time, there's no reason that I should feel sad again. Nevertheless, he always avoids being alone with me; there's an awkwardness, something heavy between us, a kind of rebuke that clings to my presence; we address the whole room when we talk to each other, he looks at me without seeing me, it's the Dutch girls' jokes and Cyrille's facetious remarks that make him laugh. I act as if there is nothing to it because deep down I know that outbursts of black humor or, worse yet, of complaint will ruin everything. The more I feel the fear gathering again within me, the more I become the most jovial, most affable, and funniest boy I've ever been. The fourth or fifth evening, I seek him out with my eyes across the nightclub. We all came together; it's very crowded, and a stylish group has just come ashore from a millionaire's yacht. He's vanished, and Cyrille's gone too. The waiters are run ragged, monopolized by the elegant tables; bronzed ladies in gold-strapped sandals and fake summer jewelry of white plastic flowers; gentlemen in tortoiseshell glasses and silk scarves who speak in loud, international voices; no one to come to my assistance; one of the Dutch girls with a little too much liquor in her shouts in my ear that she saw them leave together, then she presses me to her bosom; I mustn't go with the boys, I'm much too cute for that, those who give in only end up unhappy, you just need to find the right girl to pull you out of it and make you forget. I abandon the contestant and make a mad dash along the entire waterfront as if I were running to put out a fire.

The full moon and its reflections off the sea shed a little light on the room. They don't hear me come in. I've imagined them so often that what I see in the shadows is already familiar to me, and almost soothing. They notice me. Cyrille plays the wise guy, cracks a few jokes, they weren't expecting me so early. He gets up and draws the curtains to make the room good and dark. It's weird, it's as if I can see him better. He unleashes his anger, heaps scorn and reproofs upon me, lets fly with terrible words that hit their target and transpierce me in the dark. I don't get it at all, he can't bear to look at me, why don't I just go away? Stuff like that, anyway, which I no longer recall precisely—it still hurts today—with cruel details and shreds of the truth that don't bear going into. And now I can just shut up and go to sleep; turn and face the wall if it makes it easier. I had chosen the bed by the wall, near the door; you can't think of everything. I shut up, I turn to face the wall, no complaints, no tears, I'll do anything he asks me, you're not always lucky enough in life to have one true love. They've started up again. I hear whispering, stifled laughter, skin on skin, the bed creaking a little, breathing, mouths, hands on body. It goes on forever, then begins again. I suddenly think of my grandmother waiting for me in her Évian villa for the summer; I never should have argued with her about the students and all the crap that brought back bad memories for her; she is so kind; she forgave me on the spot, she must be wondering where I am, and she is certainly missing me. I'll send her a card tomorrow, I'll send it to her first thing, and I'll choose it with great care to show her how beautiful Greece is; I'll write her tender words to make her feel how much I love her, soothing phrases in which I'll describe the fine summer, good friends, and my eagerness to be with her again as soon as possible to tell her everything. Évian is depressing with all those old people shuffling along the lakeside, its dreadful stores, its parks that are deserted by six o'clock in the evening, its chary Savoyards with their horrible sleepy accent. It's really boring there, except for my grandmother's: the pretty, timeless house, the books and massed hydrangeas, the well-raked gravel, and the family meals in the cool shade of pines planted by her father. It's only with her that I'm not ashamed to lie because she understands what I'm trying to tell her, and she'll make tea or stroke my hair as if I had actually said it. Her cool hands always in motion, the beautiful sapphire of her wedding ring, the subtle perfume worn by the ladies of long ago—all natural, just the essence of flowers. Her age has no hold on her: "When one has ceased to please one must not displease," and the girlish laugh that goes with it—"Yes, yes, do the math, I really am quite old;" the fear of falling when she leans in to close the heavy wooden shutters; the yappy little dog: "my last fiancé"; the delightful notes she slips under my pillow at bedtime. Her handwriting is quite bold and defiant for such an even-tempered woman: "Tell me, darling, tell me all about your travels. How I should have loved to come along!" The card will take too long—mail sometimes gets lost in this country—I calculate how long it would take me to get to her before the card does: the ferry ride, the night train from Athens, a night, a day, another night, Yugoslavia, Trieste, Saint Gotthard Pass. It won't be dreary to travel alone; I'll meet people and there will surely be lots to see along the line to Lausanne. The paddleboat across the lake is much prettier in this direction as you move toward the mountains, their dark north face; the French bank is much wilder. I'm sure I'll get there first, the card's late delivery will be like a surprise. I open my eyes in the dark, they're still going at it, no matter how I focus on the sound of the waves raised by the wind just beyond their bed I can still hear them, there's no reason for it ever to stop for that matter, I get up, put on my clothes and leave before he has the chance to react; go ahead, my love, insult a closed door, give it to someone who's not there to hear it. Dawn is breaking outside, cats chase after each other with such eerie howls that one is almost persuaded to believe that they have a share in people's suffering. I immediately feel a sense of utter liberation; I know precisely at that moment, in that empty alleyway of white houses, I know with dazzling lucidity, among those screeching cats wrapped up in their own ordinary grievances and indifferent to my presence, I know with unparalleled acuity that, from that moment on, I have begun to love him less.

I have to get away; I walk with no other aim than to be somewhere else, I leave the white houses behind, I plunge into the countryside along narrow paths lined with low walls of gray stone. Everything is still drowsing in the peace and silence of the early morning, and with every step I feel a little less bad. In my haste to leave I forgot my watch, the sun is already high when I reach the monastery that dominates the island. A young Orthodox priest sits at a table near the entrance in the shade of a fig tree; he says something to me that I don't understand and, no doubt struck by my air of misery, in a gesture of kindliness that I will never forget he points to a chair beside him and offers to share his frugal morning meal: a bowl of milk, a little bread dipped in olive oil, a few figs. We sit at the threshold of the monastery, gleaming white in the morning light, looking out over the entire island profiled against the sea below, on wooden chairs at a blue table with rough linen checkered napkins, and never has breakfast tasted so delicious to me. The young priest watches me, nodding his head and smiling broadly; he has figured out that I'm French and breaks the silence by saying "de Gaulle, the Eiffel Tower, the Champs-Élysées," adding "Brigitte Bardot" with a look of mischievous complicity. He points out the surrounding hills as he names them for me, along with the beaches just visible at the bottom of each little valley and other islands not yet blotted out by the summer haze. A bell rings, he rises, gives me a friendly slap on the back and disappears within. I am left alone with the blue table, the checkered napkins and the biblical landscape. I tell myself that I could stay there forever, awaiting the damp winters when the sky is heavy with gray cloud, and go entire summers without swimming or tourists, I'll make myself useful, I'll become his assistant, I'll learn Greek and what I need to know of the liturgy, I'll be the little brother convert, somewhat out of the ordinary, whose presence recalls that many are the paths that lead to the Father's house. They're singing inside the monastery, he doesn't return; despite the shade of the fig tree I can feel the heat of the sun beginning to bear down hard. I'll come look for him tomorrow and thank him by bringing him postcards from Paris, which I'd been clever enough to bring with me, a habit learned on other trips that never fails to please. But the next day the monastery is closed and an old woman chases me off with piercing cries, as if asking to see the priest were a sacrilege. She throws my Eiffel Tower and my Champs-Élysées to the four winds. No doubt I should have gotten up earlier to see him; one is not always lucky enough to start the day with a sleepless night.

I climb down toward the beach below the monastery, longer and harder than I'd foreseen—a goat path, overgrown with brambles, that snakes between great boulders under a brutal sun. It's around noon when I reach the beach; it's deserted with its ribbon of pristine sand, very beautifully nestled in an inlet of red stone and a little scary, too, with its coral reef glittering among the waves a few hundred yards off shore; it must be a marvelous place for sleeping out in the open. I've heard that Mykonos is pretty much destroyed now with its airport, its discos and jet-skis, dirt bikes on the roads and tourists throwing beer cans over the path walls; there are no more hidden beaches, and this one is no doubt swarming with the gay nudists who have staked a claim to it. The salt water stings my abrasions and I shiver for a while after I get out because I have nothing to dry myself with. I've kept my boxers on, it's odd, I can't quite bring myself to swim naked, perhaps because I have yet to come to terms with the little scene outside Patras. I suddenly hear a

few sharp reports, meaning I'm not alone on this strand at the
end of the world, good thing I'm in my underwear; yes indeed,
it's gunfire; in the old days wicked peasants would light bea-
cons on the reef to lure boats in and then plunder the wrecks,
I prepare myself for a Greek version of the Dominici affair; let
them play the fool back in their room when they hear that my
corpse has been found on a remote beach. I find myself face to
face with a big, rather good-looking redhead in frayed shorts
and a faded old polo shirt, who appears out of nowhere and
tells me he's working on his rifleman's skills by shooting at tin
cans. He seems as surprised as I am to run into someone, more
or less his own age at that. *Mr. Livingstone, I presume.* He's an
Anglo-Irishman from Belfast, sleeping in a cabin down by the
reeds, living on tomatoes and grilled fish that he catches himself, and relying on his Winchester as his principal link to the
modern world. I don't have the nerve to ask if he's planning to
do some target practice on Catholics when he gets home; everybody knows you don't engage in humor with foreigners. Even
so I seem to make a good impression on him; I'm sure he feels
like talking, what with being alone so much. He tells me that
he has a companion to whom he's very attached, a little donkey
that quietly waits for him at water's edge when he goes for a
swim and brays for him to quit when his tin-can shooting sessions go on too long. The beast carries him to the village once
a week to buy the necessities, it's not much to tell the truth, the
most important things are batteries for the transistor radio and
matches for the oil lamp; he spends his evenings reading Joyce,
Henry Miller, translations of the Greek poets, he quotes Cavafy
while staring me straight in the eyes, but I've never heard of
him, that's how far I have to go; he writes poetry himself, and
adds that they're of no interest to anybody, laughing in a childlike and altogether charming manner. When I ingenuously ask
him whether all this isolation doesn't weigh on him, he answers

that he's been there two months and that he's eager for winter to set in; he's not afraid of a little wind, rain, and cold. Nobody bothers him, an occasional passing fisherman or shepherd, he knows enough Greek to ask them for news of the outside world; they don't give him much, ever since the Colonels all people talk about is the weather; he's met the young Orthodox priest and likes him, he's renting the cabin from the monastery, but according to him you can never get too chummy with church folk, and in any case he's not especially sociable, a little rough around the edges, in case I hadn't noticed. He laughs at himself again in the same charming way. I, on the other hand, find him rather easygoing; we've been chatting here, our feet in the sand, for some time now. His voice is that of the young people you see in English movies, the scions of good families who set fire to their venerable old schools and go off to become communist spies. With his hair falling into his face, his *Lord of the Flies* look, his strong body, and copper skin, I find myself increasingly attracted to him, and I can tell he's noticed. I'm a cork bobbing on the waves, a castaway reaching for a lifeline, you can do with me what you will, I'm ready for anything. Earlier in the day, for just a handful of figs offered in charity by a young priest I'd have buried myself alive in a monastery; incense and chastity; now, standing before this Robinson Crusoe and squirming under his wolfish gaze, I dream of becoming his man Friday; I, too, will await all-drenching winter, I will buy him pens and notebooks for his poems, I'll wash his sweaters, I'll sweep his quarters, I'll learn to shoot a rifle, I'll lie beside him and keep him warm, and I sense that my boxers are already beginning to betray me. He tells me to follow him to the cabin, he wants to show me his digs, the books, the little donkey; the invitation is brusque, eyes averted, his face suddenly flushed beneath its tan, he's all business now, and he's not doing it to put me off. We head off. The sun beats down furiously, I've put my shoes on so as not to burn my feet on the sand, the sounds of the sea swell in my ears, the beach seems less pretty to me now, almost mournful, with dead tree branches scattered about and shells crunching beneath our steps. He walks ahead of me without looking back, he holds the Winchester barrel down by the action, pressed against his hip like a hunter tailed by his dogs after a successful shot. It suddenly tears through my mind—this guy is kind of weird, I'm crazy, it's dangerous, but still I waver, I can't seem to break away from those beautiful, well-muscled, and golden legs, that sinuous step leading me who knows where; what am I risking in the end, I'm already half dead, at least let him kiss me there in his cabin, beside his donkey, before he finishes the job. I'm terribly hot, this beach goes on forever, he keeps walking ahead of me, his powerful, handball player's back rippling gently to the rhythm of his gait beneath that colorless polo shirt. They always play handball, these demonic young lords in the Public School movies, but he's moving too fast, faster and faster, he won't let me catch up with him, he refuses to reveal the hidden profile that might just reassure me, he's the ferryman of the underworld leading me toward my final breath. I stare at his delicious neck as if to say good-bye. When he disappears into the reeds, I let him go. Birds explode into the air, and I flee in the other direction as fast as my legs will carry me. I catch sight of a kind of path, I run toward it, zigzagging as if I were in his sights, my heart is beating, fit to burst—exhaustion, desire, fear, out of one hell into the next—I wonder if I'll ever manage to break free, and yet I put every last bit of my strength into it. I climb the path at top speed like a panic-stricken kid goat, he's lost some time, he didn't see me go, I'm in the hollow of a little valley hidden by the brush and the first cork oaks, I hear him firing at random, he's looking for me, the shots grow fainter, that nutcase really wanted to kill me, while I've lost all desire to have done with it. He doesn't catch up with me; perhaps it was the little donkey that saved me; the hunt was hopeless or went on too long. I hear it braying, calling him back. When I finally reach the port, filthy and worn out, the shadows are lengthening and my tormentors have forgotten everything. They want to take me out to dinner, clucking over me like one does for the seriously ill.

I pack my things without a word; they sigh as if it was just another whim. I buy the card for my grandmother and take great care over the style and descriptions to please her; I return to the port to mail it, telling myself that I should probably stay a few more days before catching the train to Athens, I no longer wish to leave on a note of utter defeat. My little gang has come to find me but I avoid them, loitering around the outdoor taverns, just enough, just as long as necessary.

Haralambos Gnelledis—a name I shall remember until the day I die—had staked me out since my arrival. He had several irons in the fire and had instinctively deemed me unapproachable, not yet ripe. He now felt that I was within reach; a price was agreed on without fuss, and he hustled me over to the home of a very kindly, matronly woman. They were in cahoots. She rented him a little room and didn't make any trouble. He was all olive tree—tan, dry, hair curly and abundant. Since that time, I've sometimes recognized him in the photographs of boys in Naples and Sorrento taken early in the previous century by the evil German baron; in the Mediterranean, as elsewhere, there are types that are replicated from generation to generation. On the first night, he'd pretended to be working the German and Swedish girls and to have taken me on as an extra, but I didn't believe it for a second. He was precariously supported by a Danish painter who sold his attractive seascapes at the souvenir shop; an English family man in eyeliner, a pleading wife and two oblivious little children at his side, tried to lure him back to London. I could just imagine the handsome little group in their cottage; they thought me harmless and asked my advice, but I was unable to assist them in their fatal decline. He himself was a chronic embellisher, and I would get lost in his complex recreations of his past—despite his youth, enough had happened to him to fill several lives. I gathered more or less that he'd been adopted for some time by a couple of rich Yankees who had eventually sent him back to Greece for reasons unexplained. He expressed himself very well in American and spoke of Miami as if he'd really lived there; thrown into the mix were a reformatory, an Italian girlfriend, street fights, a Belgian decorator, an unknown father and a runaway mother, no family and too many protagonists, with me at the very end; guys like that are always orphans, anyway. He was a little thug who hated humankind and made love quickly and reluctantly, and for whom more was never enough. But he held me with heart-rending intensity in his sleep as if he hoped never to wake up, and at odd moments he occasionally demonstrated a kind of offhand and vaguely protective friendship for me that did not jibe with the provisions of our arrangement. Between the petty thefts, settling of scores, and drunken binges that took up most of his time, he set aside an odd little place for me in his life, not unhappy to have me share his room and quite cheerful whenever he recounted his adventures, which I was careful not to judge severely. I had my own little corner for my stuff. The matron washed my clothes, she approved of me, I brought her magazines with pictures of princesses and singers; she made us excellent breakfasts at which they talked about me in voluble Greek that, although I didn't catch a word, was clearly without hostility or derision. She surely made him see that it was in his own interests to hold onto me. I'd made up with my two traveling companions but it was of little importance; in any case, they'd ended up quarreling with each other before going their separate ways. Cyrille was having fun with our little gang, but the other wanted to move on. I said my good-byes while helping

him to the ferry with his luggage, he'd hugged me with the awkwardness of an old friend, he'd wanted to tell me something,
but frankly he didn't know what it was. I can still see him distinctly on the deck as the boat pulled away, his face unreadable
as he waved broadly. As for me, I believed that he was leaving
with a pair of pants that I had loaned him and that he'd failed
to return. In any case, I wanted to stay. He sent me a long letter
two or three months later in which he wrote that he was sorry,
and it seemed sincere to me, and also that he'd decided not to
return to France and that his parents had agreed. So he stayed
in Spain, where it all worked out better for him. I don't remember when Cyrille left.

I'd run out of money, so I found some work at the nightclub,
where I worked as a kind of assistant to the disc jockey, who
was completely out of his depth when he wasn't playing *sirtaki*,
and as a kind of public relations man to the fashionable crowd,
who liked my style; the owner said I was a status symbol; I was
paid in tips like a hostess. My little pimp came for me at closing time, skimmed his percentage, and left me about enough to
live on; everyone was happy. I bought the paper looking for a
picture of my mad marksman, but his rifle must have been out
of commission; time sped by; I hooked up my hoodlum with a
rich American, which was perfect since he spoke the language; I
promised to come back the following summer and then I high-
tailed it for my grandmother's, aiming to get there for her birthday. I traveled second class, it was one of those old-fashioned
trains with a dining car that served elaborate dishes and families
wandering the corridor in pajamas. In Skopje, the city was still
in ruins from the earthquake, the building facades had all col-
lapsed, and people were living like bees in a hive; you could see
women bustling around their mid-air kitchens in their slips. The
young Yugoslavs were often very attractive, very sociable too, it
took an effort of the imagination to remember that this was a

communist country; Tito was very handsome himself, he must once have been like the boys on the train, and in the pictures of him that hung in the stations he looked like a sort of millionaire king. Approaching Belgrade, I was again seized by the temptation to escape; his name was Kim, he was dressed in a cheap white tracksuit and white loafers without socks, my age, an angelic smile and gorgeous eyes ogling my Lacoste shirt, my genuine blue jeans, and my fine watch. Winking, he pointed out the suburban housing projects along the track; in the light of a summer's evening they were no worse than those in France; that's where he lived and where he invited me to follow him; he slung his athletic arm over my shoulder, we would have kissed if the corridor hadn't been so crowded, I was trembling like a leaf and not with fear. But I was thinking of my grandmother's birthday, and I'd pretty much lost the heart for taking risks. On the platform, I gave him my Parker pen, which he pocketed like a thief. I couldn't understand what he was saying in his meager English over the foreign gibberish blaring from the loudspeakers. He was probably still trying to win me over. Through the window of the train as it pulled out, I saw his expression harden and turn sullen. He looked around as if he were on the prowl; maybe he was waiting for someone else.

In Évian everything was just as I'd left it. I got there just in time for cake, and my grandmother was happy to have me back. She thought I was very skinny but otherwise looking well; I crammed for my exams in October and we talked about the Parthenon.

Haralambos Gnelledis and I had promised to write each other. It's one of my foibles, I never know when to quit, if something has gone reasonably well I always want to prolong it. That's why I tend to hang on to all these little affairs that no longer make any sense. So I received a letter from him, but it was only a request for money, with dreadful penmanship and a few intimate photographs that were not worth the paper they were printed on. The threat of blackmail was so unsophisticated and clumsy that I felt a little sorry for him. I should have answered to teach him a lesson, and sent him what he imagined he was extorting from me, but I couldn't find the address. I don't forget, but I do lose track. One must always write a return address on the back of the envelope. That's really how it came to an end. He is the first in a very long series. It was with him that I developed the habit of paying for boys; I've had all kinds, but he's the proto-type for them all; the only difference is that he must be dead by now with the life he led.

An actress who was very fond of me and often scolded me because she knew perfectly well what I was despite my disincli-nation to confide in her said to me one day: "There is something deeply sick about the desire to pay." I totally agree, and I've had a lot of time to think about it through all the years I've tried and failed to cure myself of it: the lies that we tell ourselves, the true reasons that we bury away. I'm a past master on the subject. I know it's been a flaw of mine since always; even as a schoolboy I was overgenerous with the gifts, and my Greek escapade only confirmed it. The ugliest thing lurking at the heart of the whole story is contempt: that of the boy for the guy who pays, that of the guy who pays for the boy, that of people in general for a form of transaction that seems to be distasteful to just about everybody. One may proudly recall that it's a practice that goes back to the dawn of time, delicately invoking its convenience and pleasures, but no matter how clever you play it, the benefits are still perverse: contempt protects the boy by making him feel undamaged, it encourages the client in his pursuit of power, and it allows each to recreate again and again his role in a farce of humiliation and shame. An old man who pays is disgusting, a young man who pays is even worse; he avoids the dangers of his own age by deploying the asymmetrical weapon of money; an imposter in seduction; a trafficker in sentiment, a cheater in love. But what's the point of harping on it? Even when we know how it works and can see the damage it causes, we do nothing about it. In any case, there's no way out of it other than quitting. So we go underground; it is sometimes dangerous, often sordid, and, unfortunately, almost always romantic; we become so inured to this secret existence that we can no longer live without it; it offers us shameful rewards, surreptitious adventures, hidden advantages, and we easily convince ourselves that the experience we gain thereby is useful to our daily lives. One awful feature is that it's not terribly expensive, much less so than other addictions like drugs or gambling, and the money we spend on pleasure is never really wasted.

Still, you have to be careful, remain alert; I have had some misadventures that could have turned nasty, and I look in both directions before crossing. The greatest dangers arise when one is too kind: the boy is troubled, he's vulnerable to feelings of sympathy, contempt is harder to muster. If he is of a nakedly bad temperament, he may take fright, fly into a rage, and fall prey to uncontainable and murderous impulses to rid himself of the troublemaker who has upset his equilibrium and routine. You can't help thinking of Pasolini when confronted with such experiences. He is the obligatory and terrifying point of reference. Maybe he, too, had been too kind to Pino "the Frog" Pelosi when he took him out for pizza and Lambrusco after having picked him up at the Termini station, too kind when he spoke to him in Roman dialect to put him at his ease, too kind when he took an interest in the little stories of the young hood from the outskirts who hooks to buy clothes and take girls out on his Vespa. He had seduced boys who were tougher and boys who were shyer, but they had also been not so lost, less generous of themselves, the kind he used as *ragazzi* in his movies. Each had had his opportunity—the one to love, the others to follow. But when you cross over into macho camaraderie, where the talk turns to football and women, you

have to be able to get out in one piece. I've run across my fair
share of Pelosi the Frogs in the sordid reaches of Paris, and there
must have been a swampful like him in the Termini station; it was
bad luck that he happened onto that particular pretty boy, all
fouled up in ignorance and vanity, and proud, too, to have been
chosen by such a celebrity, of whom even the most dim-witted
call boy around had some sort of opinion. Everybody knows
that famous people are stinking rich, so it's no problem taking
a little *passegiatta* to Ostia and complying with a kinky request
or two; it's normal, the predictable course of a good business
deal. But this wasn't really an ordinary client, he didn't behave
in the usual apprehensive, hunted way. Friendly and attentive,
he exuded unfathomable charm and sympathy. Pelosi the Frog
was jolted from his role as professional con who thinks he owns
the streets just because he can pull guys whose picture he's seen
in the papers; nobody asked him if he wanted to be turned into
something different by some guy the likes of whom he'd never
met, a guy who talked to him as if they belonged to the same
world. It was something new, complicated, confusing, and he
had no intention of taking shit from some fag who wrote books
he would never read and made movies he would never see. There
are probably better things to do than speculate over the death
of someone we admire, the sordid end of a remarkable life, but
on at least two or three occasions I myself have been afraid of
meeting the same fate and I have since become much more cautious. I know I'm not the only one who's haunted by that crime
and everything it leaves unsaid.

The theory of a fascist plot against a hated enemy is equally
credible; its flaw is that it happens to suit all those who would
appropriate the murder for political ends while sweeping under
the carpet everything that is specifically aberrant and beyond
redemption about it—the normal business of hustling and its
strong ties to the traffic in boys. Whatever the case, even if there

had been no Lambrusco or banter in dialect, even if unknown co-conspirators had taught the kid his lines and waited in ambush on the beach with all the muscle necessary to murder a sturdy man with no known suicidal tendencies, the thug certainly needed no incitement to commit his crime. Inexhaustible hatred led him to kill the one who had offended him, to crush the menacing beast that had threatened him. At his trial, Pelosi the Frog, who for months had been charging 10,000 lira a pop for letting himself get blown in the Termini men's room, swore that he had never sold himself before this. For once he was telling the truth—renting is not the same as selling.

The best era for me was that of Madame Madeleine, who kept a little specialty hotel just off Place Pigalle. The whole atmosphere there was one of well-heeled civility strongly reminiscent of the underground establishments that flourished before the war. In fact, I've found spot-on descriptions in Jouhandeau, Cocteau, and a few others of the quality and faithfulness of the clientele of that honorable institution, to my knowledge the last of its kind surviving in Paris when I first began to patronize it. Madame Madeleine, already aged and almost immobilized, resembling a slovenly Mistinguett, was enthroned in her front office on the first floor, attended by a court of cheap old fairies as starchy as palace footmen. A permanent odor of good old-fashioned *cuisine bourgeoise* wafted among the plastic holy virgins, goldfish bowls, lace doilies, and postcards of kittens sent by grateful regulars. It was charming, very Prévert and Doisneau, and Madame Madeleine could have swept every prize for model concierge—the kind who harbors Jewish children while sending anonymous letters to the *Kommandantur*. Her poor legs being no longer capable of carrying her to the upper floors, she delegated the distribution of keys and towels to a small coterie of balding majordomos who sighed with nostalgia at the memory of visits by Jean Sablon and André Claveau and only rarely vacuumed the rooms. The linoleum was cracked, the beds sagged, the plumbing spluttered, but the rates were modest and the house was always bustling. Animated by a fierce devotion to and respect for social hierarchies and an atavistic suspicion of loose women, who never fail to upset the given order, Madame Madeleine treated her exclusively male clientele with the consideration she reserved for men alone and adjusted the ostentation of her welcome depending on her gimlet-eyed assessment of their background and comportment, as if they were coming before her as before the reception desk of an opulent Swiss hotel. My glowing good health flattered her snobbery, my youth reassured her of the excellent prospects of my repeat custom, and she treated me like the family pet. The service was equally old-style: the VIPs, the family men, and the shy ones went straight up to their rooms following the customary courtesies, and Madame Madeleine gave her orders through one of her minions, a powerful, confident fellow by the name of Monsieur Jackie who paced the boulevard nearby. Monsieur Jackie was the ever-reliable pilot fish; to him she whispered the identity of the visitor, whose preferences were as carefully catalogued as a police case file, and Monsieur Jackie set off to find the rare bird or its nearest equivalent. Between the local bars and game rooms the circuit was highly organized; the client seldom had to wait in his room more than fifteen minutes between the moment his order had been taken and delivery by the diligent sidewalk impresario. When business was heavy and there was a crowd to attend to, Monsieur Jackie tended to scurry about his affairs and to compromise on quality rather than risk losing a gratuity. I saw veritable ogres passing through the front door, paunchy, decrepit former thoroughbreds of the profession with gold teeth and sparse, dyed blow-waves with gray roots. Sometimes bitter complaints were made to Madame Madeleine, who assumed a penitent air while promising that Monsieur Jackie would surely locate little

Rashid or sweet Marcel the next time. She had their number: ashen and shifty-eyed, the plaintiffs were already reassuming their civilian personas and all they had in this world on which to hang their dreams of escape was her address; they always came back. I also saw a few Venus flytrap–types pass through there; they were enough to make you shudder and attested to Monsieur Jackie's professionalism when he was willing to go to the trouble. I myself preferred the more modern technique of going straight to the middleman on the street in order to preserve my right to choose. In this way I was able to introduce new recruits to Madame Madeleine, who sized them up with a critical eye so they would understand that there was to be no funny business and that she was boss in her own house, but also to take careful note of their attributes for future opportunities and future customers. My propensity for choosing from the crowd, out in plain sight, had other drawbacks: although almost no one was able to resist Monsieur Jackie's sales pitch, I was often in the dark when it came to past histories. I have occasionally come across the picture of one of my transient boyfriends on the "news in brief" page, which only goes to demonstrate the reliability of Madame Madeleine's security system.

The ascent of the socialists dealt her the fatal blow: the new admixture of behavioral freedom and police prudishness rendered all that underground traffic obsolete; cruising became ubiquitous, she didn't know any of the new commissioners, her business went into a tailspin, she was hounded by the tax authorities, and they finally shut down her hotel. She died of a broken heart a few months later and was buried with all due rites, in accordance with her wishes, mourned by her little court and a few of the nostalgically minded hiding behind the church pillars. I sometimes run into Monsieur Jackie on the boulevard; he's working freelance now and with no fixed port of call, the business has changed, he complains that all he can find nowadays are young

Arab boys and disparages them as attractive but unreliable, the commissions are not exactly rolling in, he's put on a lot of weight and smells of alcohol, it's all pretty grim, he's been locked up a few times after swing parties have turned ugly; he hates gay pride and rich liberal queens, and mutters against the new civil contract for same-sex couples, which he deems deeply immoral. Things haven't worked out so well for him, either.

I miss Madame Madeleine and her sweet little enterprise. I loved its secret-society atmosphere reeking of beef stew, the rituals of a cursed race chronicled in pulp fiction and popular song; it still had that aura of the police blotter, the tattooed legionnaire, a whole world down at the heels. The modern marketing of gays, nightclubs full of mustachioed queers, the dramatization of hysterical gayness that so fascinates straight people, the politically correct model of cute little gay couples, and the whole high-minded rant about the sacrosanct difference leave me more or less cold. Aside from the abominable disease and its victims, I have only a dim sense of solidarity. So I've done a lot of rambling without ever finding the one who could make me stop. The Portuguese on the Avenue de Wagram, the Yugoslavians in the Galerie des Champs, the North African kids on the Square d'Anvers, other guys and other places, little hotels and half-baked schemes, the unpleasant glances and nasty encounters, drugs, the harassment and the muggings, the constant vigilance and the occasional blossom that fades or vanishes with depressing alacrity: the market moves on and one does not necessarily enjoy the time or the means to participate indefinitely; everybody is familiar with that sort of thing nowadays, movies, books, the media, and television are rife with it. Ultimately, it gave me a hell of a headache and I ran out of steam.

I am hardly the first to have looked further afield, and endless jokes have been told about how it all goes down in other countries. The Maghreb solution does not exist; the transaction seems easy enough, if somewhat crude, which is not necessarily unpleasant, but there is no sense of transgression; the boy is merely a replacement woman and a bankbook; these handsome kids show up like they were going to a sports event, with the idea of saving up for appliances for their future marriage to a cousin chosen by their mother. Compulsive old queens find it quite to their liking, there can be some fun and even a little emotion in it, but it doesn't take long to figure out that the families are in charge and always come out ahead. If you fall for someone you have no choice but to switch sides; you become a big brother, protector, faithful friend, mediator of conflicts, tutor, and concessionaire of mopeds and refrigerators. You resign yourself to it fairly easily by telling yourself that, after all, it's just another kind of love exchanged among human beings. And then the boys suddenly disappear, spirited away by their new in-laws, now comfortably furnished and on the watch for backsliders. You may run into them from time to time, children at their sides, thick in the middle and with an empty look in their eye, having forgotten everything. Others are more than willing to replace them, but you have to reckon with the fatigue that curbs your appetite to go on. The boys of Moscow are jolly and bright red in the deep freeze of winter, but then there's the alcohol, the amphetamines, and the violence; in New York, the whole Internet and credit card thing is a little depressing, but with the price of the dollar you don't have to pay through the nose to get yourself a little Bruce Weber; they're *muy caliente* in Cuba, for sure, but the cops are everywhere, along with the dreadful poverty and the awful Fidel. You push on, ever further, but the white man's hang-ups thrive on all this misery and won't give an inch. The unlucky ones are arrested, the rest of us swear off that kind of love, at least that's what we'd like to do and don't. In any case, you can never bring anyone home with you, the airlines don't issue visas, no matter how hard you work to convince the consular officer; even if you make a good impression, the pretty boy stays behind. But what if there were another Madame Madeleine hidden away somewhere?

I'VE SEEN him again from time to time. In the early days, I would go to Madrid, where he welcomed me very kindly, we'd go out with his friends, his cousins, really gracious and forthright boys and girls; this was toward the end of the Franco years and there was a feeling of artistic ferment in the air in which I pretended to be interested so as not to be paralyzed by overwhelming grief and resentment, the remnants of irrational hope that I still dragged around with me. All my efforts were in vain; I might have been able to fool his little gang, but I was incapable of sliding into the role of good old buddy, of which he was equally skeptical, and he was well aware that I was adrift. Ultimately, we had nothing left to say to one another; in keeping us apart, our new lives also distanced us from our past, and there was nothing exceptional about that. In the evening I would return to my hotel, a sort of lugubrious caravansary that I'd chosen among all options with the unerring eye of the depressive, more lonely and more lost than ever; up and down those endless corridors, where I kept expecting to meet the ghosts of Raquel Meller and Alfonso XIII, who in more prosperous times had their own connections to this crumbling ruin, according to the old bartender, and in my glacial and dilapidated room the absurdity of these visits to foreign soil weighed upon me even more heavily. I tried it two or three more times, then gave up.

WE SOMETIMES speak on the phone, it's almost always he who calls and takes me by surprise; his voice, his laugh, his jokes are still the same, and each time it's like a blow to the heart that sends me reeling years into the past. We promise to speak again and time passes as we wait. When we saw each other in New York it was practically by accident, and when he happens to be passing through Paris he's between flights and I'm not always available. I've followed his career, he's aged quite a bit all the same, nowadays he looks like one of those diplomats well versed in weighty matters that you see at international conferences on TV; I must be the only one left who can still see that incandescent young man of yore inside this ambassador who adheres so faithfully to his family traditions. I dread his being assigned to France, an entirely plausible eventuality given the importance of his responsibilities and his lofty position in the hierarchy of his ministry. It's a posting for which he is certainly under consideration, but I don't know what he thinks about it. I haven't had the nerve to ask him; if he does come, I shall assume an air of ironic sophistication at official functions.

He recently sent me a picture taken in May 1968. Despite my reluctance to pick over the details of that time, I remember very well the circumstances in which it was taken. It was his sister's wedding, held in that very apartment on the Avenue Marceau, spacious enough for such a ceremony and well removed from the chaos then reigning on the streets of Paris. The guests, the usual crowd found in the finer homes of the wealthy neighborhoods, were mostly Spaniards and Latin Americans, for the bride was marrying a Guatemalan with the physique of a polo player, an ill-fated guy who was assassinated a few years later during a civil war in his country. There is no sense of tension in the photo; in the background some very respectable ladies are chatting amiably among themselves; in the foreground are we three, looking like the kind of well-bred young men who know how to match their tie to their suit, in the company of his mother, who seemed to me at the time to be of the appropriate age but who now seems to me to be considerably younger than I am today. The picture is in black and white, but I clearly recall being struck by her lovely dress in multicolored silk, an innovative style at that time. She is speaking to us, and whatever she is saying must be funny, because Cyrille is smiling broadly at her, glass in hand. *He* is not listening, or only distractedly, because he is looking toward the photographer, or not exactly that either, as it seems to me even now that he is looking off slightly to the side, at something that we will never see as he did. I'm almost positive, for that matter, that he is wearing contact lenses, which I caught him more than once in the process of putting in, the kind of intimate and familiar gesture that suddenly made me want to embrace him even more.

I don't quite know what to make of this picture; I will surely keep it with the others but it makes me uncomfortable. On the back, in his fine penmanship he has written in blue ink that he finds it very poignant. I do too, and even more poignant to me is the fact that he can still be moved by such a keepsake and that he should wish to share it with me thirty-eight years after the fact. I'd love to know how he came upon it; maybe he, too, has boxes stuffed with old papers that he brings along every time he moves. And yet, his memory and mine are not entirely in sync; in his mind there are always three of us, and being required to return to a moment long ago that he remembers with affection, I am reminded of the pain I felt then, the fear that he would abandon me, and the certainty that he might do so at any moment, entrenched deep within me without my daring to acknowledge them. In the final analysis, what strikes me most in the picture is his isolation; he is among us but not of us; it is not only his gaze that is drifting, he himself is already half gone, and I can't help feeling that it is precisely that which he finds so touching— this image of him in his solitude and his flight, this image that he prefers over any of his family, his children, or highlights of his career, so hidden and protected that even Carmen has been unable to extract it from him. As for me, I don't think I look too bad in the picture, not as handsome as Cyrille or him maybe, but not so bad all the same. I always have the same sense of amazement when I look at pictures of myself from that time: he was a nice boy, things should have worked out better for him. I will never know why I hated myself so much, to the point of falling in love with someone just like me who wouldn't love me either, nor why I had to wait until I was on the threshold of old age, when it was far too late, to see that it was a mistake to hate myself so obstinately when I was just as capable as anyone else of finding someone to love me.

quentin

quentin

quentin

quentin took them all with him: Christine, his ex-wife, with whom he had some kind of arrangement, even after the divorce; Sacha, their son, who lived with his mother and was going on fourteen; Bronia, the young Yugoslavian au pair who was his occasional mistress. He went after they did. My older brother told me the news by telephone; it was nine o'clock in the morning, it had happened in the night, maybe toward dawn, in any case it had just happened. He didn't know any more than that, but his voice was expressionless. After the police, the doctors registered their findings, but no one around me was willing to go into the details. I didn't see anything about it in the press. I think I heard that he had killed the child last, with a knife, before turning against himself the firearm that he had used on the two women. I don't know if he slaughtered them as soon as

he entered the apartment or if he waited, engaging in a disturbing monologue, or if there was an argument, attempts to reason
with him or to flee, pleading, if he lingered or died instantly.
Nor do I know if he awakened his son or if he stabbed him in
his sleep. One might suppose that the boy awoke alone in his
room to the sound of unusual noises, cries, gunfire, and that
they talked to each other. Whatever the case, I have a very hard
time imagining the scene, nor do I care to; it is unimaginable.
What is certain is that he intended to kill them when he left his
home in the middle of the night with the revolver he kept in his
drawer, without alerting his lover, whom he did not harm. She
was sleeping peacefully when they called to inform her. I wonder if he had the key or if he rang. He paid the rent himself, he
was very generous that way. He only took those he loved; he
had loved Christine since they were teenagers, and ultimately
she was the only woman for him although he'd had so many;
he loved Sacha not only because he was his only son, which in
itself was of inordinate importance to him, but also because the
child was beautiful, intelligent, and fully responsive to his affection; he loved Bronia because of her kindness, the pleasure she
gave him, and the adulation in which she held him. Perhaps he
loved her a little bit less, but she was there and was such a part
of the lives of the others that they had never considered going
their separate ways. He could have taken his mother, but either
he didn't think of it or he preferred to leave her to suffer. Plus she
was not there, he'd have had to go from one place to another,
you can't go on in that frame of mind for hours on end and
there's no insistent drumbeat urging you on. He could also have
taken each of my brothers, who had meant so much to him,
but he chose to settle things differently, taking instead the wife
of one and the associate of the other. As to his own brothers,
they no longer counted for anything; the middle one had already
been killed in a car accident and the youngest was hardly better

off, a chronic junkie who would not last much longer. So Quentin took the core group.

It seems he had been considering it for some time. In fact, he had told his partners that his son was gravely ill and that he would soon take him abroad to consult some specialists. He also told them that his son was incurable and that he wanted to retire from business to devote himself entirely to the boy. It was all oddly vague, however, and the partners put that ambiguity down to anxiety or reticence and did not dare to question him on the subject. They may even have felt that such a painful blow to such a hard and formidable man might humanize him, and they probably discussed it quietly among themselves. Little Sacha was apparently in perfect health, and Quentin's personal assistant, having gotten wind of the rumors rampant throughout the company, was astonished to find the boy in fine form when he called his father or stopped by to see him at the office, which he did often. The assistant also noted his brief episodes of abstraction and violent fits of fierce anger, which she attributed to overwork, unable as she was to confirm her own personal apprehensions, which were both indistinct and changeable. Like everyone, she admired his outstanding success and was susceptible to the extraordinary power he had over people; moreover, she was not afraid of him. At the inquest, she testified that she had considered speaking to him on several occasions but had finally thought it best to wait for a more opportune moment. In all likelihood, her heavy workload and her strategic position within the group prevented her from analyzing all the signals that had disturbed her. In any case, they were the sort of clues you only think back upon afterward.

He was a man of resentments, possessed by despair, cynicism, and the will to power, but it was impossible to identify the precise moment when that which had served him so well in his career tipped him over into murderous insanity. No one knows whether or not he was aware of having crossed a red line when he began concocting his false confidences and withdrawing into morbid mental constructs, or if he tried to pull himself together. There is no indication that he consulted a psychoanalyst, kept a private journal, or wrote a suicide note. His exceptional intelligence must have made him alert to his condition, but he may have thought that he had a certain leeway to toy with his neurosis, without realizing that it was insidiously entrenching itself and would ultimately overtake him completely. It would have taken an enormous effort and required a complete turnaround of which he was no longer capable, despite every appearance of a leading dazzling life; by dint of being subjected to sarcastic comebacks every time they tried to have a serious conversation with him and of being humiliated whenever feelings were at stake, people had stopped listening closely to what he said and were wary of him; they assured themselves that he was solid enough to stand on his own two feet, but the life he had led had isolated and exhausted him.

The only ones who understood, more or less, were the three who shared his little bubble, but they could do little for him but pursue their own tranquil lives, the three of them together, and demonstrate how happy they were thanks to him. In any case, neither they, nor those who were with him every day, nor even his lover, a beautiful, intelligent, and gracious woman whom he intended to marry, had the least prescience of something so horrible and monstrous.

Deep down, it was his own death that he was focused on; he could have embraced it alone by killing himself at the office after the last employee had left, for instance, or by holing up in a hotel when his lover was momentarily occupied elsewhere; any number of arrangements would have done the trick. But he had high expectations of his death, he was hoping precisely that it would tear him from his isolation. That is surely why he designed it with such cunning and violence, and why he required the assistance of Christine, Sacha, and Bronia, who would accompany him and remain forever at his side. It took only the first murder to make it irrevocable. It was certainly easier after that, he was getting somewhere and was now sure that they would come along with him. As for the rest of us who remained behind, our love for Quentin had long since become insufficient.

The families wanted a religious ceremony. Virtually no one believed in God or had set foot in a church for ages. Quentin had always been a virulent atheist, giving himself with pleasure to anti-religious and blasphemous provocations; the three others knew practically nothing about it and attached no importance to it. His relatives, both near and distant, and his friends belonged to that fringe of the dechristianized bourgeoisie that maintains only the most tenuous and indifferent connection to religion. But the horror of the massacre was so unbearable that people must have hoped that the Catholic rite would represent some sort of return to normalcy, something that would allow the unspeakable to be spoken and passed off as an accident. What seems stranger still to me is that the families should have asked for a single ceremony for all of them: the four coffins in one church for a joint commemoration. The murderer and his three victims side by side, together. I don't know if there were discussions about it, doubts, if anyone tried to repudiate such an arrangement. Maybe they thought it would be better for little Sacha. Everything fell into sharp focus when little Sacha was in the picture.

Quentin had had more than just his mother and his poor junkie brother, who had been too shattered to make any kind of demands on him; he also had several half-brothers and sisters who were much older and despised him, cousins who had had to turn to him at one point or another and who spoke of him all the time as the devil and the future patriarch of the family, and it just kept on going like that in ever-widening circles. In the older generation, for obscure reasons of inheritance some had even denied him the right to bear their somewhat illustrious name, but they had withdrawn their claims in the face of his brilliant success. On the other hand, those who were gentle or shy, especially women, had nothing bad to say and were devoted to him, it was as if he had avenged them by being the brightest of them all and using it against the others. In any case, their group could only cling to the "accident" theory and try to confirm it by following the appropriate rites; it was only natural. Christine's family was in the arts; her father had worked in the movie business and his second or third wife was an actress who'd once enjoyed a modicum of fame in Italy; I know very little of her mother, she was said to be exquisite, remarried to someone well known, an intellectual or high-end designer. There were fewer of them, and they were less visible. They could have refused by right, but I'm inclined to believe that it was they who ultimately decided on the shared liturgy, again for the sake of little Sacha, who belonged equally to them, and because Christine had loved Quentin and they loved Christine. And after all this time, Quentin had exerted his charm on each of them at one point or another and they may even have considered him almost as their son. As for Bronia's family, someone surely called Zagreb or Belgrade and failed to make any contact or gave up too soon. Language, distance, etc. Anyway, there she was, a cross on the coffin, flowers, the whole baleful show. Clearly, Quentin had been able to exert his powers of domination right up to the very end and without restraint. In his own mad way he had been right; he had won, they would never be separated again. Despite all the aversion I felt at the time for his postmortem victory and cruel excesses, I've always believed that such funerals are still the least harmful option, and if I'd been asked my opinion I would have said that it was the right thing to do—the most generous and humane. But I obviously had no say in the matter; I had never been anything but a helpless witness to Quentin's fearsome ascendancy over us all, a lowly extra discreetly submissive to his direction, a kid who had pretended to hate him in a naïve attempt to conceal his own confusion and desire to one day be favored by him above all others. So well aware of that was he that he occasionally toyed with my troubled emotions when he had nothing better to do.

I don't know how the priest was convinced to do it, or by whom; I didn't hear whatever it was he found to say in his homily because I did not stay in the church, which was crowded to capacity. I sat in a little café across the street and waited for it to end so I could leave with my brothers. I had my own memories and didn't care to share them. But I saw Christine's mother leave long before anyone else. She didn't know me, and I went up to introduce myself. She was a tall, blond woman, still beautiful, deathly pale and all in black. She leaned on her chauffeur for support, she held a handkerchief to her mouth to stifle her sobs, and her eyes were brimming with tears. Stooped over, unsteady on her feet, her face a ruin, she was the very embodiment of the most heartrending sorrow. Her man helped her into the car with the utmost care, as if she were in danger of breaking, and pulled away very quickly. Whenever I think of the pain that can be inflicted on a person and the grief it causes, the malice it engenders, and the toll it takes, whenever I think of absolute suffering that can never be consoled, it is the vision of that woman I see, a manifestation of woe more poignant than any other I have encountered in my lifetime.

IT'S AN episode that no one talks about any more, literally buried in a big black hole; and yet my family and Quentin's are related to each other. Little Sacha would be a year or two over thirty by now, the same age as his cousins, his friends, my brother's children, but he is barely remembered at all. The business was liquidated, the relatives went their separate ways, the only one left is Quentin's mother, retired to a little apartment in Nice. She has lost everything: her three sons and her grandson; she is old and very sick. My brothers go to see her from time to time, but they have very little to say about their visits. She wrote me a few years back to congratulate me on something or other; I'm not sure if I ever wrote her back; yet another act of cowardice I should like to redeem, but I don't know how to go about it, perhaps just drop her a line to let her know I'm thinking of her? I've kept some photographs that I stole from my brothers: Quentin, Christine, their radiant beauty, before Sacha and Bronia, the discord, the money issues, and the whole tragedy. I look at them quite often.

I don't know where or when or how my brothers met him. Not at school, but some time in the years before graduation, maybe when they were hanging around Jean-Pierre Rassam and his whole little gang; that would be Quentin's style. My brothers had been raised to respect traditional values, duty, and work, as well as slightly provincial customs—vacations in Charente or Évian, Saturday night gatherings—but our parents' divorce and remarriages had given them a certain freedom of action and they soon took to new ways espoused by progressive young lions who read Kerouac, Malcolm Lowry, and Fitzgerald, prowled for liberated girls, disdained the narrow-minded dilettantes of the sixteenth arrondissement who knew nothing of Antonioni and Godard, hitchhiked down to Saint-Tropez, took to the ski slopes in jeans and aviator jackets, and had pledged to succeed in whatever field before they hit thirty. No need to point out that they were boastful little snobs of pathetic ambition, but this was long before 1968, leftist unrest, and humanitarian causes, and in the somewhat conventional social order of the self-confident bourgeois business world they passed for rebels. Besides, my brothers were having a bit of trouble finding their path, they dithered, unable to make a clear choice between the standards they had absorbed as children and the promise of adventure that seemed just within reach; they needed a guide. Quentin had a bankable name, lived freely and as an adult without having to answer to anyone, took advantage left and right, bagged the prettiest girls, and acted like a guy who respected nothing and no one. He was an outstanding student, which scored points with all the parents, and he never seemed to work at it, which attracted the attention and envy of his peers. He could make a show of perfect politeness and horrify with bad manners, behave like a considerate, well-bred young man or like a complete boor. He was astonishingly cultured for a boy his age, informed and curious about everything; he was almost never caught out in a serious conversation, he had a gift for putting out irrefutable arguments and scathing rejoinders that always hit their mark and left his interlocutors speechless. His intelligence was feared by his intellectual equals, who sensed in him a potential rival, and by imbeciles crushed by his natural superiority. He was able to take an instant reading of anyone he had to deal with and, depending on his interests of the moment, decide then and there whether to make himself loved or despised. For his chosen ones, there was something indefinable in his implacable personality, his lifestyle, his gaze, and his laugh, somewhere between melancholy and injury, something very secret, deeply buried, like some inaccessible truth that made you want to devote yourself to him with impassioned solicitude. On the other hand, it was somewhat difficult to judge the extent to which the superhuman competitiveness with which he was already completely imbued freed him to go to any length not to lose a woman, an acolyte, or money; soon it was mostly about money, which in his system of unbroken and barbaric isolation was a tool to corrupt and manipulate. But he was also cautious, crafty, careful never to put himself in danger without cause, and his incredible charm swept away whatever was left of doubt, fatigue, and hesitation. His physical seductiveness was the subject of much discussion, no doubt on the same grounds and by the same people who feared his intelligence. For a variety of reasons my brothers never referred to that allure, the one because he was surely susceptible to it and the other because he didn't give a damn. Rather tall, slim, blond verging on ginger, high cheekbones, blue eyes . . . but there's little point in describing him; from my little corner, all of thirteen years old and painfully withdrawn, the moment I set eyes on him I found him irresistible.

My brothers began talking about him long before he made an appearance, and with such appreciative elation that I could already feel his presence. They were also laying the groundwork for our parents, whose reaction to him was unpredictable; Quentin himself was surely no stranger to such circumspect maneuvering. Our friends had always been the kind to toe the party line; they could be hot-blooded, no one made a fuss if they had a little dissipation or a blunder or two in their past so long as we knew where they had come from and whether they could be trusted to adhere to the short list of acceptable behaviors—work ethic, appropriate education, a social life that was not excessive. Now, having caught an inkling of the stories my brothers told of their new hero's high exploits, my parents were growing increasingly concerned. Quentin really came from somewhere else; although his name had a prestigious family history behind it, his father was dead and his mother lived in dubious standing somewhere outside Paris with two little children and a journalist lover at least fifteen years her junior; nobody knew where Quentin lived, whom he lived with, or what he lived on. There was something makeshift and anarchic about it all. At the very least, his involvement in their lives would entail a change of routine: my brothers' schedules, social lives, and interests had already been affected,

creating unanticipated tensions. As the threat grew more con-
crete, my parents asked to meet him. The tactic worked to perfec-
tion, and when the meeting finally took place they were greatly
relieved. He made a powerful impression, as expected. Since
my parents lived apart, the wooing operation took place in two
phases. At my father's, I remember very clearly, it felt like a veritable seizure of power. Father was captivated by his intelligence
and my stepmother bewitched by his charm. They took to him
immediately, to the point of naming their soon-to-be-born son
after him. It was a little more difficult with my mother, in part
because the rumor of his recent triumph made her even more
reserved; he couldn't get away with mere scintillating conversation and charisma, and she wasn't unduly impressed by his gifts.
He proceeded by little strokes, making her laugh with his savage
quips and showing her that he was not afraid of her. Mother
liked capable men, and this kid before her was one. She conceded
his commanding personality and stimulating intellectual powers,
and that was all. It was enough for my brothers. She acknowl-
edged that her sons were growing, and she didn't want to stand
in their way. Provided he didn't take go so far as to presume himself her equal, she could accept him as an inevitable and perhaps
even necessary evil. Things between them remained rather odd
for some time, apparently friendly and relaxed, collusive even,
but she didn't like him and he knew it. Intuitively and probably
a little out of jealousy too, deep down she was always wary and
on her guard with him; he avoided complications, making himself scarce when she was hostile and backing down when she
became inflexible. With the passing years, they saw less and less
of each other and stuck to topical small talk when they did. And
yet she never spoke ill of him; he was an adversary who intrigued
her. Having gained admission, he became a familiar face in both
households and, at the same time, an intimate friend of my brothers, who were beginning to spread their wings. For my parents,

at any rate, the important things were secure: everyone was pursuing their studies and Quentin's influence was apparent only in their spare time, on weekends or holidays. As for me, I had no access to their world, I did not participate in their lives, I was too young, the little brother sent away to his play his kiddy games. I picked up scraps of conversation, rumors of outings, fleeting images where I could.

Quentin and Paul are in Italy, they travel by thumb and by train, they score with some chicks in Capri, they sing *"Venti-quattro mille baci"* like Celentano and visit Malaparte's house. On his return, Paul uses new expressions borrowed from Quentin, it bothers me, I feel like I don't recognize my brother. I try to talk like him but it doesn't work; my school friends make fun of me, they don't know Quentin, they don't get it. He and Charles party with the fashionable young crowd; tuxedoes and hired bands, it's crazy the kind of money these people are prepared to blow to marry off their daughters. My oldest brother is very elegant, very well mannered, the mistresses of the house find him irresistible. Despite his name, Quentin is on no one's list, he receives no invitations, but Charles gets him in everywhere. He sows confusion by flirting with the untouchable girls, the closely guarded fiancées, those destined for big-money alliances. They yield to him, he drops them, it starts all over again. Scenes, trouble, bad reputation—Quentin could care less, and my brother continues to open doors for him. When the parties begin to dry up, they move on to Castel's or Régine's. They don't have the wherewithal, but with Quentin in the driver's seat they always seem to get by.

He and Paul are in England this time. They're trying to buy an old Jaguar; it's all the rage at the moment. It's not expensive and they're sure they can find some little mechanic in Paris to keep it running. They get it all wrong, of course. Their expedition takes them all the way to Glasgow, where they wind up in a queer bar;

the guys move in on them, murmuring "a kiss, give me a kiss." Paul is still laughing about it, and Quentin, seeing me perk up, leans over me, a hideous grin on his lips: "Let me show you, a kiss, give me a kiss." I howl, of course, but I'm not sure what I'm howling about. Charles has a fling with a married woman. Forty years old, beautiful and rich, a friend of my mother's. They meet secretly in hotels. Quentin has seen her, he thinks she's a dog, of course, and heaps scorn on Charles, but he can't help prowling around the affair like a caged lion. He persuades my brother to introduce the woman to him and he's on his best behavior as the bashful, smitten best buddy, but friendship is sacred as everyone knows. The woman sees straight through him and gives him the cold shoulder. But he manages to introduce such ambiguity into the situation that he shows up for their next rendezvous in the place of his dear best friend. The woman refuses and breaks off the affair. Charles is furious. A looming confrontation with the traitor, who's gotten out of worse jams than this; reconciliation on the theme "Nothing and no one can separate us. We'll have a good laugh about it one day." Charles forgets all about the woman, Quentin catches up with her on the sly, dogs her, turns her head, and drives her mad; she gives in, falls hard, takes risks. The husband gets wind of it, threatens to smash Quentin's face in, and takes his wife back. Quentin could care less, he got what he wanted. It isn't until years later that we learn the final chapter of the story.

In Mégève, at a wayside chapel, Quentin pisses on a crucified Christ through the oratory grille; he wants me to do likewise and cruelly mocks my horrified refusal. In Charente, at the home of my dully virtuous, provincial cousins, he lulls the parents into a false sense of security, plays the "Rondo alla Turca" on the parlor piano, praises the charms of the countryside, quotes Jacques Chardonne, whom no one has read, and takes an interest in the ups and downs of the cognac market. General admiration:

he enthralls the boys of the family, gropes the daughter of the house, and sleeps with the maid; he makes his getaway, leaving chaos and insurrection behind him. After he's left, I explain to the mother that he's actually very nice despite it all; she looks at me as if I'm crazy and I clam up, red as a tomato. At dinner at my father's, a guest stares fixedly at him; he's a handsome old fellow with a reputation as a ladies' man. Quentin plays the innocent, all shy, and participates timidly in the general conversation. The aging playboy literally devours him with his eyes and practically does cartwheels to impress him. Collective blindness all around, but I've seen something that no one else has: he gives me a complicit wink, which makes me horribly uncomfortable. As we're leaving, he tells me in the elevator that he can tell a fag straight away and how much fun it is to make them drool and give themselves away. The elevator is cramped, we get on at the sixth floor, I count each one and can think of nothing to say in response.

We visit my uncle, a sporting type who also dabbles a little in the movie business and has just pulled off a major coup by hosting Anita Ekberg for the weekend; everybody's very excited and Quentin tries his luck. He does a good job of it: he's seen her best movies, speaks more than passable English, and even slips in a few words of Swedish, souvenirs picked up from au pair girls of the past, no doubt. The star plays it gamely; she lets down her hair and dances with the young Frenchy who thinks he's in *La Dolce Vita*. But her boyfriend is an Apollo out of an epic movie, and my uncle is looking increasingly grim. The two men corner Quentin, who deems the odds against him and hits the road. He later explains that Anita isn't so hot; there was no point in fighting for her against two guys who don't know their ass from their elbow. I keep my thoughts to myself, but I'm very glad that it didn't work out for him.

One Sunday night, we're in my mother's kitchen; she's out for the evening. Having emptied the refrigerator, a whole gang of us

are having dinner. I'm with my dog, a black cocker spaniel that I
adore and that adores me back. Quentin, who's never given the
dog a second look, pets it and lowers his head toward its muzzle
while holding it by the ears. The dog wags its tail submissively,
as if it's pleased, but I can tell that it's nervous. Animals always
clearly sense when something isn't right. Quentin continues to
cajole it as he draws nearer and nearer, almost as if he's going to
kiss it. Everyone around the table gaily follows his little game.
I know something horrible is about to happen; the dog whines
a little, it wants to please and to escape. Then Quentin spits
right in its face, a fat gob all over his eyes and muzzle, the string
of spittle gleams on its fur. The dog howls; it knows that it's
been humiliated. Everyone bursts out laughing. No one had ever
shown the least interest in my pet; they'd accused me of being
too attached to it, and now it had been made to look ridiculous.
I leap up to rescue it, I take it into my room sobbing with rage.
I could kill Quentin.

I have dozens of memories like that. Nothing particularly
momentous, ultimately, the childish pranks of a nasty brat, the
provocations of young people who like to think of themselves
as freethinkers; each time, my brothers say he's gone too far but
that's a part of who he is, approving of him makes them feel that
they are freer. If I complain they turn on me, and I myself sense
that I'm not so different from them; I struggle silently against my
excruciating attraction to him, and if I act as if I hate him it's only
because I have no other way of making him notice me. I'm never
surprised when I awake from a dream of him; in my sleep, he is
always very sweet, very affectionate, he has no interest in girls
and fusses over me as if I were his own little brother. I've seen
him once or twice in his white T-shirt and American boxers, in
keeping with the fashion code of the diabolical threesome, who
shop mostly in American army-and-navy stores, the latest thing
at the time. They share their exploits while they slowly dress

themselves. There's an atmosphere of carnal triumph or incipient epic bender in the air, and there I am among them, like a burglar caught red-handed. I also saw him once, just once, in a bathing suit, at the Évian aquatic center, a dreary, rundown place where his presence was particularly incongruous; they must have been truly inseparable for him to follow my brothers to a spot like that. He's got a nasty look in his eye, he's probably unhappy having to bare his body, especially in such a bleak establishment where all his charm counts for naught. My embarrassment at seeing him in his undergarments suddenly turns into virulent repulsion. That redhead's skin of his, all pale and freckly, surprises and disgusts me. Seeing him half-naked like that, I imagine that girls must feel the same repugnance; it would be impossible to touch such skin and not feel sickened. But at the same time, I have trouble tearing my eyes away, and I know myself well enough by now not to be surprised by my own reaction. In my dreams that follow soon after, his skin is as lovely as porcelain, wonderfully delicate and fresh, it smells so good, it is like no other when he rocks me gently in his arms. The fact is, I know very well that he would only have to brush by me for my strange aversion to evaporate on the spot.

One day, he pretends to try to rape me as a joke for his buddies; I try to tell them yet again how awful their cynical little games are, but collective inhibition has been thrown to the wind. He's much stronger than I am, he pins me to the ground with the full weight of his body against mine, he leans in and tries to kiss me on the lips; I shout, I struggle like a madman, I twist my head this way and that to avoid his mouth; he understands perfectly well that this is no game for me, my panic is my secret laid bare, the trap I have feared and into which I have fallen. The English kiss, the spitting on the dog should have put me on my guard. I won't get out of it this time. But the diversion soon palls, or my distress moves him, and he loosens his hold on me; I get up, hurl insults at my laughing tormenters, and flee the room. In my mind, I replay the farce of my irredeemable injury, but I can't fool myself for long, I prefer to acknowledge the truth of how dearly I long to be alone with him and let him start over. I know it will never happen.

It's not always so miserable, and the entertainment is not exclusively perverse. Quentin's great hunger for life electrifies everything he touches; very likely, my brothers' friendship helps bring out his remarkable gifts, and my parents' welcoming attitude moves him to be less callow. I'm captivated by everything the three of them have to say about their reading, girls, nightlife, even their studies. Together, they finally manage to buy their legendary old Jaguar; as expected, the purchase is ruinous, but in my eyes it confers upon them an incomparably romantic prestige. It's quite true that they have the prettiest girlfriends and that they themselves are the most stylish and the sharpest young guys I know. Everyone else—their hangers-on or the older brothers of my school friends—lead drab and boring lives by comparison. I'm impatient to grow up and leave my morose recriminations behind so that they'll accept me. I'd show them how I could keep up. Even today, I can see their provocations in perspective; those silver-spoon hooligans had rare power, originality, and curiosity. And sometimes, too, Quentin could be quite considerate and disarmingly thoughtful: with my parents, to whom he penned affectionate letters; with my brothers, whom he heeded when they sought to restrain him; with me, protecting me and pleading my case when my grades were poor. I've lost all count of the books he advised me to read.

I must have been sixteen when Christine came into his life. Without abandoning any of his customary cynicism, he became as dependent on her as he was on my brothers. She was assuredly deep in love with him and immediately understood what she must and must not do. She accepted his cheating and having to share him—that was the only way to hold on to him and deepen his attachment. Christine and I never had a particularly intimate relationship; I was just an obscure and sullen satellite in the constellation Quentin; she took us on board as a group, she got along very well with my brothers and occasionally gave me a light dusting with her hand, like a trinket that it would have been unseemly to neglect entirely. In any case, little brothers—kids who hang around, tag along, and slow you down—are just pests who get in the way and make love a chore. Me, I was both the brothers' little brother and the kid who was always staring at Quentin. Even so, I think she was very fond of me, probably because Quentin had appropriated me along with the others and, when all was said and done, gave me a lot of attention. I thought her very pretty, the Deneuve look of those years suited her, and when I close my eyes I can still hear the crystalline timbre of her voice, her indulgent laughter at Quentin's wisecracks and misdemeanors. Still, I held back; with a flirt like him you never knew who was going to last, although he proved me wrong in this case. And also, she belonged to the realm of boyish love life that was closed off to me and that I observed with my nose pressed up against the window. One night, in fact, I overheard a conversation on the street, spoken in exaggerated whispers that allowed me to follow precisely what was going on. Quentin asked Christine if she was feeling all right; the question was unusual, and he sounded both a little worried and absolutely determined to feel no sympathy for whatever was wrong with her. A little as if she were undergoing some sort of initiation ritual, successfully passed by those girls who were able to hold onto a guy and decipher his code of conduct without being a pain in the ass about it. Christine answered with a laugh, as usual, that she was a little tired but that she would be fine. Quentin dryly ordered me into the Jaguar, and they kept talking a while on the sidewalk. On the road, they were silent; the radio was on, Christine had fallen asleep, and Quentin told me I was a little asshole who would do best to mind his own business. In those days, abortion was mysterious, scandalous, and a very serious offense. You heard terrifying stories of sinister old hags, infected knitting needles, and girls dying in hospital emergency rooms. Quentin was never mistaken about me: the little brat sitting so quietly in the back of the Jaguar kept close tabs on his opportunities to cause trouble and would certainly not pass up the chance, one day or another while the grown-ups were chatting among themselves, to suggest knowingly that abortion was an abominable crime.

When I think back now on the way Quentin laughed off my obvious hostility and allowed me to insert myself as much as I possibly could into certain episodes of his life with Christine, without my brothers being even fully aware of it, I feel overwhelmed with tenderness for him. I'll never know what place I held in his life in those days—no doubt modest and minor—yet the fact is that he did not ignore me, even when he was treating me cruelly. I was present, and he did not shove me aside. I remember, too, one evening during our winter break in the mountains when Christine and I had to return to Paris on the same train. I don't recall how it was that I found myself yet again alongside the two of them, but I'm sure I was careful not to complain about it for fear that I'd be fobbed off on someone else. We were running late; Quentin had wanted to keep skiing until the slopes closed. He took us to the station on a snow-bound, icy mountain road, as usual driving at top speed like a madman. I sat in the back; from time to time Christine would ask him not to go so fast. "Stop Quentin; be careful, Quentin; Quentin, please," but he wasn't listening and continued to rocket around the bends. It was obviously really dumb to take unnecessary risks, but I said nothing, I trusted him, I wasn't afraid, I felt fantastic, exhilarated to be in his charge. We made it to the station only just in time; everything with Quentin was only just in time; that was the way he lived, always pushing the envelope. While the train was about to pull out, he lingered on the steps kissing Christine—long kisses on the lips with his eyes closed. When the train began to move, we opened the window of our compartment and he ran alongside as long as he could; he skied like a pro but he ran badly; he called out laughing, *"È pericolo sporgersi!"* and then: "Take care of that little jerk, I don't want anything to happen to him!" He'd almost killed us in his speed-wagon, but he seemed genuinely unhappy to see us go. I remember him like that, too, so handsome on the station platform in the middle of the night, dangerous and tender, kissing with his eyes closed, and the little jerk who needed to be taken care of. In fact, I was the one who ended up taking care of Christine: she couldn't find her ticket, and I soft-soaped the collector by saying that I was her little brother and that I was the one who had lost the ticket. I could be very convincing, and he didn't press the matter. I was proud to do it for Quentin. The next time I saw him and told him what had happened, he didn't give a shit and treated me hatefully. With Quentin, you were never ahead for very long; that boy lived in another world to which none of us really had the key.

Quentin had lost his father, and the fact is he never had one. In his passport he bore his mother's maiden name, but there was no reason to see his passport. Except for my brothers, who had gotten hold of it in the course of their travels. They had been unable to conceal their astonishment, and Quentin had told them the truth. The unknown father had been a right-wing member of Parliament of a certain notoriety who had abandoned his mother when Quentin was born and subsequently cut off all contact. They had nevertheless met when Quentin was a teenager, but the meeting did not go well. The man had drawn a line through his past and shown the door to this painfully radiant and hurtful reminder of a youthful lapse in judgment. It would seem that they never saw each other again. Quentin spoke of him only reluctantly and resentfully with my brothers, while I, of course, was supposed to know nothing about it. I often wonder what that gentleman, reputable in every respect, must have thought of the outstanding success of the son whose very existence he had denied, or of the dreadful tragedy whereby that same son ended a life for which he had abdicated all responsibility. This was a practically absolute taboo subject with him, not to mention the love-child aspect; Quentin's real and false half-brothers continually revealed little snippets of his story, sometimes out of malice toward him and sometimes out of sympathy, which comes to pretty much the same thing. It's a complicated story, parts of which remain mysterious and will never come to light: the hunger for respectability, wealth, and inheritance played a role in it, as they do in all family sagas, but bohemia, emotions, and Quentin's luminous personality muddied the waters further still. At the very least it was horribly cruel for the child victim who only wanted to be loved and avenged himself as he grew. The famous name that Quentin touted everywhere, and managed to append to his student IDs and bank statements—no doubt at the cost of painful and humiliating scheming—was that of the imposing old man who had married his mother after his birth. A military engineer and an industrialist in the finest tradition of feudal capitalism, he achieved considerable renown from his early career, but his work, like his fortune, had undergone an irreversible decline. He had long been widowed, with sons and daughters who were older than Quentin's mother and had married and had children of their own; one can only imagine the welcome extended to the second wife, young and saddled with an illegitimate child, especially as she happened to be the sister of one of his daughters-in-law, who turned out to be a good soul, Quentin's only ally as he was caught up in the family imbroglio.

Although he did not go so far as to legally recognize the bastard, his stepfather treated him as a son, with affection and enthusiasm for his precocious gifts; in return, the boy was deeply devoted to the man, who was old enough to be his great-grandfather. No one doubted that he would be remembered in his will. Two more boys were born of the new union; it was soon understood that they were the fruit of the young mother's wandering affections, but the patriarch was decidedly broad-minded; they assumed their legitimate place in the ranks of succession. It all drove the first-generation heirs crazy: the improbably close harmony between the spouses, one unpleasant surprise after another, the dwindling estate divided into ever-smaller portions. Quentin, the Trojan horse of the scandal, was the catalyst of their fury and animosity. He was twelve when the old man died; he lost in a single blow the man he thought of as his father, the identity he thought was his own, and above all a model of generosity and benevolence whose absence he felt almost immediately. I have always been convinced that it was loyalty to his memory, first and foremost, that drove him to cling to the name he had been permitted to share throughout his childhood; then, too, it was to make himself feared and respected by all those who were infuriated by his claim; moreover, it was convenient—although very soon nothing remained of the industrial empire, the name alone continued to strike the imagination.

I have a very lovely photograph of the patriarch and the three children on the terrace in Saint-Germain-en-Laye. It's wintertime, and they are looking in the direction of Paris. The old man is magnificent in his black coat and felt hat, wing collar, and fine white whiskers. The very picture of old-style chic, as seen in history-book photographs of great men of the last century. The children are dressed English-style, very shipshape in their little round caps, a little distant, a little bored. Quentin, while also in schoolboy's clothes, is bareheaded and pokerfaced and appears to be deeply focused on something; he is leaning into the old man, pointing out something in the distance for him, and wears the decisive look of someone who is listened to. We sense the intimacy, affection, and trust that bind them. Quentin is about ten years old; at that moment he is with his father, the true son of the true father.

I was shyly in love with Quentin's mother, guilt-ridden that I might be betraying my own. She was fabulously beautiful, with a style all her own. She gathered her auburn hair in great tortoiseshell combs, wore muslin shawls and rhinestone necklaces. This romantic, Old World look was viewed askance by other women, but it was perfectly natural on her. She had a British complexion, deep blue eyes, sublime hands and legs. Everything about her was expressive of poetry, indifference to material things, a passion for love. When I knew her, she was living in Le Pecq, in a house that had once been substantial but was now falling apart, with a journalist lover almost half her age who was equally charming and consistently good-humored. She was also very gay, sophisticated, lively of step and imagination, cooking up old-fashioned, half-forgotten recipes, botanizing in the countryside, voting communist because she liked the candidate's beaten-up old sheepskin jacket, whisking her brood off to exotic vacation destinations where there was no danger of running into other tourists—Formentera, a little-known Balearic island, or the Col de Tende, where she had discovered a fairytale castle without running water or electricity and where they bathed in the rivers. It seems she was badly shortchanged when the estate was parceled out; she lived on modest means and drove an old black Rover that we considered to be the height of elegance. As a mother she was flighty, treating her sons as if they were her lovers, incapable of exercising the least authority but passionate in her feelings; squabbles and reconciliations, scenes of jealousy and compulsive clinging—no one ever knew who had started them; the young lover was careful not to intervene to patch things up; they always seemed to patch themselves. She made valiant attempts to meet with teachers, to oversee allowances, to hold up my brothers and me as models of good behavior, but her efforts were somehow so inimical to her nature that nobody paid them much attention, which made her furious and then made her laugh. Quentin's two younger half-brothers made the most of the situation; they worked just hard enough to avoid the threat of boarding school, which in fact was quite minimal; they took full advantage of a very elastic schedule, ransacked their mother's handbag to finance their childish recreations, and declared their undying adoration while criticizing her roundly. Quentin was her man, her one and only. She spoke of him broadly as a monster, amassed imaginary grievances against him that had little connection to his very real wickedness, and caved in faithfully to his every demand. They quarreled regularly, but even at the height of their arguments there was something radiant about her that betrayed the joy she felt in his presence, her pride in having such a son. For his part, Quentin never discussed his love for her. Such sentimentality would have been a confession of weakness, but he talked about her often, casually and spontaneously. He protected her, he watched over her every move, theirs was a relationship of mutual potentiation; his mother was his very substance. It is likely that she inherited a share of the self-hatred that gnawed at him and that that is why he spared her when he closed out all his accounts—to make her pay for that first separation of having brought him into the world. Strangely, there were no pictures of the patriarch in the house; while he had been of such importance to them, it was now as if he had never existed. Maybe in her bedroom, but I never went in there. All in all, in those days they formed a self-contained world of bohemia and carefree existence that enchanted us; we took advantage of all Quentin's comings and goings to tag along with him to Le Pecq and bask in the atmosphere of freedom that his mother encouraged. Later on she moved into a little cottage on the far side of the Saint-Germain forest, which she decorated with exquisite taste and which we took to visiting every Sunday. I spent more and more time with my brothers on the pretext of my new friendship with the second brother, who was my age and with whom, in actual fact, I didn't get along especially well, though I never let it show.

My two brothers were crazy about Quentin's mother—one because he entertained the fantasy of a romantic liaison that she coquettishly dangled over his head, the other out of a desire to be transgressive and freethinking. My mother took their rapturous descriptions as critical comparisons, but she was clever enough to conceal her irritation; she had an amusing way of sending up her arch-rival as Blanche Dubois, heroine of *A Streetcar Named Desire*, and was very cordial to her when they happened to meet; urged on by my brothers, she even acquired a black Rover that she hated driving and that was always breaking down. For her part, Quentin's mother never tired of heaping praise on ours, who was doing such a good job raising her sons while, she claimed, she herself was having so much trouble with her own. The exchange of courtesies allowed them both to come to terms with a rather unusual arrangement, whereby Quentin and my brothers had defined the identity of a new family, hybridized and sturdy. What interested me the most, after Quentin, was his little brother, the youngest of the three.

He was about ten when I first met him and was still called Sweetie, a nickname he claimed to despise but willingly exploited to pull the wool over everyone's eyes. Beneath a graceful, cherubic façade that seduced me from the start was the barely concealed character of an evil seed, ever alert to the makings of a wicked deed. His alacrity, intelligence, and precociously perverse sense of humor reminded me of the demonic fair-haired boys in the English horror movies I saw at the Cinéma Napoléon, which struck a chord with my as-yet-inchoate masochism. A tantrum-thrower, a liar, and a thief, with all a child's fragility and need of affection, he was just like his brother and allowed me to picture what the latter must have been like at the same age; he was my own miniature Quentin. I had a gift for provoking his worst impulses and of ensnaring myself in his little plots; he was quick to grasp the motives behind my clumsy indulgence of his wicked-ness, which only whetted his appetite for hurting me. He sys-tematically thwarted my every attempt to make myself noticed, which was already hard enough in itself; his hands were always in my pockets and he was always swiping the records and books that I'd been stupid enough to bring with me; he hid needles in my orange segments and at table insinuated with a look of disgust that he knew I was a fag and could prove it. Initially, his "proof" was of the vaguest sort, and his mother cut off his explanations with a scolding, ineffectual as usual, begging my pardon for having given birth to such an evil specimen. For me, however, it had already become a sensitive subject, and I splut-tered in my attempts to vindicate myself. Then he'd flash me that triumphant half-smile that made me want to hit him and kiss him at that same time. I would sometimes get back at him, always within the confines of that cruel little Eden in which we battled; if I was able to catch him, I was stronger than he was and could knock him down, but once I was on top, my knees pin-ning his shoulders while he cursed and tried to bite me, my face hovering above his, I couldn't think of anything else to do but spit on him, which was becoming an odd family quirk. Another way I took my vengeance on him was to strip him of his bathing suit at the beach and to make fun of his outraged modesty from afar. I didn't stare at him for long while he heaped insults upon me, his naked and slender body paralyzed by his anger at being exposed, before I returned the bathing suit to him, though now

he was in no hurry to put it back on and twirled it over his head
like a slingshot. He always foamed at the mouth with feigned
fury, and I awaited the inevitable retaliation in a new cycle of
criminal activity. In a word, he understood me perfectly, and we
were always happy to meet again the next time.

Our relationship changed with adolescence. His was just
beginning; mine was coming to an end. By now I had fully
grasped the significance of certain games, and I monitored
myself strictly; he, too, grew less and less hostile. Like me, he
was hooked on history and the movies, we were able to talk to
each other normally, I eased into the classic role of big brother
contributing to the intellectual awakening of the younger. I was
still deeply scared of what I was, and I deluded myself with a
lot of such reassuring twaddle. Not to mention that Sweetie
had so extended his malicious vocabulary in my respect that
I was afraid to take risks. In our dull conversations on matters cultural, I avoided such scabrous subjects as "lifestyles of
ancient Greece" or "the ambiguity of pretty boys in Visconti's
films," but it was precisely such topics that interested him most,
and I had nothing to teach him that he didn't already know. We
coasted along without pushing it; we had become most cautious
and reasonable. At the same time, I sensed that he was expecting
something from me, and the more clearly it was defined and the
closer it drew, the more afraid I grew of confronting the truth. I
needed more time to shed my inhibitions, and he was in a hurry.
I also needed to feel less hemmed in by so many people if I were
to set my scruples aside, but he was as indifferent to them as
he was to my fastidious conscience. I was in the grip of a full-
blown romantic reverie, and he wanted something else—to have
fun, feel his own strength, explore his freedom. He surely didn't
get it, and he soon made other arrangements; that sort of thing
was easy for him. I regret it, have always regretted it; I wasn't so
bad, he probably wouldn't have stayed with me for long, but he

would have enjoyed himself with me and that would have done me some good; we would have remained close; you can go on to do a lot when you start off with such little secrets.

One evening, I'm reading by the fire in the living room of the country house; Sweetie has fallen asleep in front of the television, everyone else is in bed. I remember it as a wonderfully mellow moment. He is sleeping so deeply that I muster my courage and decide to carry him to his bedroom. On the stairs, he drapes his arm around my neck, his head lolls against my shoulder, I feel his breath on my cheek, his eyes are still closed but I'm convinced he's faking it. I set him down on his bed and take off his shoes; what I really want is to undress him, just his pants and shirt, say, so that he'll be comfortable under the sheets. He remains still and I hesitate; when you're really asleep and somebody puts you to bed you turn over, you move around a little; I content myself with watching him, little Sweetie is still so young, I turn off the light, go out, fall into a deep sleep. At some later date, I've just passed my driving test and I'm behind the wheel, we're not alone in the car, he's sitting in the back, as I did when Quentin drove. We're listening to Les Chats Sauvages on the radio, he sings in my ear "blah blah blah, you talk too much," yes, I know, I should talk less and act more. The whole time we're driving I can feel his hand up against my back. When we get there, he has friends his own age waiting for him, he throws me a mysterious smile before he heads off with them, I remain alone with the feeling of his handprint on my back. Another time, he joins me in the room I'm staying in; he's heard I'm good at Latin, he sits beside me at the little desk so I can help him translate— *rosa* the rose, that was a whole other life, I don't remember a damn thing about the Gallic War, I've forgotten all my Latin, and that's no exaggeration, but he could care less, that's not why he's here; he presses his leg against mine and stares right at me, that mysterious smile playing on his lips. Okay, this is the real thing, no point resisting, my blood is singing in my temples. But someone knocks at the door, he withdraws his leg, we plunge into Alesia; his mother has made tea, there are guests, it would be nice if he could come say hello. I think, whatever happens, tonight I'll go see him in his room. I count the passing hours, but something happens, I don't remember what, and I have to return to Paris that evening. In any case, my seeing Sweetie depends on my brothers and Quentin, on my so-called friendship with the brother my own age; I can't very well admit that I go to Le Pecq or the country house to see Sweetie, nor can I ask him to come stay with me in Paris; I dream up schemes involving excursions to the movies or homework assistance, but they won't wash; at this point, any desire I might express to be alone with Sweetie would be really weird. We're together only with the rest of the family, one-on-one only for fleeting snatches; I try to proceed craftily, by innuendo, but it doesn't get me very far; I am very careful not to give myself away even when I manage to pull off a moment of covert triumph now and then. Just watching him grow and develop among us is a source of endless frustration and nagging pain to me, locking me into absurd fantasies and forcing me to hang around as much as I possibly can with Quentin and my brothers, who've given up trying to shake me, all the while concealing the real reason for my visits.

Once, however, I manage to meet up with him in Paris; he must have been about seventeen and had begun spending weekends here with various friends, like Quentin used to do. He doesn't go by Sweetie anymore, he's recovered his real name, he's not as talkative or insolent as he used to be, and not at all aggressive. Despite the unbridled freedom that his mother gives him, he's top of his class and surprisingly erudite for a boy his age. People say he's some kind of genius who will take the world by storm; they were already talking that way when he was little, but now it's been confirmed with a sort of general sigh of relief because he's become a nice person while losing none of his charm. It's New Year's Eve, we've gotten a little gang together that he's somehow attached himself to; we go party-hopping, our little group gradually dwindles, it's just the two of us, I bring him home, he doesn't say a word but that's the way he is nowadays. My mother is still up, she's a little surprised to find him with me, but she's also very happy to have a chat with him; he's changed a lot since the last time she saw him, when one of my brothers married his first cousin and the two families were brought even closer together; she's heard all the good things being said about him, she congratulates him, questions him about his studies, he answers very sweetly; she's probably thinking he's another Quentin, but a good deal less dubious and more pleasant than the original. It makes me happy to see them together, the emotional confusion I felt throughout all those years of running from one house to the other is soon allayed by such calm, informal conversations as this, but it's not really the ideal atmosphere for obtaining what I desire, and it would be just as well for me to go straight to bed and forget all about it. Outside on the street, idiots are celebrating the new year by honking their horns furiously, and suddenly I feel very tired. My mother gives us sheets, the apartment is enormous, and we'll be pretty isolated down at the far end of the hallway, he in one room and me in mine just next door; I leave my door open. I hear him getting into bed; he laughs as he talks over the night's events; I sit on my bed, still fully dressed, and my cheery answers ring false; the only thing between us is the open door, but it feels impassable to me. He turns out the light and wishes me good night in the tone of voice of someone who's about to fall asleep. Darkness and silence. He will not come to me, and I dare not cross the threshold of his room. It's been several months since he's gone over to women, and the fact is I've suspected as much all evening. I've missed my chance.

If I ever see his mother's handsome lover again, I will try to ask him if he was kissing Sweetie that morning when I came upon them in the shed at the bottom of the garden. This happened around the time of the Latin translation, when I thought I was the only one dreaming about Sweetie. I hadn't thought of the shed as a place to bring him to, a place where practically no one ever went; I don't remember what I was looking for when I burst in abruptly. There was a brisk flurry of movement, that awkward yet casual show that I know so well. I pretended to have noticed nothing, and we never spoke of it again. But I am firmly convinced that they were kissing. It's a memory I have kept to myself, a vision that hurts a little or thrills a little, depending on the day. His mother and her handsome lover separated before the tragedy, I never knew why; they seemed to get along so well. I think he lives somewhere in the countryside; it wouldn't be difficult to track him down, but the truth is I'm not sure I'd have the courage to ask him the question.

Over the years, and as the two families gradually fused into one with the marriage of the cousin, the birth of children, our widespread and common tendency to mind each other's business, relations between Quentin and my brothers insidiously deteriorated and eventually broke off. The stockpile of grievances had become insurmountable, and although it was certainly difficult to acknowledge that Quentin seduced the wife of one and tried to sabotage the other's business, I understood that he had suffered far too much to be able to believe in family harmony; he surely experienced it as an obstacle to his rule of solitude and his will to dominate. He remained the dark heart of the clan, but no one ever saw him anymore. Messages passed back and forth between Christine, whom he had married, his mother, and even little Sacha, with whom she spent a lot of time now that she found herself alone. My brothers were very loyal to them. Personally, I'd retained all my affection for Quentin, but I was elsewhere

too now, I had a different life. I hardly ever ran into Sweetie or
the brother my age; they'd come into their inheritance, invested
part of the money in Quentin's business, and were methodically
throwing their youth away with the rest of them, living the fast
life, driving sports cars, dating beautiful girls, tagging along with
the rich kids on their endless travels, and getting more and more
involved with drugs. For Sweetie, the descent into hell was particularly fast. People said that this suited Quentin and that he
was more than happy to let it happen, but I don't believe that at
all. It wasn't his way to harm the feeble.

Once when I was in need of a large amount of money and
could find no one to oblige me, I called him to ask if he could
lend it to me. He'd already made a bundle, but I was not at all
certain of his response. He came to the phone right away, teased
me about being the same little jerk who was always in trouble,
and arranged to meet me the next day at the hotel where he was
staying in the Cap d'Antibes. He would be leaving for the United
States in two days without stopping back in Paris. I was in a hurry
but didn't have the money for the airfare, so he gave instructions
for a ticket to be left for me. I had the very distinct impression
that he was eager to see me, although our last meeting had taken
place a good ten years earlier. He received me in a white bathrobe by the Eden Roc swimming pool. He was accompanied by
an American supermodel, deluxe category, and surrounded by a
bevy of pseudo-millionaire wonder boys with 3,000 teeth apiece.
Black Porsche sunglasses, Calvin Klein bathing suits, and plastic
Mickey Mouse watches, which they found hilarious. He'd put
on some weight and was extremely handsome; he exuded success, energy, and power. I recalled his miserable showing at the
Évian aquatic center and felt ill at ease in my Sunday best, in this
technicolor Hollywood movie set, where I feared running into
someone who knew my brothers and would tell them they had
seen me with Quentin, which would certainly displease them.

He asked about them in a peremptory manner, invited me to a sumptuous lunch in the grill room with the supermodel, who was very sweet and very much in love, all the while questioning me about my dealings and reasons for needing money. He was no-nonsense and specific with his questions, no doubt his usual business manner, and I cut a sorry figure as I sat before him muddling my answers; the reasoning I had rehearsed on the plane to convince him to help me might perhaps have played on the sympathies of other poor slobs like me, but he was in no doubt whatsoever that I would have a very hard time repaying him. The supermodel, who knew the score, focused all her attention on her crab salad; I had nothing left to hope for but the old routine of sardonic quips to signal the end of the discussion, and I was eager to be on my way. Instead, he gave me a friendly slap on the cheek, smiling and with a glimmer of affection in his eyes that I will never forget, and pulled from his bathrobe pocket a manila envelope that he set down on my plate. Cutting short my expressions of gratitude, he spoke of his regret that I had not had more influence over his younger brothers; he was distressed by their lifestyle and worried about the risks they were running; I promised him that I would try to get back in touch with them, but he was dubious that such a line of attack would be helpful, and I caught a fleeting glimpse of a dark and hopeless fatalism at work in him. The supermodel dived into the pool, I was running late for my plane, and we barely had time to say our good-byes. When I turned back toward the hotel along the broad pathway rich with the scent of sun-drenched pine and bay, I saw him at the pool's edge, facing away from me. I was still quite near. He had removed the bathrobe; his shoulders were still covered in freckles. That was the last time I ever saw him. In the plane, I opened the envelope; it contained all the money I'd asked for in new bills of large denomination; it occurred to me that he must have gone to some trouble to organize everything so well and that I ought perhaps to have asked him for more money the day before. It was an unworthy thought, but I believe it would have amused him. I can't remember how I did it, but I managed to repay him with appropriate dispatch by sending a check to his office. He responded with a brief note in handwriting that was hard to decipher; it said something about a little jerk who could always count on him. It's the only letter he ever sent me, and I keep it in a secret drawer in my desk.

Sweetie died a few months later. No one ever answered my many phone calls, but I received plenty of bad news nevertheless. At the height of a bad acid trip, he had a very serious accident in his car and part of his foot, I'm not sure which, had had to be amputated. His rehabilitation went badly, he was in a lot of pain, and he limped. Drugs helped him to ease the pain and live with his disability, but he was also trying to quit and began abusing the replacement drugs. He was also drinking heavily, which was a whole other vicious circle. One night, he called his mother in a flood of tears. She begged him to come join her in the country: she was making up his room, she wouldn't go to bed, she'd wait up for him. Sweetie was driving drunk, and his speeding car left the road on the rising approach, at the final hairpin turn just before reaching her house. His mother heard the car as it flipped over and over down the slope and crashed at the bottom. I've always had trouble making up my mind to write her.

howard brookner
howard brookner
howard brookner

he had shot a movie about William Burroughs, and back in the early 1980s I was running a small chain of art houses for experimental films. He'd come from New York to find a venue for his movie in Paris. It was a low-cost production that he had financed himself with borrowed money, and he was counting on Burroughs's literary renown in France, as well as on our reputation as cinephiles, which was still intact at that time, to give the film an extra boost and maybe open up some festival opportunities. It had run at a theater in SoHo for several weeks and garnered enthusiastic praise in one review. The movie was filmed as a work of reportage about the American writer and included documentary sections in which he'd interviewed people who knew Burroughs, visited the writer's usual haunts, and dug up archival footage, as well as fictional sections inspired by his

writings, in which Burroughs played himself with the rather terrifying indifference of a sleepwalker. It was a very good movie,
cold and detached, which was just the right tone for capturing
Burroughs on film while avoiding the potential pitfalls presented
by the writer's unprecedented active participation in front of the
camera. I only became aware of all that later, when I actually
saw the movie, because when we first met I only had eyes for
Howard Brookner himself, and I took to him from the start.

He must have been about my age, thirty at most; he was not
very tall, his hair was thick and dark, his eyes were blue, his face
handsome and regular of feature. He wore an American-cut raincoat, like Paul Newman in Mark Robson's Cinemascope movies,
the type of suit worn by a banker or a lawyer, a very 1960s-chic
shirt and tie—a squeaky clean look, but not at all affected. In a
word, his style was a mix of American and European at a time
when none of the filmmakers I knew from New York to Paris
dressed that way. He spoke slowly so I could fully grasp what
he was trying to tell me, since my English was decidedly weaker
than it is now. I continue to struggle in that respect, but I believe
that our brief relationship drove me to make serious improve-
ments because I enjoyed talking with him so much. There was
nothing arrogant or in the least vain about him as he showed me
his reviews and explained his film to me. I'll never know why he
was so determined to come to me when there were other, more
prestigious and flourishing houses in prime locations in the heart
of the Latin Quarter. He merely told me that he'd done the full
circuit, Pariscope in hand, and that my theater, with its adjacent
restaurant and book store, had struck him as the best suited to
air his movie. He had been captivated by the atmosphere of the
place, a warehouse recycled as a cultural center, and by the constant flow of people among the bookshelves, the crowded tables,
and the screening rooms. In any case, he was not familiar with
Paris, this was his first trip, and he wasn't in it for the money; he

preferred a limited distribution with a guaranteed run of several weeks without the threat of being unceremoniously bumped if attendance was poor. He was wary of distributors in general and trusted me to attract some good press and to promote the film in the best possible way with the means at my disposal. In addition to the indefinable charm that he exuded—calm, precise, and reserved—I was touched by his trust. Within half an hour at the very most we came to an arrangement; even if I'd never heard of him before and had not yet seen his movie, a documentary about and featuring William Burroughs was exciting in and of itself. I saw the film shortly afterward and considered myself lucky.

The fact is, I knew little about Burroughs. A bit about his life, his legend rather than his work; I was one of those clever hipsters who could pepper his conversation with references to Jack Kerouac, Neal Cassady, Allen Ginsberg, the years of wandering, Tangiers, the *Naked Lunch* scandal, the deep undercurrent of homosexuality, drugs, the accident that killed his wife when the gun-crazy Burroughs shot her in the course of a drunken reenactment of William Tell—the whole romantic surge of the 1950s that had had a powerful effect on my brothers, whereas all I had ever done was glean tidbits from books or newspaper articles about the Beat Generation. A patently excessive crank, this ageless, rather unappealing man with thin lips and the physique of a clergyman held little attraction for me; he struck me as a kind of guru of an impenetrable and morbid universe to which I did not have the key. But I understood his impact on contemporary literature and sensed the fascination he held for his devotees; shallow as I was in those days, that was more than enough for me to stake my claim and make my humble contribution to attracting a wider audience for the iceman in the fedora.

Howard Brookner was staying at the Louisiane, a storied hotel in Saint-Germain-des-Prés that has seen many of its residents go on to fame and that is home to the delightful Albert Cossery—a lifestyle choice very much in keeping with his own work. Now, every time I pass by the Louisiane, I think of him with a pang in my heart; one of these days I'll rent a room there just to check it out, before Albert Cossery makes his exit, since it's a sure thing that Howard Brookner will never stay there again. We chose a date for the opening, and before he left for New York I stopped up at the Louisiane two or three times to take him out to dinner. We'd arranged for him to return to Paris for the few press screenings my meager budget would allow; we figured it would take about three months for a new print to be made, the subtitling finished, and all the other work necessary before the launch. He seemed in a hurry to return to the States in the meantime, which is why I saw so little of him on that first trip. In any case, at the time I was involved in a typically impossible affair, in which I loved without being loved in return; any assignation with someone I barely knew would have struck me guiltily as a kind of betrayal. The fact that I was in no danger of being discovered made me all the more afraid of being caught red-handed.

He was always on time, and so was I; I had only a moment's wait on the second-floor landing, with its worn carpeting and desk clerk shouting into a phone that had seen better days. He was dressed as ever in a raincoat, blue suit, button-down Oxford shirt, and nondescript tie, and possessed of elegant manners and a drawling, pleasantly resonant voice. We went to little neighborhood restaurants, and he took very naturally to Parisian ways, menus, and cuisine. He'd read Gertrude Stein, Janet Flanner, and Mary McCarthy, and he moved about the city, where he'd only just arrived and knew absolutely no one, as if he'd lived there all his life. He did not drink alcohol, ate little, and was discriminating in his tastes. He hardly spoke about himself at all; our conversations were limited to movie talk. He had no particular emotional connection to Hollywood, was indifferent to the politics of *Cahiers du cinema*–type writers, and although he was amused by the "camp" style, which I knew inside out, he wasn't especially interested in the classic stars of black-and-white movies, their tortured lives and scathing wit. His main interests lay elsewhere; he loved Robert Flaherty and the great documentary makers of the 1930s, the old Warner Brothers social-theme movies, Italian neo-realism, Warhol, Steve Dwoskin, and the oddballs of the 1960s New York avant-garde. For a young American director, his knowledge of Third World filmmakers was astounding. He also questioned me about my profession, the life and times of a Parisian cinephile, the film I'd made in Somalia, about which he'd heard in passing. His opinions were colored by uncommon insight and sensitivity and always expressed with his characteristic reserve and lack of emotion. I put this odd detachment down to American pseudo-Puritanism; it was, perhaps, that typically aloof Yankee way of dissecting life and art with equal parts diffidence and perspicacity. Aloof, but not cold; with his blue eyes upon me and a half-smile on his lips, I felt him to be very present and affable. Dazzling in his judgment, reticent about himself, mysteriously linked to me in some way. Still, a guy who had spent several months with Burroughs and was intimate with Kenneth Anger and the films of Satyajit Ray must have had more in common with me than a predilection for endless movie talk. But his admiration for Burroughs, which in truth was somewhat circumspect, told me nothing about his past and shed no light on what had happened to their relationship once the film was finished. I sometimes had the impression that there was more than one meaning to his words, which he enunciated slowly so I could understand him, and at other times not—we were simply talking about the films we loved. I also took a tentative stab at seducing him, very cautiously because his self-sufficiency was so impressive and I was afraid he might clam up, get to his feet, and leave. But he never moved, maintained his smile without reacting, and, ignoring my discreet attempts at footsie, went on talking about the cinema in his tranquil and reflective manner.

Ultimately, it came out in dribs and drabs that he'd grown up somewhere on the East Coast, Maryland or Delaware—not exactly the boondocks but not a center of sophistication either—and that he'd gone to college in New York and decided to stay rather than strike out for the Hollywood studios; but I had no vision of what an American youth might entail and it was all very indistinct to me. I couldn't tell, for instance, if he had a family or friends or even if he liked men or women. At that point, frankly, I was hoping that he liked women, since my every attempt at charm had failed, but I still felt myself attracted to him. In the end, I came to enjoy all this uncertainty as much as simply being with him.

He wrote me several times from New York. American-style letters, one typewritten page on yellow paper with his name and address in a handsome font at the top and a signature scrawled at the bottom. His first name only, preceded by "love," also handwritten, but it didn't mean anything; "regards" would have been too impersonal and "yours truly" decidedly businesslike. *Love* was for the dinners we'd shared and our very correct cordiality; I was happy enough to get that much out of him. I was preparing to launch the film, and his letters focused on our work, identifying the excerpts to be used for the television trailers and the Burroughs scholars to be dunned for articles. Not a word about what he was up to in New York at the moment, and no further specification about when he was planning to come back to Paris. I'd grown used to the absence of personal information, but I was surprised to get no sense of his return schedule, and I wondered what could possibly be keeping him in New York when he'd been so meticulous and methodical in preparing for the release of his film. I tried several times to reach him on the phone but always got the answering machine with a generic greeting, and my messages were not returned. I also had other concerns, between my sorry love affair and ongoing money problems, and started to think that the film would have to be launched without him. It had received some good notice in the press and selected excerpts had run several times on television, attracting a lot of interest, particularly the one in which Burroughs, firearms in hand, gives vent to a gory persecution fantasy. All in all, I'd done a pretty good job and no longer needed Howard to draw attention to the movie. Nevertheless, I was very sorry about our broken contact and his inexplicable absence; never, I believe, had I been so eager to win a director's trust or simply to please someone I barely knew.

He arrived without warning the day after the film's release. As handsome as ever, impeccably dressed, serene, staying at the Louisiane. He referred in passing to some vague problems to explain his disappearance, but I deliberately chose not to question him, which he seemed to appreciate. In any event, I was glad to have him here and made use of his presence to schedule a number of interviews with journalists. He pored over the articles that had already come out, assessed the reactions of the early audiences, and monitored the quality of the projection, which he declared to be good although it was not, but I thought him oddly reluctant to meet with people who could have been of use to him. I was used to the demands (not to mention whims) of directors, but he found everything to be perfect and made everything easy for me, except for his increasingly explicit refusal to grant interviews. His growing reliance on and trust in me was so touching that I could hardly insist, so I left him in peace. If he was sick and tired of always having to answer the same questions, the answers to which were all in the press kit anyway, that was his right. I was hopeful that the time thus saved might allow me to arrange at least one of our ritual dinners in the Louisiane neighborhood, but things did not work out that way. Other than the times he showed up unannounced in my office—never for very long—he was incommunicado. The desk clerk at the Louisiane made awkward excuses to avoid putting me through to his room—he was either asleep, or on the line, or not there; in any case, I could never get him on the phone and he never called back. I didn't want to be too pushy by laying siege to his room. At the end of the week, the desk clerk informed me that he'd checked out and returned to New York—left without even saying good-bye. We'd had none of our talks about the movies, having only discussed the details of the film's release. Our conversations, friendly and interesting as always, had been confined to the minimum. His attitude was totally unfathomable and left me baffled. On the other hand, the film was doing quite well, a fact that he'd had time enough to register.

Some months went by with no news of him. My attempts to reach him in New York remained fruitless; a letter, in which I explained that, following five weeks of excellent receipts, I could keep the film running indefinitely at one showing a day, remained unanswered. Knowing his orderly mind, I imagined that he'd found a way to get *Pariscope* in New York and to follow the daily box office on his film. Could he have had other ways of keeping himself informed? There were a considerable number of young Americans among the film's audience. And after all, it was always possible that he had French friends he'd not told me about who could keep him abreast of matters. I sometimes went into the theater to see some part of the film again and listen to his voice and commentary; it was my only means of contact with him. Then the day came when no one attended the daily screening. I had only one print, and it had been requested for screenings in the provinces; I took it off the billing and sent it off to live its own life. I was hoping that he'd come forward when he noticed that it was no longer being screened in Paris. And that's what he did.

I received a letter from a woman who introduced herself as Howard's assistant and informed me that Howard was unable to write to me himself for *"motifs personnels"*—"personal reasons," set down like that in French—but that he was deeply grateful to me for all my work and for having kept the film running for so long. The assistant asked me to send her the accounts, if it wasn't too early to settle them, and suggested that I try to negotiate a television sale in the wake of the critical and public interest expressed in the movie, even if, given the obvious marginality of its audience, I could not secure any great price for it. Such instructions, that sense of practicality and unpretentious pragmatism, were definitely Howard's style. He must have dictated the letter or at least overseen it down to the last detail, but who was this assistant I'd never heard of, what were these obscure "personal reasons"? At the bottom, the word "love" was written beside the signature, in a different handwriting but just like before. The letter was definitely from him. I worked up his accounts; in fact, there wasn't much left over after the publicity expenses, and when the print came back from its tour, I sent it around to the television companies with few illusions about the chances of a positive response. I informed the assistant by letter of the final accounting and of my dealings with the TV people, and signed it simply "truly yours" as a formulaic courtesy. At the end of the day, I may have been growing a little tired of the whole story. The assistant must have evaporated into the ether, because I received no answer from her.

Howard showed up in my office a few weeks later. I'd almost forgotten about him; I was very busy and he reappeared like one of those people you meet while traveling or on vacation and whom you find you don't have much to say to when you see them again. Actually, it wasn't exactly like that either. I was feeling a little resentful toward him—something in me was smoldering still—but rather than bombard him with pointless

questions, I told myself that all I need do was settle our accounts
neatly and have done with it, each goes his own way, back to
the daily grind, at least until the next film. He clearly grasped
the situation and took a seat in a corner of the office, his back
to the window, while looking over the press clippings and the
receipts from the out-of-town screenings, while I attended to
more urgent business. This should have been quick work, since
he'd already read most of his press on his last trip and the list of
theaters outside Paris was rather short; but he seemed absorbed
in his reading, taking his time, calmly making himself at home,
as usual, as if we'd seen each other only the day before. And
again, I was totally befuddled by his manner; I pretended to
work but I was just spinning my wheels, and I felt the aura that
surrounded his mere presence gradually take over the whole
room and envelop me entirely. And yet he was sitting absolutely
still, his eyes focused on the paperwork. I glanced at him surreptitiously from time to time. He had changed, almost imperceptibly, but changed he had—he was thinner, with rings under
his eyes, some gray at the temples. It's been eighteen months
since we first met, I thought to myself; we grow old in phases,
that's what's happened to him, and to me too no doubt. Finally,
he raised his head while I happened to be looking his way, and
he smiled at me in a way that melted and dazzled me all over
again. I asked him how he wished me to settle what I owed
him; he answered that a small cash advance would tide him
over while he was in Paris but that he didn't want to trouble
me if things were tight; there was no real hurry for the rest. In
any case we trusted one another, ours was a brotherhood in
the jungle of moviemaking and commerce, there was no need
to worry about these little things between the two of us. He'd
said "brotherhood" in English, I'd heard it as clearly as I'd
read "love" in his letters. Again that smile, the blue eyes, no
tie but his collar open to a powerful neck on his shoulders. I

would never understand him at all, that was for sure. All that remained was for me to make a pretense of tidying up my desk and take him to lunch. Which I did forthwith.

I'm coming to the heart of the matter, or at least to something that may well seem unimportant to those who are not interested in such things, but that I recall often with abiding melancholy. He'd planned to return to New York very quickly, and we had only three or four days to spend together. And even then it was only the evenings. I had work to do, but I could have made time for him; he was busy, he told me, in the mornings and the afternoons, he preferred that we see each other at night, in dim lighting; he laughed as if he were making a professional joke. And yet I felt that he was as lonely as ever, immersed in a bottomless solitude that colored the indefinable aura of his presence, and when I went to pick him up at the Louisiane at nine o'clock, I had the impression that he'd spent the day asleep in his room, which was odd for someone who could not be said to be slovenly or lazy. I owned a black Austin Mini, an almost perfect archetype of the English compact car of the 1960s that had been immensely popular in its time but was now decidedly out of date. I'd bought it, as I imagined, for its snob appeal, commensurate with my modest means, and it suited me very well as I only drove it around the streets of Paris. I used it to take him beyond the Latin Quarter to the sixteenth arrondissement, where I grew up, or over toward the Bourse and the Palais-Royal, having carefully chosen a pleasant restaurant where the tables were not too close together and we could talk at our ease. He really liked the black Mini, which he thought very exotic and brought out a kind of childlike glee in him. Its pokiness, its wooden steering wheel, its brutal gearshifts and suspension were the very opposite of the enormous gliding American models. We almost never talked about the movies, and since he was still as private about himself as ever, I told him about myself, never overstepping the bounds of modesty but also leaving no stone unturned. Telling my life story seemed as good a way as any to get some insight into his. He couldn't get enough of it, asked me lots of questions, and revealed himself only in sweetly ironic remarks suggesting that he had certainly had many of the same experiences. Unfortunately, mostly the worst ones. We had a whole ritual: at the restaurant, I would begin by talking about very general things, usually concerning the routines and customs of life in Paris, then move on to more personal topics as I drove him back to the hotel by roundabout detours. We drove the black Mini at length through the haunting streets of late-night Paris. I felt him at my side, tremendously alert, miraculously congenial, as enigmatic as a taboo, his handsome, half-smiling face turned to me, glowing in the headlights of a passing car or at a red light. *Brotherhood*. It took us a couple of hours to get back to the Louisiane. At times we remained silent; he wanted to listen to Édith Piaf on the cassette player and asked me to translate the lyrics when he didn't understand them. In fact, he got along pretty well in French; I tried not to touch his knee when I shifted the balky gears; and he had no plans to make another movie, at least not at the moment. These were delicious moments, the kind that mark the beginnings of an as-yet-unspoken love, when life expands at a dizzying pace, the past disappears, obstacles fall away, and death ceases to exist. The black Mini sped us toward limitless horizons; I could have driven that way until dawn and through the next day, and the next night, and again and again if he had asked.

The last night—I didn't know it was to be the last, since the issue of his departure no longer came up between us—I suggested that we go see the boys on the way back. I'd confided that the black Mini was pretty good for cruising, not as good as a Porsche or an Italian car, but the manicured, outmoded English look had its fans. We wrote a song, "The black Mini strikes again," that we sang as we cruised the Rue Sainte-Anne neighborhood, where there was a hustler every fifteen feet in those days; the only people on the street these days are those heading for the Japanese restaurants that have replaced the gay bars. This must have been in the late spring, because many of the boys were in shorts and some were even bare-chested; there was something for everyone; some were very good-looking indeed. I played the regular, discreetly pointing out the boys I knew, who hailed us with their usual shamelessness. Howard stared at them thoughtfully; he hummed *The black Mini strikes again* quietly to himself, but I could also see that he was growing increasingly glum. A storm cloud had suddenly opened up over him; he turned all grim as if his sadness had erected a wall between us. The Rue Sainte-Anne hustlers had been a bad idea in the end, so I headed for the lights of the Avenue de l'Opéra. I apologized for my mistake; he told me there was nothing to apologize for. He relaxed and we turned Édith Piaf back on. "Les Mots d'amour," music by Michel Rivgauche and words by Charles Dumont, as she herself announced before each song; he loved that courtesy of hers, how even the way she spoke their names was a kind of song. According to him, in America only Frank Sinatra was her equal, and not always. I wished he wouldn't go home to America, but obviously I couldn't say so, although I was sure he could hear it in my silences and feel it in the car. The song, yes, the song: "It's crazy how much I love you, how much I love you sometimes, sometimes I want to scream because I've never loved, I've never loved like this, I swear it's true, if you ever went away, went away and left me, left me forever, I know I would die, I would die of love, my love, my love."

Later, I dropped him at the Louisiane; he had already reached the foot of the stairs at the threshold of the hotel entrance when he turned back toward me, leaning over the open door of the black Mini. Although this happened twenty-five years ago, the image is burned so deeply into my psyche that I could film it right now, frame for frame. The door, the pallid light of the entryway over the street, the ever-present raincoat, the blue eyes and the smile, hesitating as they drew near. "You'll come to me tomorrow night," he said to me in French, then kissed me very quickly, very lightly on the cheek, adding "to sleep, only to sleep," and in English, "no body fluids." I was so happy I didn't know how to answer except, oh yes, his French had really improved, which was a stupid, kindly, and not entirely true thing to say. I was also thinking, "Why not tonight, right now?" but it was a perfect moment, there was no need to ask for more. *No body fluids, no body fluids.* I didn't see him enter the hotel; I was in a bit of a daze and staring straight ahead. At that moment, in the film, there will be nothing but an exterior night shot of the deserted street spread out before the black Mini.

The next day he was gone; he must have changed his mind at daybreak. I never saw him again, my calls and letters went unanswered, I never again heard the sound of his voice. *No body fluids.* The print of the Burroughs movie was somehow lost in the vast chaos of the television studios, and I've never found that again, either.

A few years later, after my movie theaters went under, I became the host of a series of television broadcasts in which I interviewed all sorts of celebrities, talk-show style. Burroughs's publisher had organized a promotional tour for his author in France, and naturally I was asked to have him on.

I had made very little headway with his work, whose power I certainly appreciated but whose icy cruelty caused me anxiety and discomfort. I supposed I knew enough to hold an hour-long conversation and make an interesting show of it, but I hoped above all that our meeting would help me understand why Howard had suddenly vanished, if Burroughs had kept up contact with him. That unexplained ending, the flameout of hope in the void, the momentum lost into thin air had long haunted me, as I imagined they do those confronted by the mystery of death—the parents who cling to the image of a vanished child and are condemned to the blind pain of not even knowing whether their little one ran away, was kidnapped, or fell victim to an undetected accident; the wives of lost sailors and soldiers; the husband whose wife has left him in the middle of the night; secret double lives that ensnare those with whom we share our existence and leave those who remain behind obsessively to retrace their common path in reverse; the dead end of unanswered questions; the labyrinth of days to come spent wondering if they'll ever return; the plots of detective novels and comic films; those pictures of kids that break your heart in airports and post offices. It wasn't that bad for me, of course—just a touch of bitterness that had not faded with time.

I needed to speak with Burroughs to prepare for the show, and I hoped to take the opportunity to ask him right off the bat for his thoughts on Howard's disappearance. An atmosphere of urbane, semi-literary mayhem surrounded the writer as he made his rounds of interviews with print journalists, signing events, and a formal reception at which Jack Lang made him a Commander of the Order of Arts and Letters. All that was to be expected, but the first time I met Burroughs I was put off by his provocative and nihilistic behavior, which I soon came to suspect was a deliberate act put on to impress the crowds and indulge the painful sycophancy of his hipster admirers. His baggy eyes wandered as, whistling faintly through razor lips, he spoke words I did not understand but that seemed to be incoherent and perhaps obscene, delegating to his publicity agent the task of informing me that he didn't give a damn what we talked about on the show. I made a second attempt to buttonhole him at the party held to celebrate his decoration, but thronged by a clucking, chortling crowd, he was too busy pretending to draw a bead on his medal

for me to take the chance of telling him my little story. I couldn't
help thinking that perhaps Howard was just like him in the end,
a younger and more lightweight version of the dedicated cynic,
and that the film had succeeded because they had found in each
other the same perverse facility for manipulating those around
them. I resented Burroughs for having inspired such a thought in
me; I came to despise him for this new self-doubt among all my
others, a kind of mark of Cain proclaiming my status as a petit-
bourgeois Frenchman incapable of appreciating the emotional
underpinnings of the American counterculture.

I approached the interview in the spirit of an amusement park
ghost ride—unwilling to deploy shock tactics, yet ready to give
viewers their money's worth. All the same, I was well prepared,
my questions were reasonably intelligent, focusing mainly on
literary technique, which even an author like Burroughs had a
stake in; nor was it necessary to be particularly friendly—all I
had to do was hold my nose and ape his flatterers, whom I'd
had every opportunity to grow to loathe. And in fact, everything
went rather smoothly. Burroughs had arrived in the company of
a kind of secretary, a dirty-blond giantess in her forties, equally
cold as ice, whose job was to answer for the master when my
questions struck him as just too idiotic. The publicist, who was
beginning to wilt after a week of bedlam, explained in embarrassment that the secretary's presence assured that we could get
through the entire interview without Burroughs growing bored
or distracted and simply getting up and walking off the set. The
secretary stayed; I looked at her, wondering if perhaps her lack
of charm had been counterbalanced by good looks in her youth.
Burroughs refused to look at me, the cameras, the secretary, or
anything else; he muttered between his teeth and the interpreter
in the control room could barely follow his train of thought; it
hardly mattered. With his spectral pallor, his bony, inscrutable
face, his hat glued to his head, his gray undertaker's suit, and his

vaguely threatening nasal twang, his presence-absence was altogether riveting—*Night of the Living Dead* after the final credits, when you're left wondering what the zombies will do once they've killed off all the living. When the interpreter floundered or Burroughs fell silent, twisting his face into a rictus that must have scared the shit out of the well-heeled book-lovers who had tuned in, the secretary performed her duties like an American academic talking down to a bunch of semi-literate schoolchildren. It was good show business, and when the interview was over the publicist was as euphoric as if she'd just emerged from the shelter after a nuclear scare. Détente. Even Pol Pot must have had moments like this after the cameras stopped rolling, tensions dissipated, and the social niceties were tacitly resumed. That was when I finally mentioned Howard—"Howard Brookner, that young guy who made a good film with you," I tried in English. Burroughs repeated the name *Howard Brookner* several times as if searching for it in the depths of memory. Howard Brookner, no, he had no recollection of this stranger with whom the Frenchie insisted he had spent several months. The studio was going dark, the crew was breaking down the equipment, and I stood paralyzed by the sound of that heedless twang which, with every repetition of Howard's name, seemed to consign him ever deeper to obscurity. The tall blonde—and now I was sure of it, she must have been a looker twenty years earlier on the beach at Tangiers—cleared the air: "Howard Brookner died of AIDS five years ago." "Ah yes, died of AIDS," Burroughs echoed, as if he were swatting a fly from his lapel. And they started to laugh. I pressed them. They knew nothing more than that, but this much was for sure: "Died of AIDS five years ago." All perfectly normal and funny too; it must have been since it made them laugh like a good joke. I stood there with my Howard, dead only a few months after *no body fluids*, and those two laughing assholes who hadn't even bothered to ask after him once he'd gone.

I have a fairly good sense of people's feelings and why they behave the way they do, but there are some things that completely stump me, closet skeletons to which I am totally blind and oblivious. Drug problems, conspiracies, sexual proclivities, money issues—it takes me a while to catch on, and often only too late, after an irreparable falling out or a tragedy I have been unable to prevent. Such gaps in my relationship with reality are no doubt explained by my childhood fear of the outside world and the future, a fear that I've largely overcome but has left traces of itself that prompt me to ignore whatever frightens me or threatens my composure and equilibrium. I'm able to act boldly in many instances, deal with difficult situations that would defeat others who might be thought more hardened than I, and I've endured more than my share of rough treatment with no long-term trauma, but I have a hard time applying the lessons I've learned to other people's experiences. When I met Howard, I knew all about the epidemic and its calamitous spread, the symptoms, miseries, and horrendous physical deterioration that precede an ineluctable death, as well as the fantastic courage displayed by so many patients; the barely credible stories of debauched New York nightlife, the specter of Armageddon that followed, the appalling fate of those early victims whom I knew by name or had even met on occasion—I was all too familiar with that convulsion of insanity and intimate tragedy. I was even better informed, more mindful and involved than most people, and yet not for one moment did it occur to me that Howard had been infected and knew his days were numbered when he came to see me in Paris.

I had assessed his absences and silences only in the light of my own disappointments and without considering that he might have serious personal reasons for withdrawing from the world: treatment, concealing his condition, exhaustion, and crises of despair. I'd been satisfied by my frivolous and superficial observation of the subtle changes in his physical appearance. Without ever questioning the bases of his extreme thoughtfulness and tenacity, I had readily ascribed his reserve, his unwavering trust in me, and his bizarre indifference to the commercial aspects of our arrangement to his eagerness to get the movie out there, while for him it was certainly his only remaining connection to life, his last attempt to leave something behind and be recognized, his final message in a bottle. His sudden attack of melancholy while we were among the boys on the Rue Sainte-Anne should have made me stop and think, instead of which I pursued my prideful, grim charade of cruising in the black Mini. I had not heard "no body fluids" as a confession or, as it may well have been, an appeal.

Twenty-five years later, I can still hear that very particular resonance in his voice as he sang along to a different Piaf song in the car—"Padam, padam, listen to all the racket it makes . . . as if my entire past was unfolding before me . . ."—and I can still see those blue eyes, from the day we met in my office to that last night at the Louisiane. The image of his death soon afterward in some bleak New York hospital, and in that fortress of solitude he inhabited, has long haunted me, as if I had been personally responsible for it. I've tried several times to contact his assistant. It's strange, but I can't help feeling that she was not his assistant, but rather his mother, and that makes me feel a little better. I tell myself that it was because she was so close to him and so overwhelmed with grief that she did not respond to me. I've promised myself that I would go to New York to inquire into what really happened between his return and his death and to determine whether I had been of help to him in any way despite my obliviousness. But the years pass, I never stay there long enough, and it must be getting harder and harder to find people who remember Howard Brookner. But since I will never forget him, I've written myself a letter in my makeshift English, a fake letter typewritten on yellow paper with an address at the top in American type and an elegant signature at the bottom with "love" next to it, and I've filed this truthful lie among the other letters typewritten on yellow paper in the file on the Burroughs movie that I saved after my theaters went bust. I take it out from time to time and find that it has come increasingly to resemble the others.

Dear Fred,

Don't worry if I decided not to stay one more night in Paris. You will know someday the reason why and you will understand then, that my only purpose was to protect you from some personal problems that I cannot overcome. We will never meet again, I am afraid, but I want you to know that I am deeply grateful for all that you did for me, and moreover since you have been the most sensitive and most charming French brother that I could have dreamed of. Would you forgive me if I did not let you know which were my feelings for you; from the first day these were feelings of tenderness and love even if I did not want to intrude in your life and bring some more strain as it was impossible for me to fulfill the hopes and the promises of my heart. Keep your share of the film. Regards to our Edith and the black Mini. Take care and please, please, "no body fluids."

Love, Howard.

tenerezza/tenderness
tenerezza/tenderness
tenerezza/tenderness

The first time was on the Rue de l'Université, in the seventh arrondissement. You were walking along happily with your little boy; I was passing on my moped. It was one of those sunny days when Paris is at its loveliest, a day that makes you want to go shopping in a quiet neighborhood of antique shops, bookstores, and boutiques selling pretty things for the home. You were wearing dark glasses and carrying a canvas bag, the child was following close on your heels, as all children devoted to their mothers tend to do; he must have been about seven; it was because he was with you that I recognized you right away. No one else was paying attention, but I took a closer look, stopping a little further up the street to watch you discreetly, pretending to adjust my locking mechanism as you drew near. I heard you talking to each other; for you two it was certainly just one of those ordinary moments that make up the fabric of happy times.

I can date that day with some precision back to the spring of 1969. Despite all the appearances of leading the normal life of a student, I was actually in a state of great intellectual and emotional confusion at the time, and had exacerbated the situation by falling into the clutches of a brooding young man of good breeding, intelligence, and depravity, who was playing the hero in the events of May 1968 and had roped me into his leftist pipe dreams. I served him as confidante, factotum, and pimp, an unpleasant role that I played to the hilt in order to please him. He was the first in my series of teases, and our friendship, which I portrayed to all and sundry as exalted, was in fact an ambiguous relationship steeped in sorrow and disenchantment. In the fog of our anti-establishment paradigms, we blithely identified the collaborationist writer Drieu la Rochelle as one of our theoreticians of armed struggle; he had me read "L'Intermède romain," a beautiful, hopeless short story about a fleeting love affair. It was the kind of reading that allowed us to make fools of ourselves by voguing as free and sophisticated intellects. Among all my youthful delusions, I also harbored the dream of becoming a movie director. When I crossed paths with you, I imagined it was the hand of fate and an opportunity not to be missed; in my vanity and naiveté, I thought you would make the perfect heroine for the screen adaptation of the short story my friend and I were writing. It wasn't an entirely idiotic notion, actually, but between an immature teenager like me and a woman like you there was obviously an entire world I knew nothing about. You were beautiful, young, and famous, and I was still profoundly childish and thoughtless. I had no doubts about anything. So I sped off on my moped to the La Hune bookstore, miraculously managed to locate a copy of the book, and went off to track you down again. I made quick work of it, finding you on the Rue du

Pré-aux-Clercs; you must have stopped in somewhere along the
way, because your son was carrying a large, carefully wrapped
package and still scurrying along behind you like a little soldier
boy all proud to be of assistance to his beloved.

I can still see your astonished expression as I suddenly
appeared before you with the book in my outstretched hands;
my heart was beating wildly, I must have been bright red with
shyness, and I stuttered as I explained that I'd bought the book
for you because it contained a short story that you would surely
love. Still and all, I was polite, I apologized a good deal and
made a great effort not to frighten the little boy, who stared at
me with eyes full of suspicion; in the end, it was all perfectly
sweet, if perhaps a little sudden, and you saw straightaway that
this kid on his moped, so eager to force his attentions on you,
was no threatening stalker. You thanked me in a steady tone of
voice, slipped the book into your bag, and went on your way;
the child fell in behind you, he did not turn around, and was certainly relieved to be rid of the tiresome intruder. It all happened
in the wink of an eye. I was a little let down that the whole
foolhardy operation—the wild there-and-back to La Hune, the
good luck of finding the book and then tracking you down—
had been completed in such a rushed and prosaic manner, but
my principal emotion was one of triumph. I hadn't screwed it
up—I'd got up the nerve to approach you, you hadn't rebuffed
me, I could picture you thinking of me as you opened your bag;
in a certain way, I had forced my way into your home, into your
life. And perhaps you would read the book and wonder who
the young stranger with such judicious taste could possibly be.
I prepped myself for a second encounter, where we would have
an actual conversation in which I would contrive to pique your
interest; fortune had served me so well, there was no reason why
it should not go to work for me a second time. My head ringing,
I sped away on my moped as if spurring on a stallion, but in the

wrong direction down a one-way street; the real good fortune is that I didn't fly headlong into the first oncoming truck.

As you might expect, nothing ever came of it, and I didn't even hazard to mention it to my friend; he would surely have made fun of me as he always did whenever I ventured something on my own; anyway, once I'd sobered up, I wasn't entirely convinced that the gloomy atmosphere of Drieu la Rochelle's chilling story would be to your taste. My pride in what I'd done gradually faded, and as time went by, I began to think that I'd behaved with shameless and foolish pushiness. What had gotten into me? I came to see, more or less, that the way in which I'd so irrationally thrown myself upon an idealized and clearly unattainable woman was linked to my fear of the girls I knew, those who were available and whom I avoided, whom I ought to have desired but did not. And I was ashamed of having used you as an excuse to continue lying to myself. Obviously, it wasn't particularly serious, I'd done you no harm, and you probably forgot all about me in short order, but what had at first struck me as an admirable act of zeal and generosity had merely been a form of selfish exploitation, even an abuse of trust. I suppose that it is through such little misdeeds and the remorse they engender that one begins to mature. Through an unplanned reversal of emotional roles, while I long avoided Rue du Pré-aux-Clercs and the remotest possibility of running into you again, you entered my life secretly, and became entrenched there forever. It is equally true that, even without knowing you, there are any number of reasons why you might come to mind. Oddly enough, the idea of adapting "L'Intermède romain" must have been in the air, for Bertolucci was inspired by it to direct *Last Tango in Paris* only three years later. It was at that time that I liberated myself abruptly from my friend's power over me following one of the cruel betrayals that he seemed to practice habitually. I saw him only one other time many years later, dazed and unrecognizable, shortly before his death from causes unknown to me, and I was never moved to reread "L'Intermède romain," either.

I no longer remember the name of the little beach club where I'd seen your sister three years earlier, in that quiet spot below Ramatuelle, which someone had predictably nicknamed Hawaii or Acapulco Beach, provincial in a nice way, and a long way down the coast from the pandemonium of Rivas and the paparazzi. My stepmother had rented a charming house in the village for the summer, filled with friends and children; we went down to the beach *en famille* and had little to do with la dolce vita of Saint-Tropez. Even so, the nonstop party atmosphere rubbed off on me; I had just passed my driving test, my father had loaned me his Italian car, and I spent my evenings mostly with boys my own age that I knew from Paris. We did the rounds of the clubs and private parties, where the mood was incredibly hot and heavy for someone who had only known the rather staid gatherings of the sixteenth arrondissement. Slim, tanned, sexy, their bodies lithe under wispy clothing—summer suited them and their youth opened every door; night after night, my friends plunged merrily into new amorous exploits, wreaking havoc among women who, in the gray days of the coming fall, would not deign to look their way should they pass them on the quad. Loosely on the prowl but inevitably awkward and timorous, I watched them make their opening moves while I stayed in the shadows, sidestepping any intrigue that threatened to involve me more directly. In any case, there was always such a crowd and such a confusion of players that my elusiveness passed unnoticed. Despite the suspicions of their dates and their painfully enthusiastic attempts to fix me up, my young lotharios were far too absorbed in their own business to ask me uncomfortable questions, and while they may no longer have been in much doubt about me, my fine car and enthusiastic willingness to act as chauffeur were more than enough to make me popular.

It was a disabling life, entirely given over to repression and frustration; I preferred it to the prospect of another joyless return to my studies, but I knew full well that the euphoria of summer vacation changed nothing, that this way of living would almost always be bitter and solitary. A simple romantic dance number playing on the radio while a couple made out in the back seat, or listening to a sentimental melody while some handsome boy whispered confidences beside me as I drove him to his assignation, could easily bring me to the verge of tears. The fact is, I sped along the peninsula's narrow curving roads, all windows open to the warm night, and nobody ever noticed a thing.

I think your sister chose our beach precisely because it was set away from all the commotion. But the young summer staff who set up the beach chairs and served drinks recognized her and flew into a tizzy; their reaction brought her in turn to my attention. She'd arrived alone with a little dog, an English griffon or a Chihuahua; in a broad-brimmed straw hat and a dressing gown that covered her practically head to toe, concealed behind an umbrella in the secluded section of the beach, she made it very clear that she wanted to be left in peace. As families gradually became aware of her presence, they craned their necks for a glimpse of her and exchanged whispered commentary about which of the two sisters was older, prettier, more talented, but she buried her face in a book and, with the little dog at her side, ostentatiously ignored the general interest. The situation was pretty strange, it must be said; we weren't used to having celebrities on our beach, and it was odd to see a young woman like her without an entourage; you had to be either truly fed up with all the artificial adulation or else be a unique sort of person to resort to such a method of protecting your anonymity. In her case, it was surely both. Our little community being relatively well-heeled, the feverish attention cooled rather quickly. Then again, it was very hot out, we were all pretty dopey in the heat, and I was daydreaming as usual that my sassy beaus had finally taken an interest in me, when we heard your sister calling her dog, which had run away and vanished. I leaped up and presented myself before her with an offer of assistance. I remember very well the huskiness in her voice and the anxious, anguished expression on her face; I was also struck by the porcelain whiteness of her skin, which stood out among all the tanned complexions around us. This was not the moment for small talk, the little creature had to be found as soon as possible; the beach boys scattered in all directions, and she grew increasingly disturbed, practically desperate. I knew what it was like to lose a dog, but people generally don't give a damn; they were going out of their way for her now but it wouldn't last long, it was time for lunch, and the families who had sat down to eat beneath the reed awnings were already getting impatient to place their orders. Since the dog had not been found on our stretch, I had the clever idea of looking in the next kitchen down the beach; there he was, being cosseted by two fat ladies with southern accents, and I took him in my arms and returned him to your sister—a somewhat perilous operation, as it happens, as he was in a very bad mood at having been disrupted in full feast. She was so happy to have him back that we chatted a while; she thanked me profusely and sweetly, and I was moved this time by the intensity of her gaze, so limpid and penetrating; she asked me my name, but I didn't want her to remember me that way and I only told her my first name. I also pretended that I didn't know who she was; I could tell that she was wondering whether to offer me a reward, but somehow, I don't remember how, I managed to suggest that it would bother me and she had the delicacy not to insist. That was it; those who had not found the dog looked put out and shot us baleful glances intimating that it had all been a lot of fuss about nothing, and I was also uncomfortable being in her presence in my bathing suit, as I was hung up about my underdeveloped body. We had nothing left to say to each other; the incident had brought us together unexpectedly, we were each happy in our way, and such a moment should not be ruined by getting bogged down in pointless conversation. With a little luck she would not forget me, I'd be the sweet boy on the beach who had rescued her little dog and had not exploited the situation to his advantage in any way, not even to beg an autograph, since he hadn't recognized her. I have no memory at all of how we parted, but it must have been hard for me to stroll back to my family nonchalantly and without scurrying over the burning sand. On the other hand, I clearly recall feeling less inadequate with my friends on our subsequent nocturnal outings. I had had my own adventure; maybe it wasn't up to theirs, but it was mine and mine alone.

I saw your sister again a few months later, and this time you were with her. I was hanging out at the time with a nice bunch of kids, not as fast as my vacation gang, boys and girls of the same age, studious and clearheaded, who had only recently flown their genteel nests and prosperous neighborhoods. Intimate friendship was more highly valued with them than erotic designs; emotional dithering was considered among them to be a rather poetic, even reassuring state of being that time would ultimately elucidate to everyone's satisfaction. This gave them the romantic notion that I was endowed with a certain experience of the alluring and esoteric world of the night, and as I had carelessly boasted of having been admitted to New Jimmy's, Régine's super-trendy and super-exclusive nightclub, it was decided that I would bring my friends there as a reward for the quiet, dutiful students' lives we led right next door, here in Paris. I had indeed once penetrated that holiest of holies of the fashionable clubbing set, but I'd done so in the middle of the week, by myself, and by slipping in among the regulars. I was terrified at the prospect of having to show up on a Saturday night in a group, confronting the ogre who guarded the door behind his peephole, and being met with a humiliating rejection; as anonymous and gauche as we were, we didn't stand a chance. And yet, contrary to all expectations, we were whisked inside; the club was full to the rafters but was short on young people that night; the alchemical reaction that produced the right atmosphere apparently required a good mix of ages, and we fit the bill, more or less. The tables at which they sat us were in a dark corner at the back, at some distance from everything else, but the dance floor in the center was brilliantly lit. I immediately recognized your sister, who was with what I took to be an older man, but one I could not describe today if my life depended on it. I stared at her in the hope that she would remember me once she noticed me, should I emerge from my dark alcove. I saw you just afterward; you were with your husband, the English photographer who looked just like the lead in *Blowup*, which I had recently discovered at the movies. Pictures of your marriage in London had been published in *Paris Match*; you had worn a short black dress, only close friends had been invited and it was all very casual. I'd thought it the height of chic. In those days we went to England quite often and sometimes to Italy, too; America was still too far away. The four of you were dancing the twist to quasi-Latin tunes, indifferent to the falsely blasé glances of those around you; with your joyous, carefree, intimate ways, you seemed to have evolved in a magic circle that outshone everything else—the other dancers, my little group, my own fumbling existence. Oddly, that night I thought your sister even more beautiful than you, with her pale skin and that inextinguishable inner flame of hers—the looks of Greta Garbo and the energy of Janis Joplin, those were my kind of reference points in those days. No doubt another error of judgment. You each simply had your own style, despite everything that was said about you in gossip and in print; and yet it was she whose attention I hoped to attract, convinced that I'd earned the right to do so by my role in the affair on the beach with the little dog. My friends and I danced all night, and so did you in your magic circle of four. At times there were fewer people on the floor, and toward the end there was practically no one but us; it was as if we were dancing together. I was tireless, and they happily followed my lead. I heard her laugh; her voice, which I'd found so moving, floated across to me in little snatches, I wore myself out trying to catch her eye as it wandered by without stopping; it didn't work, she did not recognize or had forgotten me. You, on the other hand, seemed to have my number. I felt as if you were staring me down impatiently, as if to convey that my persistence was inappropriate in a place like this, but perhaps it was just an impression; I had already developed a tendency to slip into my fantasy life at a moment's notice.

I don't remember how it all ended, but it doesn't matter since the important thing is still here in me. I can see her dancing, I could almost talk to her, she is a physical presence. And in any case, it was a fantastic night out for my little gang.

Every time I take the highway south along the Côte d'Azur toward Nice, I think of her. I'm not sure I know the exact spot, I read it somewhere but I've forgotten. Anyway, the closer you get to the airport the more dangerous it becomes, with all those trucks barreling along madly, the lights from the suburban sprawl merging with the headlights at dusk, the anxiety of arriving late and missing your plane. I once did the trip on the back of a motorcycle at twilight with a friend driving 120 miles an hour; it was late summer and the scent of pine and bay mingled with the gas fumes, I thought I was going to die like her; it was really dumb, you might even say pure insanity. It was ugly too; I had no business mixing up my childish deliria with a real sorrow that was not my own, that cannot be consoled, and that will never pass.

In the 1970s, when I was running my little network of movie houses, which enjoyed a certain reputation for their programming,

I became friendly with some of the famous actors who passed through our lobby. I've wracked my memory but I don't remember seeing you there, or else it was my bad luck to be out when you came. But I continued to dream of knowing you and to mistake my desires for reality; one day I told some journalists that you had once manned the box office as a favor to me. I'm not especially inclined to tell tales; you must have really held a special place in my mind for me to lie like that. When I saw the story picked up in print, I was horrified at having been so stupid and feared that you would react angrily, but nothing happened, either because you never read the article in which my weird fabrication was repeated, or because you shrugged your shoulders and decided that you had better things to do than pick up the phone to put yet another phony in his place. But I had frightened myself; my desire to make contact was decidedly irrational and threatened to go too far; I would have to take myself in hand if I were not to become one of those neurotic fans who stalk their idols with obsessive and sometimes dangerous tenacity. More often than not, these are rather ordinary people who lead gray and joyless little lives; mine was not so sorry, but it had a depressive side that I hoodwinked by compulsively watching movies, especially yours, which obviously complicated my efforts to exert self-control.

Unfortunately, it was inevitable that I would run into you at some point. It happened in a private screening room to which I'd gone to pick up a print, and where you and a film crew were watching the rushes of one of your movies. I knew and liked its director, a delightful and friendly man who would certainly not have hesitated to introduce us if I'd asked him. Instead, I hid out in the projection room and then hustled past you when the lights came on, my motorcycle helmet on my head and the can under my arm like a messenger to whom no one pays attention. Even so, I had enough time to notice that you seemed very pleased with the rushes, and I remember thinking that the director, with whom you'd already made several movies, was a lucky man to be able to work with you. At the same time, I felt that stubborn sense of sadness as I passed by you; for me, everything that concerned you felt like a sort of party to which I would never be invited. And yet, according to something you wrote in the course of a single page, and without making a big deal about it, in a book that I always keep by my side, that happened to be a time of problems and anxieties for you as you went through the trying ordeal of a lengthy "blackout," as you put it. Still, in the eyes of those who know you as little as I do, your career was as wisely managed and scintillating as ever, an abundant harvest of interesting and sometimes excellent films and often outstanding filmmakers, and you lived discreetly with a man one cannot help but admire, despite his rather unknowable quality, the father of your daughter and a fabulous Italian actor who starred alongside you in the very film whose rushes I'd glimpsed. Obviously, only we ourselves can say when our darkest nights have dissipated and allowed us a moment's respite, but I believe that you have never really been free of doubt, anxiety, and a sense of vulnerability, and that everything you have made and offered to the world is the result of an enormous exercise in self-discipline on your part, pursued with intelligence, dignity, and modesty, and of a vital energy that cannot be explained but that separates those who wake up every morning from those who spend their whole lives asleep on their feet. Having heard the stories of those who have been rude or rash enough to try to break through your reserve, and of the cold shoulders, the tongue-lashings, and the occasional brutal combination of the two that they have received for their troubles, I have no illusions concerning your opinion of these pages, should you happen to read them. I imagine that you have little empathy for the fantasies you inspire, of which this, my intrusion into your life, would certainly appear to be one. But you see, I've spent so much of my life thinking about you that I had to come out and tell you about it one of these days. Just this time, just this once, and never again. We have but rarely crossed paths, and then only at a distance, but after all these years of a dialogue that has never existed, I beg your indulgence since, instead of trying for the umpteenth time to get closer to you, now I am simply trying to tell you good-bye.

We can't help taking an interest in the private lives of those we adore in secret or noticing details and signs that no one else does. In the little restaurant of the hotel La Fenice in Venice, for instance, a few framed photos of you hang in a cluster over the banquettes where people eat their meals. They don't occupy a prominent place, but represent rather the owner's intimate display of friendship for loyal customers. They must have been taken in winter—you are both wearing warm clothing—and they are relatively recent. I seem to recall that the two of you had long been separated and had only reunited for a brief interlude; whatever the case, the number of years that had passed between the films you shot together and those photos allowed me yet again to appreciate the strength of the ties that bound you; as I looked at them in the midst of all the hubbub and general indifference, I felt as if I were projecting myself onto memories that were not mine yet were as precious to me as if I'd spent time with the two of you in some other life that was far more beautiful and interesting than my own. Venice in the winter, a damp fog over the lagoon that forces you to bundle up good and warm, a couple that has reconciled for a few hours or a few days, far from the prying eyes of tourists who have sought the sun elsewhere; they are fairly ordinary snapshots, but to me there was nothing ordinary about them at all. On the other hand, I was able without much effort to resist the temptation to steal one; they weren't very firmly attached and I could have come back when the restaurant was empty, but a curious aspect of my obsession is that I have no trophy-hunting instincts.

I often think, too, of another moment, captured by the cold and soulless eye of television, that I found all the more moving because you refused to relinquish one iota of yourself to that gaze. It was when you and your daughter arrived at the building where her recently deceased father lay at rest. The entryway was besieged by photographers and the cameramen hounded you shamelessly, but you ignored them all completely. You wore a shawl and dark glasses; your daughter was bareheaded but her face was as impassive as yours. You broke through the circle to enter the building, your daughter went ahead of you, the horde seemed ready to follow you right up to the elevator door, you were both already moving away, but I distinctly heard you ask her to wait for you. It was almost the cry of a woman in flight, a very human reaction of anger toward them and distress shared with her. But what moved me most was that you had spoken to her in Italian, the language that the three of you—mother, father, daughter—spoke among yourselves, and the language that you spoke to one another as lovers, the language of the child you brought with you, the language and its circle to which your pursuers had no access. *"Aspetta, aspetta,"* and you added your daughter's name, it was even more radical and intimate with the name. But I'm not writing down any names—some will get it and some may not.

HER NAME, for instance. She died just recently, not far from here, in Normandy, where I went to spend the weekend with the child. Everyone loved her, that is so rare, truly everyone: her friends; those who knew her a little, like me; those who knew her only through her books or through what they'd read or heard about her in magazines or on the television; and even those who criticized and badmouthed her but did not put their hearts into it as if they'd anticipated that it wouldn't take. Her son, too, who adored her, as I would soon discover, and who clearly understood his own special role in her life, in that secret heart of a life of extremes, hemmed in by celebrity and the rumors, flattery, and lies that go with it; she had been running on empty for years. Everyone knows that charisma cannot be explained, that you could set forth all its nuances without ever identifying how hers acted so powerfully upon others. Freedom and intelligence, talent and elegance, depth and impertinence—all these key elements might help explain lesser personalities, but they entirely miss the mark in her case. You could throw in the kitchen sink without being mistaken; putting all the pieces together would still be a highly complex problem, entertaining in a way that society intrigues no longer are, as disturbing as everything that resists analysis, impossible to resolve. She left behind hundreds of trails for us to wander along blithely for as long as we wish, but she took the map with her.

The young woman who lives with her son warned me that the end was near. This young woman was a very sweet, pleasant person whom I met through work; she was clearly devoted to her and spoke to me of her, I thought, in the same way she spoke to her of me; it was yet another subtle link between us, although I saw her only rarely and even less since I'd learned she was ailing. I was still traveling in her wake, but far back; our lives were very different, and I experience anxiety bordering on panic when I'm with sick people; it's even worse with those I love. And yet I felt a tenderness for her that we usually reserve for a very close friend, which she was not, and for a soulmate, which she had been since the moment we crossed paths and throughout the years during which she was openly affectionate with me every time we met, as if it was the most natural thing in the world. I admired and was also intimidated by her, two attitudes that she challenged by making light fun of me, which loosened me up a little in her presence. I was fascinated by her energy, her humor, her vivacity, the interlacing of life and poetry that made me feel that everything around her sparkled, including me. I took her on my motorcycle, she took me driving at top speed in her car, we often spoke, as they say, lightly of serious things and seriously of light things; we shared very Parisian meals and others tinged by sadness, which were sometimes the same; we met on television and the radio as if going on vacation together, we had a lot of fun together. She had the rare gift of making you laugh but never at someone else's expense. Our intimacy no doubt flattered my vanity, but she struck me above all as marvelously imaginative and sensitive. Basically, we really looked out for each other while maintaining a certain formality.

I did not yet know her at the time I walked by you disguised as a messenger, but I readily associated my image of you both with the same romantic impulse. A few years earlier, you had filmed an adaptation of one of her books, in my opinion the best of them; in it, your stunning beauty and sense of the right tone and appropriate gesture came together perfectly with the ineffable grace of her style. I remember going to see it with my grandmother. She left the theater very pleased; she'd enjoyed one scene in particular, when you sit on a bench in the charming little square in front of the Atelier theater and a group of fops, observing you at a distance, breaks into an improvised refrain: "Ah the lovely lady, ah the lovely lady!" My grandmother said: "I understand them, a young woman so pleasant to look at. If your grandfather were still among us, he'd certainly adore her." My grandmother had the enthusiasm of a young girl, which was sometimes astonishing in someone apparently so wise and rea- sonable; she was even a fan of Marilyn Monroe. Nevertheless, despite the quality of the film, which both of you must have appreciated, I gradually came to suspect that relations between you were not especially close. Admiration, surely, and a certain

friendly respectfulness when you happened to meet, but it probably remained ill-defined; I have a hard time picturing the kind
of intimate friendship that you each had with others. You had
little in common and you moved in parallel worlds. I'm sorry
about that, as perhaps you are too now, but I've learned not to
expect perfect match-ups; parents divorce, friends fall out, some
never reconcile; that in no way weakens the strength of my feelings for any of them. However, since she is no longer here, I will
probably think of you even more often. The desert is encroach-
ing, and I've lost many of my landmarks. Of her, I have my fine,
delicious memories; of you, the years to come and my silent,
almost clandestine attention.

B UT IT is still far too soon to fall back on memories and their
bittersweet consolation. I heard the news that night on the radio
while I was on the road, just before arriving and just as I was
thinking of her, as I do every time I take the little road that leads
to my mother's place and can also lead to the house where, it
was said, she lived as a recluse. I went straight to bed, taking
refuge in sleep; there was nothing to say, it was fate. Today, all
day since the morning, I have felt growing within me the pain
that awaited me when I awoke. At the television station I run,
I ask those on duty to rebroadcast a special about her; I read
the papers, filled with long articles and pictures devoted to her
life and books and their very special magic. As it often does,
Libération does the best job of it; there are also lengthy analyses
of her legal troubles, her drug and money problems; I know all
about that and at the same time I don't recognize the person
they're talking about. I watch the news, but the other items,
dramatic as they are, seem to fade into the background. People
everywhere seem to be taking it hard, and their pain mitigates
mine to a certain extent. The broadcast interviews are decidedly
less polished than usual in such circumstances, they express a

sincere sense of loss and confusion, a kind of remorse at having abandoned her, alone and practically penniless, in recent years. We don't hear from those who were closest to her, they must be in hiding, a significant portion of their own lives is gone with her; I try to reach some of them, I leave messages on answering machines, including that of her son's girlfriend. Her death brings to mind those of her friends who died before her, a little circle of people who seemed to enjoy the good life, to share the same sense of curiosity, and to reject self-pity; they were brilliantly witty, sometimes very rich and very famous, but certainly less creative, less anxious, or less clear-sighted. The characters in her books were modeled on them, and I moved among them with some frequency while always staying in the background, eager to please them, reluctant to follow them, observing them without belonging to their world, and admiring them without letting on. What could it mean to them? Now they're dead and I cannot shake their memory, though it has faded to the point of disappearing. Finally, I can't stand it any longer, I don't want to regret later having done nothing while she is just next door; I go to her house without knowing what I'm looking for, I don't know what I'll find there. I'm not even sure they'll let me in. In any case, I'd promised to come see her last time I was there, exactly one month earlier.

It's a lovely estate somewhat set back from the narrow lane; you have to know the way and head deep into the woods to find it. The house is at the center of a vast glade; the long drive leading up to it is bordered by large trees that have stood through countless storms; the sea is just nearby but not visible; there must be a path through the barrier forest that leads down to the beach. I'm sure you can smell it at high tide, the scent of kelp and salt spray rising through the beech wood; I should have asked her, but I didn't think of it at the time and we had so much to talk about. The style is not that of a half-timbered Norman

manor house but rather that of a bourgeois family home built in
the nineteenth century, free of all ostentation and with a view to
comfort and pleasant proportions; built by lawyers or doctors
from Honfleur perhaps, who invested a portion of their assets
buying up land worked by tenant farmers, as the surrounding cottages and barns would seem to suggest. Not quite up to
Madame Bovary, but quite Flaubert all the same; one thinks,
too, of André Gide's house across the Seine. After the men of
means came the artists: Alphonse Allais and Lucien Guitry lived
here; it was surely one of them who added the large sitting room
at the front and the bedroom at the side; the effect of these addi-
tions is muted by Virginia creeper. And there was also Lucie
Delarue-Mardrus, a whimsical poetess in the lyrical-exotic style
fashionable in the belle époque, a bold lesbian who put Natalie
Barney and Colette to shame and who retired here after the First
World War before fading into obscurity. We amused ourselves by
invoking her memory the last time I was here; the house creaks,
perhaps it's her ghost at play. I'd promised to find her memoirs
at a secondhand bookseller, but I didn't have the time.

Standing at the padlocked gate, I am not alone; several
paparazzi are on the stakeout; I'm hardly big game for them, but
they buttonhole me with a professional familiarity that I am in
no mood to indulge. They tell me there are people in the house;
they've seen them coming and going but haven't recognized anyone. To get in, I climb the low wall beside the gate; it's easy—
she wasn't the type to surround herself with fences. One of the
paparazzi snaps a photo without much enthusiasm; that's one
useless picture that won't earn back its costs. As I approach the
house my heart is pounding, I'm overwhelmed with grief, and
I'm struck by the intense thought that she is here somewhere,
close by. At the same time, I don't want to be pushy; just because
I was here four weeks ago doesn't give me the right to come back
today. I know that no one will say so, but I resolve to stay but

a short while; it is unlikely that I will ever return to this house. Cars are parked haphazardly on the lawn, you can tell there has been some commotion. But I see nothing else. Everything is calm and quiet. I ring, I knock at the door, gently, then harder; there's no answer. I set off around the house, looking in at the windows; it's a little embarrassing, I hate feeling like an intruder, but at this point I can't help myself; furniture, personal effects, a raincoat on the sofa; they're certainly not far, maybe on the second floor. I raise my head but hear nothing, and as I continue past the windows, room after room is empty. I've come almost full circle when I suddenly see her, stretched out in the solitude and stillness of death. At this very moment, she is the subject of speculation throughout France, the international press is already devoting lengthy pieces to her, memorial broadcasts and tributes are being prepared at every television network, and here I am before her, separated by a single pane of glass, alone at the window of her room and of her apparently deserted home. I'd had the same sense of ineffable strangeness when I found my grandmother at rest in a room that she still occupied with her presence, but from which life had fled to pursue its existence elsewhere. Perhaps the dead are no longer watched over as they once were. I wonder what happened to the little dogs that used to have the run of the place; even they seem to have taken shelter in some hidden refuge. I continue prowling around the house; I'm so anxious not to make noise and be taken for a thief that my footsteps on the gravel make me feel like I'm walking on crystal. I find myself again at the front door, which I very gently push open. I'm familiar with the layout, the front hall, the little parlor, the hallway, the second door on the right. The television is on with the volume off, all that's missing is a steaming cup of coffee and a cigarette smoldering in the ashtray to make you feel like you're in an outtake from *Pandora*. I enter the room, I sit beside the bed, and I realize that I have never seen her asleep. Her lovely, sudden shakes of the head, as if she were preparing to let loose; the smile and fragility that made you want to take her in your arms, which I would never have done as she was propriety itself and in no wise informal; the equal measures of merriment and sadness in her gaze; that very courtly, lighthearted way she had; everything about her that conveyed the idea of friendship and her pleasure in seeing you—I had been privy to all that. But not sleep, that token of absolute truth that we reward to and share with our chosen one—I never saw her in her sleep. The sheet and thin eiderdown cover her entire body, revealing only her face; she's sunk deep into her bed like a little girl who's gone to sleep after a rough day and is chilled to the bone. Eyes closed, blond hair, bird-like profile, no trace of pain or finality; you could almost convince yourself of what you tell children, that she's gone to sleep forever. But there's also an absurd impulse to wake her up, to rise together from a bad dream and hear once more the little voice that once tossed out words, exclamations, and amused queries like tennis balls. But there's nothing to do but stay there at her side and wait a while, wait for nothing.

When you get right down to it, there were two last times. One on her birthday earlier in the year, when the child took her a little book about Chekhov on my behalf; she was said to be very sick, much diminished, and I didn't have the heart to see it for myself. I'd parked at some distance from the house and told the child to give the book to the first person he met inside, but he'd run into her in the parlor. She was delighted by the attention, the gift and the sweet, mysterious emissary; he'd had the presence of mind to tell her he'd come by bike, and she had not questioned him further. In the car on the way back, he'd been proud to have accomplished his mission so skillfully, and although I was a little sorry in the end not to have gone in myself, since she had not seemed so very ill, I was pleased that they'd met; to love the child is to love what I would like to be. She called me later to thank me, and having chatted as cheerfully as we always did, we agreed to meet at the end of the summer, when I would come in person; that would be our truly final encounter, but I had no clue of it at the time. It was rumored that the atmosphere there was stifling, that she was ruled over by a ubiquitous and imperious patron, that her supporters were drained and demoralized—all the dark burdens of dependency—and I'd been warned that she was decidedly not well. It's true, she was not alone, she was being watched over like a person in danger. And yet my visit took place in pretty much the same climate of jollity as in the past, and nothing especially morbid or worrisome occurred. Perhaps the conversation was a little more disjointed, although a certain poetic rambling had always been customary. She was thoroughly exhausted but altogether present and as quick-witted as ever. In any case, I was not of her intimate circle, it was not my place to ask questions or to poke my nose where it did not belong, and I'm sure she expected me to behave as if all were normal and nothing had changed, as before.

I did my very best to make myself agreeable to her entourage; I knew that she would ask me back, and I didn't want there to be any fuss because they barely left her alone for a minute. I didn't stay long, not wishing to tire her further, but I was heartsick as I left. She was being taken down the drive in her wheelchair, her words were tumbling over themselves at an even more rapid-fire pace than usual, I couldn't tell if she was trying to say good-bye. When I called Saturday to arrange my next visit, as promised, the governess in dark glasses, who had not said a word during my visit and had inspired in me an instinctive sense of trust, spoke of a relapse and told me it was impossible. She had that soothing tone of voice that one uses on the very sick. I took her at her word and did not venture to pry further; I allowed myself to be reassured, like a coward.

The sun brightens the prettily furnished room. The patron,

who had saved the house from the clutches of the tax authorities, had had everything redone tastefully and simply, the bedroom along with the rest; hanging above the bed was a painting of a nude, the kind you find at antique stores specializing in the minor Montparnasse masters of the Roaring Twenties. I wonder who chose it, she or her watchful friend. The painting is rather beautiful, but there is something odd about that sensual, triumphant female body overhanging the inanimate one at rest beneath the blanket, probably too ravaged to be seen. Then again, a Christ on the cross or a Virgin in majesty would have been grotesque. My thoughts are wandering; it's time to go. Leaving the house, I find myself face to face with the caretaker, who tells me that her son has gone to Honfleur to attend to the formalities; he should be back shortly, I'll see him if I wait a moment or two. I've only met him once and liked him immediately—charming, devoted to his mother, and attentive to all her needs—but I'm ashamed of my intrusion, I wouldn't know the right way to behave in his presence. The patron, who hasn't been to bed in days, is asleep; people are expected this evening, the faithful inner circle no doubt, those who have always stood by her. The caretaker suggests I go see her room. I dare not tell him I've just been, and I find an excuse to flee. In the car, my mind drifts back to the photograph of my uncle François on his deathbed. He had been her friend, but she had had the tact not to refer him to in my presence, since our relationship did not admit of such intimacy. The picture had been taken by a stranger and its publication had caused an uproar, although it had been considered perfectly natural to photograph the deceased not so long before. I could have taken one just like it—no one would have been the wiser—and kept it for myself. This vulgar idea perks me up, restores me to the world of the living. The fact is, I don't enjoy looking at the pictures I took of my grandmother; I've stashed them away in a drawer that I never open.

I SAW you more often in the 1980s, and we even exchanged a few words now and then. At the time I was very close with little Célia, who worked at the fashion house that dressed you; she belonged to the inner circle of its two founders, to whom you were always faithful out of admiration for their talent and affection for themselves. This group excelled in any number of creative fields, held enormous sway in the fashion world, made its mark in business, and branched out into the media; you were naturally associated with it, and it seems to me that you took Célia under your wing. Enveloped in Célia's love for me and always made to feel welcome, yet shy and preoccupied by my work, I tended to orbit the outer reaches of the enchanted sphere. Célia tactfully avoided talking much about you around me; I sensed your presence in a turn of phrase or by allusion; I saw you float past at the private parties, collections, and film events I attended with her. It wasn't enough to get to know you, but at least we were able to chat briefly, at a superficial but friendly level. I was a vague presence on the landscape, like a satellite in your nebula, apparently unassociated with any possible encounters we may have had in the past, none of which, I noticed, seemed to have left you with the least recollection of having met me. I was careful never to refer to them. I still have some photos from that time in which I can be seen with you; they remind me today of those snapshots in which strangers surreptitiously inch into the frame with celebrities and then flaunt them to prove how close they are with people who were barely aware of their existence at the time and forgot them entirely a moment later. Anyway, you were less on my mind in those days; I was completely taken up with Célia, we clung to each other like two survivors, but unfortunately from two different shipwrecks.

Petite, very pretty, and well built, with a porcelain complexion and the tiny hands of a doll, she still bore an incredible resemblance to her childhood portraits even as she approached forty.

She was of South American origin, and those pictures show her as the diminutive heiress to a mysterious fortune, ensconced on a velvet sofa in a vast Buenos Aires drawing room just like those found in the Haussmann-era townhouses of the wealthy districts of Paris. She did not talk about her father, and I never found out why; her mother brought her as a teenager to Paris, where they lived extravagantly for a while, adopting the mores of what was still called "café society." Her intuition, stylishness, and a very confident sense of taste endeared her to all sorts of brilliant people, but she never lapsed into the triviality and snobbery that might have been used against her. When the money finally ran out, she went to work for the famous fashion designer whose clothes she and her mother could no longer afford to wear, and she did so the way one returns to the bosom of one's family, without bitterness but with unspoken nostalgia for the prodigal years. She'd had a few lovers, all handsome and remarkable, and had even briefly been the talk of the town when, before a horde of astonished reporters right in the middle of Orly airport, with her own slender little hands she had pried from the clutches of some KGB goons a Russian dancer with whom she was in love and who would soon became famous the world over. But she had never married, not having the mindset for the kind of grand social career that should have come naturally to someone like her. She was more Left Bank and Tuscany than Avenue Foch and Palm Beach, unable to renounce her freedom or, ultimately, to sacrifice her privacy. Outside the comfortable cocoon of the fashion house—which, by the way, was not entirely immune to abrupt mood swings—she led a solitary life in a charming apartment on the Île de la Cité that she could not afford, her only company a little dog that went crazy when she came home every night and sat quietly beside her on the banquette when she took her mother to lunch at Prunier's every Sunday. She knew a lot of people but had only a handful of close friends, often the same people I knew from a distance. She loved Paris and enjoyed all it had to offer as only cultured outsiders can, but her favorite thing was always intimate dinners at one of the sophisticated bistros on her inexhaustible list. She did not linger late into the evening, preferring to leave early for the little dog awaiting her at home. Oddly, she'd never given up her nationality or country of origin, to which she'd never returned but where she might have found long-lost relatives and vestiges of her vanished fortune. She was bound to it by secret ties and memories of the childhood that was still so alive in her features; everywhere and always, subtly and without making a big deal about it, she was an outsider. In the early days, I was in awe of her romantic lifestyle, but I soon came to love her deeply, with a love that endures even though we don't see each other as often as we used to. But mine was a love without desire, whereas Célia wanted me all to herself. My inability to sleep with her didn't discourage her; it offered her a kind of guarantee that I wouldn't be drawn to other women, and in that sense she was right. I even considered marrying her, though I was wise enough not to ask—I believe she would have said yes.

I have always loved women. By the time I met Célia, I had long since given up any idea of conforming to any kind of heterosexual stereotype, which I would have to have worn like a disguise, or of adopting the kind of aggressive and showy homosexual mannerisms that repelled me. My friendships and emotional relationships were open to all takers and compensated for my stubborn rejection of the kind of labels and touchstones that seemed so necessary to so many people. And even my fierce attractions, which all pointed in a single direction, were not without their surprises; I was susceptible to the allure of the female body and sometimes dreamed of it at night. I had learned to be wary of peremptory, possessive, and castrating women whose hunger for power and dominance played perversely on the genuine or supposed vulnerability of their status and the social inequity of their condition, but I had no trouble distinguishing between them and all the others, and I'd had enough experience with selfish, paranoid, and destructive queers to cherish any further illusion about the officially ecumenical unanimity of their community. It certainly helped that I identified with movie stars—preferably those whose past was riddled with stormy love affairs and scandals—rather than with soccer players or heavy-metal rockers; it allowed me the invaluable theatrical freedom of feeling like Ava Gardner or Liz Taylor as I stood before some office tyrant who imagined he held my future in his hands, and to float alongside them toward some distant prospect of adventure and fantasy whenever some good-looking simpleton misread my interest and tried to tell me about his girlfriend. At the same time, I was not at all the right companion for a lonely woman looking to talk about clothes and heartaches with a Virgin Mary. Such alliances strike me as suspect: ersatz men for aging, unhappy women who used to disdain gays but now, in the wilderness of their declining years, find them useful; ersatz women for fairies looking for a mother and willing to settle for a wicked stepmother. Even so, I had seen it work sometimes; there are so many ways for people to come together, and we all get by the best we can. Before I met Célia, my tendency to act kind of manly but without masculine arrogance, falsely presenting myself as a sensitive straight man, had set me along a path toward hetero affairs that quickly degenerated into listless associations as it became clear that the initial misunderstanding and mutual self-discovery cancelled one another out. The moment always came as I was undressing, when the decision to make love was abruptly invalidated by my absolute inability to do it. After every failure, I reproached myself a little bit more for the pride and willful blindness that had led me to lie to myself and to hurt my friends with my thoughtlessness. And if she had a brother, a son, a boy of her acquaintance to whom I'd taken a liking, my sense of guilt was all the more burdensome and opaque, magnifying the dread knowledge that I would soon give in yet again to the same old fantasies and start the whole thing over with the next woman willing to fall into the infernal trap with me. The list was a long one, steeped in a feeling of inexorable misery and regret. When my life became entwined with Célia's, I finally began to see that loving is not necessarily the same as being in love, and that needing is not always the same as desiring. She, too, had learned it, but perhaps she was not quite as vulnerable and damaged as I was, and in her passionate affection was always willing to defer the question of what was to become of us. This forward-moving retreat even exacerbated her immoderate attachment to me, rooted in her perpetual fear of being abandoned: the anxiety of the poor little rich girl who, when she looked into her bright Parisian mirror, saw the penniless exile whose father had run off and who had been forced to play mother to her own mother. Available yet untouchable, without realizing it I had provided her with a kind of ideal brother, and the more I cared for her and protected her, without being able to give her what she also needed from me and pretended not to want, the closer we were drawn to each other, she by yearning and I by remorse.

We had a good time together. Célia's sense of humor was the kind I like, making fun of everything without being unduly hurtful, picking up on the incongruous or ridiculous detail in a situation or behavior that good manners might normally exempt from critique; she went at it with razor-sharp perspicacity and a light, buoyant touch devoid of malice and any propensity to humiliate. Nor did she spare her own foibles or mine. They were right up there with current events, tales of overweening ambition, gay follies—all cultural pedantry was fair game. Sensible people thought our conversations trivial and that we spent too much time watching television, whereas it was they who were too serious, and we were protected by Boy George, Jacques Becker, and the other heroes of the day. Free as a high-born dropout yet as conventional as an émigré never fully convinced of her permanent status, Célia cast an ironic eye over a world that she feared would be taken away one day for some obscure reason she hadn't anticipated. It was a pretty good match for my own deeply covetous and apprehensive social persona and my general sense of living perpetually under a suspended sentence. Through her, I held an increasingly secure place in that magical little club whose every member was assuredly interesting and exceptional, but which also felt like a gilded cage to me. My work, my inability to afford the kind of lifestyle I craved, and other envious impulses made me unhappy in a way Célia could understand very well yet refused to acknowledge. She took my attempts to gain some perspective as personal betrayals, and her mounting panic only increased her demands on my time and attention. The fact is, she was right—by seeking to put some distance between us, I was calling her entire way of life into question. And yet I had a hard time resisting her because I loved her as much as ever; her unhappiness touched me, and I had come to depend on her charm, her uniqueness, our way of sharing exactly the same thoughts; nor did I have any intention of cutting myself off from her group of friends, people who were like no one else in the world and whom I will always admire with genuine affection. But while I never seriously considered leaving her, none of my promises, vows, or proofs could lay to rest her increasingly agonizing doubts. We had come full circle, back to the lost child in her Buenos Aires palace; I suppose she had to relive the entire sequence of events, from the earliest need for love to its loss. The mechanism had been set in motion, from argument to reconciliation, indictment to breakup; the bistros grew insipid, dates became a chore, we always brought someone along with us to avoid confrontations that ended in tears. On the day I caught her just as she was about to place herself in great danger—certainly without realizing it, although you never know—that day I finally understood that we had gone too far. I think that if I'd managed to sleep with her we would still be living together to this day; it may not have been essential to her, but it was to me.

I DON'T know if you still see each other. Célia stopped working, the fashion house was sold, there are fewer opportunities for the two of you to run into each other. I never could tell whether her affection for you was more than professional or whether it was simply just another feeling that made your association especially easy, without spilling over into the kind of private friendship that leads to nights at the movies or antiquing sprees. She did occasionally have dinner at your place, and it was odd that she never once asked me to go with her although she took me just about everywhere else. I'm sure you're just like her. People you don't know—and there are so many of them everywhere you look, people who talk at you and whom you feel obligated to respond to, people who ask things of you that no one else can even begin to imagine—all those people annoyed and exhausted her; you must have thought I was one of them, and perhaps she wasn't sure enough of me to convince you to make an exception of me. I dropped her off once or twice beneath the bright windows of your apartment, which was said to be very beautiful, and then I drove off as fast as I could. At those times when she managed to do without me, I had appointments with boys who were not very savory in hotels that were even less so. I believe you must have been very fond of her, I don't see how it could have been otherwise, but I could sense her basic modesty and fretfulness merely in the way she spoke your given name the way one speaks of a relative one admires and does not wish to disturb, as well as that uncivilized, essentially disinterested side of her character that allowed her to drop all contact with you once the fashion house was sold, the enchanted circle gradually dispersed, the little dog died. The truth is I know nothing about it, but I've seen the way she files things away, keeps only the bare minimum, turns every page; she has that neat side to her that is just like you, and that penchant for fatalistic thinking that is so unlike you.

They recently broadcast a documentary on television about the fashion house that was shot shortly before the end. It has quite a lengthy opening sequence—clearly unrehearsed and filmed on the fly, as if the camera crew were there by surprise—in which you can be seen choosing dresses and trying them on. It's a delightfully lively moment of pure cinema as in the old American comedies, the kind no one knows how to recreate in today's films. Célia does not appear, probably because she is so camera-shy, but maybe because she's already left the company, which would soon change beyond her recognition; yet I can feel her presence at every moment, you were with her and she with you, each of you permeating that gracious universe with your charm, embodying its peerless style. It was almost as if the two of you were taking your leave with a smile and a rustle of fabric, closing the curtain on all those years that I now miss so dearly, years in which I see you as one in my mind's eye. Ultimately, the sequence invalidates my assumptions; now that I think about it, I would be willing to bet that you are closer now than ever before; you're not the kind of people who throw out their memories along with everything else. Besides, the other women that I love are your friends; when they speak of you it's with a touch of admiration, and I would even say respect, so rarely heard in the compliments one woman offers another, that leads me to suppose that you hold an important place in their lives. Anita, Pascale, and Dora; those aren't the real names, but almost—at least close enough that they might mean something to you.

TALITHA GETTY also knew you. She would sometimes call me very late at night, and half asleep I would have to tell her about one of your movies. She took the opportunity to suggest that you two were casual acquaintances, had met at parties in London and Rome; you weren't close friends but you lived in essentially the same world. She slipped these allusions surreptitiously into our conversations. I did not respond to them, but they stayed with me; they bothered me as if they were indiscretions. Our relationship was very strange in any case. I couldn't remember having met her, I couldn't put a face to her warm and friendly voice, I wondered how she'd gotten hold of my phone number; she mentioned a winter vacation when we'd skied together a few years earlier, mutual friends whom she declined to identify. It was all very vague and muddled. Then again, she knew quite a lot about my work, my pastimes, the people I socialized with; she spoke naturally and casually with me, as if we saw each other all the time. But we never saw each other at all; sometimes in the course of our nocturnal chats we'd discuss getting together for what, by her lights, would be a reunion at which I'd recognize her immediately; we'd even set a time and a place, and then she would abruptly disappear for several weeks, leaving a message on my answering machine at a time when she could be sure I would not be at home, claiming another pressing engagement, a spur-of-the-moment trip. She never left a phone number where I could reach her. All I could do was wait for her to call back; far from embarrassed at having stood me up, she quite relished her vanishing act. I had no idea what she wanted from me, but she'd managed to insinuate herself into my life by catching me at moments of extreme exhaustion and loneliness. For me, our whispered, disjointed conversations evoked other times when I'd been equally tired and alone; I had the feeling that she'd been through some hard times herself, there was always an edge of anxiety to her sense of humor, she told me that we read the same books and went to the same shows, that was enough for us to compare symptoms and pretend that we understood each other intuitively. I'm the kind of boy who opens his heart to strangers on the train and has no fear of upsetting office relationships with sudden, misty-eyed declarations of love. I have to admit that these weird phone calls from someone who was both so present and so elusive gave me a kind of grim, excited pleasure; they were like communications from the beyond, the kind you see in movies about trances and possession. Obviously, I continued to be baffled by the amnesia that had erased her from my memory and by her repeated disappearances, but I let the mystery play itself out because I like secret doors, indecipherable signatures, messages in bottles. Besides, I was both flattered and intrigued by her calls.

Getty was the legendary name of the oil tycoon, said to be the richest man in the world, who before his death had built a fabulous museum to house his art collection. He was famous for his capricious existence as a reclusive billionaire in an English castle; his misanthropy; the pay phones he made his guests use out of avarice; the enormous ransom he ended up paying to the Mafia after they'd cut off the ear of his grandson, a teenager led astray by Roman drug dealers; his mournful, haughty appearance; the power and complexity of an all-encompassing rapacity that had terrorized his family and provided him with an incalculable fortune to bequeath; the tabloid fate that continues to captivate biographers, art lovers, and romantics like me. But I knew no more than that, whatever miscellaneous anecdotes I'd managed to pick up in the papers; maybe I should have applied myself to the books I'd bought about his life, which in my usual indolence I'd barely skimmed. I knew even less about Talitha except that I loved her exotic name; she was the patriarch's daughter-in-law, and what with her palace in Rome and her *riad* in Marrakesh she was living la dolce vita with a whole troupe of "beautiful people" and gilded fairies. I vaguely recall some gossip in the press, the paparazzi, and articles in the interior decorating magazines about the glamorous refuges of the hip, gregarious superrich. There was also a lot of talk about drugs, orgies, feuds, and reconciliations with the old crocodile, who treated her with an indulgence that he showed no one else. It was all pretty hazy in my mind and outdated; the clock had stopped in the1970s, when I myself was young and eager for the kind of excitement that was beyond my means—a period that is already rapidly fading into the distant past. Talitha was sparing with the details; she hated rehashing the past and offered me the barest tidbits, but they were enough to fire my imagination; I listened to her the way poor people stare into high-end window displays. My self-esteem was flattered by being the object of interest of a genuine jet-set princess; waking me up over and over again in the middle of the night was her own way of being faithful; our nebulous, clandestine arrangement melded with my dreams. Plus, she was very good at dropping unverifiable intimations about her encounters with you; half-asleep at the end of the line, I was hooked. My daytime hours offered no such pleasures.

All the same, I finally found out one day that Talitha Getty had been dead for twenty years, cut down in Rome by an overdose after a night of sordid scenes with her husband. My nighttime companion, my cohort in drowsiness, the attentive and perceptive confidante to whom I unburdened myself in the loneliness of my darkened room, was nothing but an imposter; our liaison—as I thought of it, despite the absence of any physical contact—had turned out to be a dark lie, an emotional counterfeit perpetrated by a mythomaniac. I'd been had, but I couldn't be bitter about it—it was just another one of those things for which I only had my own naiveté and carelessness to blame; I only felt a little sadder than usual. I let her call me a few more times without telling her I knew she was a fraud; I was still

clinging to the tatters of the fable we had created together, me
out of thoughtlessness and she out of madness, or maybe vice-
versa. Then I finally grew tired of it, and I took the opportunity during one of our silences to tell her the story of her own
death—the fight with her husband, the syringe, the street kids
heckling her at dawn as she lapsed into a coma; the *carabinieri*,
the ambulance, photographers, scandal—the whole deal. She
was mute at the other end of the line. I knew she was still there
because I could hear her panting harder and harder like an animal at bay. Then she simply said goodnight, very softly, and
hung up. I was convinced that she would never call back; she
had left me standing like a murderer over the corpse of a lover.
I thought of you at that moment and of how you must have
had far more experience than I with all those nut-jobs who are
attracted by fame and sometimes turn very dangerous, which
Talitha was not. And I told myself that the difference between
you and me is that there are times I feel so low that I'm ready
to throw them the key. It's like the scene with Vivien Leigh in
The Roman Spring of Mrs. Stone, when she looks down from
her terrace at the vagrant below, who's been following her for
days and days now; you think she's crazy and that he'll do her
in for sure. The funny thing is, Vivien Leigh took the same risks
in real life, those joyless nights when she invited taxi drivers up
to her room . . .

YOU AND I have been on casual speaking terms for about
fifteen years now; like acquaintances who barely know one
another, we talk quietly about trivial things that we never
remember afterward. Well, I do remember, actually. Just once,
I happen to mention your son, whom I run into occasionally;
of course, I refer not to the little boy on Rue du Pré-aux-Clercs
but to the man he has become, who is as handsome as his father
was when he played cards with André Gide down near Grasse. I

can sense your hackles go up, and I back off; we return to polite banalities. It is only by chance that we've come together, but chance dictated by mutual proximity and custom. Paris is your oyster, as it is Célia's; we live in pretty much the same neighborhood, we socialize with the same people; our jobs and interests bring us together. Sometimes I feel as if I were dogging you, but I'm not; I don't look for opportunities to run into you, I don't interrogate our mutual friends compulsively; I only listen very attentively to the things they say about you, it's not very difficult to get them talking, they're hardly aware of it. They're very discreet, I promise, but the fact is they tend to be just as smitten as I am, and you're no Garbo either; there's no vow of total silence. So, as if in a dream, I trail in your wake to Saint Petersburg, Portugal, or southern France, and I watch your movies as if I'd been present at your shoots. My vigilance is like that of anorexics or drug addicts who hide their dependency so well; no need to worry, I've been doing this a long time, I have great self-control. I find safety in my affection for you as others find it in drink, except that affection is a mutual feeling, whereas I have to run the question-and-answer sessions alone during the times I can't see you or there's no one around to talk about you. Then again, you know, I have an excuse: not a day goes by that I don't come across a picture of you or an article about you. There's that book that just came out; in the bookstore where I bought it, and where I'm sure you shop often, the sales clerk handed it to me with a sardonic smile I didn't care for; one of those posers with his finger on the pulse who sneers at everything and treats the whole world with a vulgar familiarity that strikes me every time as a slap in the face; everyone thinks like an entertainer these days, and in the end it makes life dull and ugly. I didn't say anything; he wouldn't have understood. Reading the book, I felt so close to you that it was almost as if you'd written it for me. I am definitely going to have a hard time getting over this. In the book, you talk about the violence of the written word, the words one cannot put down, the sense of propriety one must maintain, the care we must take not to hurt others. I read what is written, and it only takes a little thought to grasp what's being said between the lines. I hope I'm not wrong about what is yet to come.

THE CELEBRATION of the bicentennial of the Revolution is to be held at the Place de la Concorde. You're one of the VIP guests: your pale blue suit, your complexion, your skin that still looks like porcelain in the light of such a summer's evening. I'm the television commentator for the big parade; I know it's going to end badly, there's a total lack of professionalism among my crew—one technical glitch after the other, my colleagues are smug, the director is full of himself and out of his depth in such a massive operation. I'm anxious and tense; you wish me good luck as you pass by, and as I remain glum you turn around and smile at me as if to say, "There, there, everything's going to be fine." One always feels very much alone in these circumstances, and only you could have made such a gesture. You are with a man whose face is everywhere these days; they say you're living together, his toadies are dithering about on the sidelines with a bevy of pretty girls, they don't hide their jealousy of or their pride in their boss. Ambitious young strivers with their cruel, anxiety-steeped fantasies make me nervous. I tell myself that their universe is not yours and that it can't always be pleasant to have to share their company. The evening goes off even worse than expected, the broadcast is unstructured and slapdash, you hardly get any sense at all of the magnificent parade. I look for you when the crowd of guests breaks up, but you've already gone. I walk home, sickened by all the waste and hating the guy who brought you along with his pack of carnivores, the perennial top dogs in a world of big business and macho camaraderie that has claimed you for itself and to which I will never have access.

TWO YEARS later, we find ourselves by chance in the same electronics store, each of us waiting for our purchases. People recognize and stare at you, it's not like the tradesmen in your neighborhood who are good at acting nonchalant. My unexpected presence helps you to ignore their rubbernecking. We chat. The store lighting is harsh, there's something oppressive about the atmosphere; you look tired, your face is drawn, and you have rings under your eyes; you are certainly aware of it but there's nothing to be done but wait it out in this hole. I could offer to take delivery of your purchases for you and then drop them off at your house afterward, but I don't have the nerve, it would simply highlight the fact that you look under the weather and in any case you would surely refuse. Your voice is as beautiful as ever, with that brisk cadence I love so much. You tell me that you're about to leave for the Far East for a movie that you have wanted to make from the moment you read the screenplay and the role assigned to you. But the prospect of a long journey and a filmmaking venture in difficult physical circumstances has you a little worried; I can tell that you're both happy and anxious, eager to immerse yourself once again in the powerful energy of a movie set, its impersonal collective momentum, the implacable, totalitarian discipline that makes you forget about everything else and leave all your bone-tiredness and perennial problems behind. I watch you as you speak; I think to myself that the cinematographer is going to need to be very careful, but then again maybe not; this may be the face the role calls for, the face of a woman being insidiously worn down by the climate and the frustrations of the old colonial life. I don't know how to tell you how courageous I think you are. They bring us our parcels, and you vanish into the crowd on the Rue de Rennes like Alice down the hole into Wonderland.

I SEE you a few months later on Avenue Montaigne; you've lost weight and look triumphant, your glow is back, and the signs of exhaustion are gone. You're in a hurry and walking fast, there's no time to put a name to the passing face, but people turn to look, struck by the impeccable stylishness of the apparition. So French amidst all the American stars in the *Vanity Fair* Hollywood photo shoot, so glamorous in the Minnelli–Donen manner on a Paris couture set; the little sister of Marlene in her late Dior years and of Audrey in her early Givenchy phase. The woman in the red dress, incredibly desirable as she throws open the door of her hotel suite and stares at Helmut Newton with an air of defiance. My film could go on forever with you in it, and I'd love to know what urgent appointment you're rushing off to. You haven't noticed me, possibly because you never look around you, possibly because you have more important things to do. I don't have the guts to go after you, but I cross the street and race down the opposite sidewalk to pass you, then cross back so I'm facing you. Ever since our conversation at the electronics store I've allowed myself timidly to believe that I've earned the right to disturb you, just a little. You can't escape me, I mumble a greeting and a polite compliment, but it's not really the right time and you barely respond; you're affable, evasive, in a hurry to move on. I chide myself for being so stubborn and clumsy; there are plenty of superb women on Avenue Montaigne when you think about it, I could take them in at my leisure, but I'm not interested in them, or in the limo driver who flashes me a smile. You got what you hoped for from the film shoot in the Far East—distance and novelty, the trust of your crew, a sense of a job well done; it did you a lot of good. I read that in a book, too, not long ago.

THE AIDS awareness gala night is broadcast live by every station. It's a high-minded project that does its best—which is not good enough—to avoid being sunk by the usual emotional blackmail and showbiz marketing: over-the-top effects, an enormous crowd, a flood of good intentions. It soon degenerates into universal mayhem, funny condom stories, coke dealers infiltrating the stage during the variety numbers. The junkies from the projects shouting their lungs out in the back rows aren't so lucky; their misery is far too subversive for the directors in their control vans in the parking lot; they'd rather turn their cameras on the stars, who have carefully calibrated their compassion to avoid making waves in the provincial bastions of conservatism. The emcee Line Renaud, the actress Clémentine Célarié, and a few others find the right words to say and the right gestures to make in all that racket; just about everyone manages to have a better time than the sick and the caregivers and the nurses hanging around at two o'clock in the morning, long after the singers have gone home. I'm fed up almost from the beginning, I shut down but I can't leave; I imagine it's the same for you, lost in this unfathomable circus. I am supposed to interview you about why you think you're here. Normally I'd have no trouble pulling it off, I've long exercised a kind of mild schizophrenia that allows me to play the professional interviewer while repressing my personal feelings, but there's nothing normal about this night. I don't feel like doing anything at all, I ask stupid questions, as conventional and banal as I can make them; you soon send me packing, one might even say curtly, a glacial exchange in a depressing atmosphere. Even so, the assistants are signaling me that it's already gone on too long, and we move on to the next thing. I had been sitting beside you and not once had we looked each other in the eye. In the morning, the whole experience seems a little less bitter to me; after all, up until that moment I had never really touched you; we'd been so tightly packed in that crowd, I could feel your body against mine: your arms, your shoulders, your breasts, the perfume on your skin. I've had this sense of abrupt physical release before, with Montand and Delon; the slightest touch made me suddenly aware of their whole body, and each time they took me by the shoulder it was like an incredible carnal force had struck me down. With you, your breathtaking gentleness was an added bonus. I can only remember one movie in which you bared your magnificent breasts; on-camera nudity is not your style. From that moment I no longer had to imagine your body, I'd seen the real thing. Maybe that's why my questions were so dumb, I was staggered by this new experience and almost woozy from the shock. And yet, my sense of having sleepwalked through the interview while millions of people watched on television without noticing a thing heightened the pleasure I take from harboring secrets in a public setting; such a sense of assured survival always gives rise to a certain feeling of jubilation, tinged with sadness in this case since there was no reason in the world that it should ever happen again.

THE YEAR 2000, one of those long weekends in May. My perennial capacity for self-punishment is in full gear: I've managed to saddle myself with work and find myself stuck in a deserted Paris. The weather is lovely; in the evenings I take my dog for a walk along the broad, empty streets. The summer light accentuates the ghostliness of the stepped buildings. I wallow in my usual bittersweet melancholy. Suddenly, at the corner where the road ends at the Polish embassy, a car runs a red light and hits a motorcyclist coming down the Boulevard des Invalides. The collision is very violent, and the unmanned motorcycle hurtles toward me, its horn shrieking like a bomb in a wartime newscast. I just barely avoid the projectile as it crashes into a wall behind me. The car drives off, the rider lies inert and broken on the ground. The suddenness of the accident in the deep tranquility of a quiet neighborhood, the explosive emergence of uncontrollable danger in the still of the evening, I've seen my own death plunge by me in flash; it happens that way sometimes, you hear stories about it, with luck and good reflexes you can sidestep it by mere inches. Luck was with me this time. My dog had a close call, too; he trembles like a leaf as he presses against me. If the iron monster had struck me head on or swept him away, how could either of us go on without the other? There are moments like this when we both have the sense of being alone in the world. I know very well that there are five or six dog years for every human year, but we are so devoted to each other that I try not to think about it. There are usually cops around here because of the embassy, but nobody's coming as far as I can see; they must have taken the long weekend off themselves. No one at the windows or out on their balconies. The motorcycle's horn sputters and dies, like the death rattle of a wild animal. Utter silence resumes; not a single car passes, my dog shakes himself as if he had just emerged from the water; I tell him to lie down and wait; he's used to it, he spends the better part of his day waiting for me. I approach the rider lying in the center of the intersection, he seems to be coming round, he groans as he begins to stir. He's a man in his forties with a little moustache, wearing a parka and velvet pants now torn to shreds—a guy of modest means, I guess, who wears his winter clothes right up to the start of summer. His helmet seems to have withstood the impact but his right leg is in bad shape—it's pleated like an accordion and turned completely back to front. I remember the old directive that you're not supposed to touch the injured in case you cause irreversible damage. I try speaking to him, he blinks but does not answer, he may have a fractured skull after all, and I look to see if there's blood coming from his ears. My first aid skills are decidedly weak, I lean over him uselessly, I walk around him completely powerless to help. There is still no one in sight other than the waiting dog, who keeps his eyes glued on me. Even on August 15, at the height of the summer heat, there would be more people. After what seems like an endless wait, I finally see a car heading up the Rue de Grenelle in my direction. It's a black Audi, not the hulking tank they make for the nouveaux riches but a mid-range model, newish and discreet, the kind suited to the urbane, sophisticated middle class, perfect for trips to a country house somewhere near Paris. I wave down the lovely car and it dutifully pulls over; you and your daughter emerge. This isn't the moment to get bowled over by the perfectly stunning coincidence, much less to hug and kiss over our unexpected reunion. I can't even be sure you've recognized me. On the other hand, you immediately grasp the situation and take charge. You open the Audi's trunk and retrieve a plaid blanket and a thermos, while your daughter inflates a rubber headrest. Dumbfounded, my arms dangling, like an idiot I peek into the trunk, where I see a set of little leather valises packed in perfect order. I wonder if you always travel this way with your daughter, a deluxe version of a Doctors Without Borders auxiliary reserve squadron, and suddenly I have a terrible urge to laugh. It's surely a reaction to having been almost killed by the motorcycle, but you can't know that and my attitude irritates you. Addressing me by my first name, you tell me to support the injured man's head as he shivers under the blanket while your daughter holds a cup of tea to his lips. I slip the cushion under his head; I still feel like laughing but I manage to control myself. I must still look completely dazed; in the space of a few short minutes I've run the whole gamut of emotions, including that of knowing that I can't be a complete stranger to you since you remembered my first name. The poor rider's troubles are far from over yet; the blanket, the hot tea, the cushion, and all that female attention have revived him a little, he's stopped blinking and keeps looking at his leg, then at the sky, then back again; when he sees you leaning over him, he passes out again immediately. When he tells the story to his family, they'll all think he was delirious. And as for me, I'd imagined this whole misadventure as a surreal bookend to our meeting on Avenue Montaigne, but now I'm afraid it will all end badly if you keep conspiring to make me laugh. But you call the police on your cell phone, the EMTs come and load the injured man onto a stretcher. The cops pay no attention to me; they help you gather your belongings and return them to your trunk with the graceful movements of intimidated bears; also, they ask you if you witnessed the accident and you point to me the way one might recall a forgotten piece of old furniture during a move. Maybe that's an exaggeration, you're only answering their question, but I suddenly feel sad and tired and it makes me obtusely sensitive; you're probably also anticipating the moment when the issue of autographs arises and you want to get away as fast as you can. Your daughter smiles sweetly at me, the doors slam, the Audi pulls away; the witness stays behind with the police officers—a sorry excuse for a witness, since I didn't even take down the perp's license plate; but I tell them the story of the careening motorcycle that almost crushed me, they whistle while they examine the debris and they see that I need some time to myself. I return to my dog, which has not moved all this time and now jumps up to greet me; at least someone's happy to see me. Night has fallen, the two of us head home, *allegro ma non troppo*. There are lives in which we wait forever for something that never happens until a surprise brings us to a sudden halt. My friend François, who loved you far more than I do, once told me with tender wisdom: "She's a little Prussian. You have to know how to take orders." I also read somewhere once: "I don't make much effort with people who don't attract me." By this time of night, the black Audi must be nearly at the country house.

ONE SUMMER'S evening I go to the theater on Rue Saint-André-des-Arts to see a Taiwanese film that's said to be very good. I'm alone, the room is half empty, the film is long and depressing; it works on me like a morose incantation and I leave the theater feeling wrung out, in a state of mild dejection in which I'd talk to anybody just to unburden myself of all this excessive emotion. This sort of thing happens to me often, and people are generally responsive, at least for a little while. A light rain is falling, the cafés are closing, the street is dark. You had been sitting with some friends a few rows ahead of me, you'd waited patiently for the audience to file out. I had recognized you from behind and by profile when the lights came up. You're walking home, you're in a good mood, the conversation with your friends is lively. I push my moped without starting it up, it's not a bicycle, it weighs a ton but I am absolutely determined to approach and speak to you. Yet again, I must look bizarre to you, emerging out of nowhere dragging my burden through the dark and the drizzle. Your friends eye me with the suspicious reserve of people who are ready to form a protective ring around their famous companion at the approach of a stranger. But you enjoyed the movie, and my presence doesn't bother you. You're curious to hear my opinion; I know a few things about the director that pique your interest, you introduce me to your friends, who are suddenly more friendly; we are all briefly from the same world. And here it is again, that feeling that we are somehow used to one another, that there is a tenuous yet sturdy thread, or a secret passage, that connects us, hidden away somewhere behind the glowing screen that preserves your image. It's the same old delusion, of course, but there's no escaping the power you exert, your openness and dazzling brightness, your moving beauty, your alluring detachment, your way of saying just the right words in just the right tone of voice, which I would recognize among multitudes even in the darkest night. I've had my moment, I don't want to ruin it, I start up the moped, trying not to be too loud. You smile as you tell me to drive carefully; again you call me by my first name—it seems that you always call me by my first name as we are saying good-bye. When I get home, I write you a crazy letter, steeped in distress and affection, and mail it right away before I get cold feet. I receive no answer, not the tiniest peep from you; I've soon convinced myself that I put you off with my capriciousness, a big baby clamoring for attention and love. Declarations of love are interesting only to those who make them; no matter how heartfelt and sincere, all that zeal has nothing to do with you and I imagine you don't even find it amusing. It's just one of those inappropriate intrusions that makes one uncomfortable, and the only thing one can do is cut it short and seek to avoid its author in the future. I picture you unhappy, perhaps even furious with me and with the indefinable unfairness of fame that authorizes strangers to use you to burnish their own image and entertain pipe dreams for years on end. That damned letter is going to haunt me for a long time, like the remorse one feels over a serious mistake, crushing under a freight of shame and angst any enthusiasm I might feel at the prospect of seeing you again.

A few months later, it so happens that I'm playing emcee at the premiere of one of your movies. It's a role I despise, reducing me to the trivial functionality that emphasizes the distance between me and real artists. I had allowed myself to be lured in out of friendship for the director and out of bravado, wanting to make a clean break of it. I still believe that I can control my anxiety and improvise depending on your attitude. Before heading to the Champs-Élysées, the film crew gathers in the lounge of a grand hotel, ringed by security goons and frenzied paparazzi.

There's a feeling of elated vitality in the air, cocktails are served, and a single glance about the room is enough to confirm that, despite being surrounded by other well-known actresses, you are the focus of all activity. It's a matter of natural authority and prestige. These sorts of ceremonies are also part of your job, and no one can deny the confidence with which you pull them off. There are still a few details to iron out, and I'm urged to go work them out with you. What could be more normal? As I make my way across the lounge, the weight of that letter makes each step heavier; by the time I reach you I'm completely paralyzed, my mind is blank and my heart pounding, and my only wish is to bring this nightmare to an end and flee. But this is probably not the right time to parade my emotional condition; certain aspects of the evening's arrangements are unsatisfactory, which you coolly call to my attention, although I have nothing whatsoever to do with the things that have gone wrong. It reminds me a little of that time of the accident, but now my first name has dropped from sight, I don't have a name, I've rejoined the amorphous ranks of those who don't do their job properly. It's particularly unfair given that I can see the organizers hiding out by the buffet, and they're a lot less susceptible than I am to the seductive power you exert even when you're angry. Ultimately, though, I find their cowardice soothing; at this point, nothing seems important anymore and I'm beyond fear; they love you less than I do, a makeshift majordomo with a whiff of insolence about him, the butler who knows everything important about you: affable or disgruntled, courteous even in disdain, distant even in warmth, attentive and inaccessible, available and secretive, passionate and restrained, bold and cautious, generous and distrustful, aware of the privileges won by your beauty and reluctant to exploit them, cultured without being intellectual, loyal to the point of possessiveness, sophisticated and simple, greedy and self-controlled, free and conventional, brazen and modest, strong and vulnerable, seeking excellence in all things and despising counterfeits, cheerful and sad, there and not there—the ties that have bound me to you for so long are too numerous to name. Given the atmosphere prevailing so early in the evening, it's a comfort to recall from the outset that your personality can never be reduced to that which you choose to reveal of yourself. Thus, I find almost as much pleasure in your reproaches as in your kindnesses, since I think I know how you feel and can claim to understand why. The price I have to pay is to resign myself to never getting close to you, because I am neither man enough, nor creative enough, nor fragile enough to make you so interested in me that you would want to be my friend. As it happens, your frosty welcome suits me, too: I take it as an answer to my letter in the guise of a work-related conversation concerning professional matters that require practical solutions. I murmur apologies that are not mine to make, and I withdraw on the pretext of having to review the night's program in accordance with your wishes. As often happens when disaster looms, it all comes out just fine in the end, I'm as chatty as if I shared in the ambient euphoria, from the corner of my eye I see you smile at my standard claptrap, and then I go home when the lights come down for the screening, skipping the dinner to follow; I'm not needed here anymore and no one will notice my absence. On the avenue, a gang of wild-eyed young North African kids ask me, "Who's the hot babe?" they saw entering the theater earlier in a storm of flashbulbs. When I tell them it's my girlfriend, they look at me half skeptical, half jealous. It's only a little lie and I've had far too much emotion already for one day.

A FEW months later, I spot you among the guests on a plane chartered by Pascaline to fly them to her party in a chateau in the Bordelais. Pascaline is an extraordinary woman—intelligent, witty, and incisively empathetic; she spends her wealth tastefully and without arrogance, but she doesn't skimp on the frills when she thinks it necessary to promote her wine business, which she runs with great competence. We are bound by a deep and enduring love that has given us nothing but good memories and abiding pleasure every time we see each other. I'm not surprised that she knows you, but I've never seen you at her place, and since I tend to doubt that you enjoy party-hopping and social events, I suppose that finding yourself jostled by all these elegant people, greeting each other effusively in the pallid light of the departure lounge, is not your idea of fun. In fact, you stand at some remove, accompanied by your faithful servant Gabriel, a boy considerably younger than me, whose picture—in bathing suit on a Mediterranean beach—I have long kept hidden away in a drawer. The guests are all geared up for the party, but you are still in your day clothes, casually stylish while everybody else is dressed to the nines. Gabriel carries the valise in which you must have packed your evening gown and everything you'll need for the next day's picnic in the country. The letter I was foolish enough to send to you is still playing havoc with my psyche, and I don't have the nerve to approach you; the moment seems particularly inappropriate to me. I don't see you on the plane, where it would be equally uncouth to roam the aisles looking for you; false anonymity is one of the rules of the social farce played out among all these famous faces. In Bordeaux, you and Gabriel are discreetly whisked away by a limousine while the rest of us are loaded onto buses; I feel like I'm the only one to have noticed Cinderella's vanishing act, unless all these wicked stepsisters are simply too well-bred to let their jealousy show. I follow you with my eyes throughout the evening; Pascaline has seated you at the table of honor with the superstars, who look decidedly wan compared to you in your stunning mystery dress. The thing is, sitting at the far end of the room in a shabby, ill-fitting dinner jacket, I feel as if I have you all to myself. The dancing begins, you float by through the golden iridescence of a forest of candelabras, and it's like the most beautiful ballroom scene from a movie you have never made. When Pascaline comes for me, you've already left for the chateau. At dawn, I fly home with Gabriel, who is taking the valise. I ask him if he's ever been tempted sometimes to borrow the queen's dresses for parties of a different sort; when he looks at me in horror I know that he's been dying to do just that. Some time later, Pascaline—who's onto all of my childish tricks—tells me that you never received my letter. I must have copied down the address wrong on the envelope, but the post office never returned it to me, either.

the old lady
the old lady

the old lady

The old lady emerges from the Rue de la Pompe Metro station carrying a parcel. She's dressed in black, as old ladies often were in those days; other than the white lace collar, everything from hr straw hat to her patent-leather shoes is black. The parcel is the size of a shoebox, wrapped in brown paper and tied up with a length of ordinary string. She clings to it with care; despite its humble wrapping, the parcel is important to her; perhaps it's a gift, pastries she's made herself, or some personal item intended for a loved one, something she picked out among whatever articles fell to hand at home—one of those respectable homes, no doubt, where nothing is ever discarded. She is also carrying a handbag that keeps bumping awkwardly against the parcel. She climbs the last few steps with difficulty; her thin fingers grasp the parcel and she cannot hold on to the banister. She's out of breath by the time she gets to the top, people rush by her, and she drops the parcel.

I'm about twelve years old and on my way home from school. I pass the Rue de la Pompe Metro station every day, stopping to scan the headlines of the newspapers sold at the entrance. I see the old lady, how desolate she looks, I bend down to retrieve the parcel. It's light, easy to carry, the old lady must be very old indeed. She thanks the sweet little boy and heads off unsteadily. The parcel falls again, she can't manage to hold onto it. Where has she come from, who let her go out alone with the pathetic parcel she keeps dropping, how long as she been enduring this ordeal? Riding the train with the parcel on her knees might just about work, provided it's not too crowded and someone gives their seat to a senior citizen, but getting off, getting on, the rushing crowd, perhaps a connection to make. I've been watching her; I pick up the parcel and hand it to her again. She smiles at me with a most gracious expression in which I see gentleness, confusion, a sort of childlike complicity, and the sorrowful confession of the infirmity of old age. She moves off once more but she has gone barely a few steps before the damned parcel slips from her hands to the ground. I take charge of the parcel; if this goes on, it will end up damaged; if its contents are fragile they could break. I tell her that I'll walk her to her destination and will carry the parcel until we get there. She tells me that I shouldn't bother, she's almost there; you can't imagine what it's like to be so clumsy, you're going to make yourself late, your parents will be worried, see it's there, right there at the corner. I seem sure of myself; she doesn't insist and allows herself to be persuaded. She puts all her trust in this well-mannered child of privilege.

She's a little confused about the corner, it's the next one, at least a hundred yards further up the street. It's probably because she didn't want to be a burden. We walk slowly. She looks so tired, so fragile, but her voice is strong and pleasant, with a hint of youthful merriment; she's someone who certainly enjoys every moment of life remaining to her. She asks me what grade I'm in, if I'm a good student, if I have good friends because good friends are forever. Questions like that, the kind old ladies ask young boys they don't know. My answers are just as trite, but in the end the conversation is secondary; we're just happy to be together. I get to feel as if I've done a good deed, she is glad that I came to her assistance; and I feel there's something proud about her, despite her listless pace, while she must appreciate my schoolboy look in blazer, flannel pants, and satchel on my back.

We arrive at a mid-size building with a paint store at street level. She tells me her daughter is waiting for her and that I mustn't go to any further trouble, there's an elevator. She rummages through her bag, she wants to give me a little something to buy candies or some other treat. I refuse, of course, but I don't mention that I'm too old for candy and that I never know what exactly might constitute a treat. Then she kisses me with a vigor that takes me by surprise; she smells fresh, powdery, violet-scented. She laughs as she thanks me again and again in a delighted tone of voice. There's a young girl beneath all that black clothing; I have no experience in that field, but it feels as if a young woman has just kissed her lover.

I hold open the glass door for her, I hand her the parcel, she grips it as best she can and disappears into the dark stairwell. I should have made sure that there's really an elevator. In fact, there's no proof that she really has a daughter, and anyway I have no idea who lives at this address. I have a feeling that the parcel has fallen again. Yes, I'm sure of it, I heard the hollow clap, and there's her black silhouette bending over to retrieve it, but I don't dare open the door and seek her out in that murky foyer. We've already said our good-byes, and we will never see each other again. I run all the way home. I don't know why, but I've always had a thing for old ladies.

bird

bird

bird

The boy walks through the night a few steps ahead of me. Dark pants fitting close at the hips and narrow down the leg; a white T-shirt tight around his shoulders and down his back; bare arms, a Swatch at the wrist, dark hair with shiny highlights, trim at the nape. An easy gait, calm pace, everything's fine, clean, impeccable. He doesn't turn around, he knows I'm following him and he is surely aware that my one glimpse of him in profile, up close and without touching, is one of intense pleasure for me. He's used to it; it's his fourth since last night. I'd had the idea of stopping by a club I'd never been to before returning to my hotel, and I'd noticed him right away. They all look alike only to those who do not desire them. He stood with the others on the little stage, his hands behind his back to show off his body under the lights, in immaculate boxer shorts, the John the Baptist stance that they all adopt instinctively and that the queers adore. But his face was sharply defined, there was some character in his expression, no vapidity in his gaze or soliciting in his smile; he had an immediate charm that distinguished him among the ranks of professional pretty boys. He made me think of Tony Leung at twenty. He laughed as if he'd won the lottery when I had them call his number, and when he came up to me I caught a trace of scent off his skin, delicate cologne and cheap soap; none of that duty-free perfume they usually drench themselves in. He really seemed genuinely happy to be going with me; I sensed that he would be energetic and fraternal. Rats swarm the alley and scurry off ahead of us, the neon lights fade into the gloom behind us, the stale smell of trash cans mingles with the muggy heat, and the deafening roar of techno from the open doors of all the other clubs enhances that sensory deprivation in which I focus all my attention on him alone and on what lies ahead. Awful, computer-generated synthesizer noise that can barely be dignified by the name *music*, but its hellish rhythms shake the whole neighborhood, keep you hovering between arousal and stupor, and make your head spin with the desire pounding at your temple. The sound level drops a little in the underground passage leading to the hotel parking lot. Its fifteen stories of mediocre international comfort rise above the tide of humanity and the jumble of clubs and greasy spoons; its guests are the modestly funded tour operation clientele who travel the city in tight packs, furtively window-shopping for a cheap thrill and a laugh or two to carry home as souvenirs before going to bed early behind air-conditioned, double-paned windows. But its roots extend deep into far more fertile soil—a kind of cavern where taxi drivers hold raucous card parties in a gambling den ambiance straight out of a kung fu movie; the cavern leads to a series of windowless rooms that usually rent by the hour but can be had for longer, even indefinitely, if you're willing to come to terms and set a price. It's certainly not the worst place to die, anonymity and discretion guaranteed. Nasty-looking youths who wouldn't stand a chance selling themselves in the clubs enjoy their moment of glory as impresarios of the pleasure caves: they're in charge of the keys, keep the lively turn-over moving, reset the meters, clean up between tricks. They can be surprisingly friendly, all things considered; they claim to know every boy by name and provide the tipping regulars with a simulacrum of grand hotel service: foil-wrapped towels, paper slipcovers for the sheetless bed, new carpeting, a chrome-plated exhaust fan, mirrors everywhere—even on the ceiling for those who want it. The "room valet," as he elegantly calls himself, attempts to show me how to work the television and, sizing up my look of defeat, offers some cassettes—to perk me up, I suppose, just in case. We laugh a little without really understanding each other, I pay him for the two hours, enough to buy himself a new gold tooth, and he leaves humming a tune. We're alone. My boy hasn't said a word. He stands before me, unmoving, his gaze as direct as ever, a half-smile playing on his lips. I want him so much I'm trembling.

THE BOY himself is not the only catalyst of my attraction; it's the whole staged setting in which I found him. In every club, the boys stand around on a well-lit stage in groups of four or six; they wear the distinctive costume of the establishment and its specialty, minimal and sexy: turn-of-the-century bathing costumes with shoulder straps, or cyclist costumes for the ath-letes; boxer shorts, briefs, or G-strings for the pretty boys or pseudo-thugs; the cross-dressers get to wear miniskirts. They stand there without moving or talking, their bodies straight and legs slightly apart, gazing into the distance or smiling depend-ing on what kind of club it is; the better sort would require them to be impassive, at least earlier in the evening, staring out into the half-light of the room below, the obscurity from which the customers watch them while sipping at their drinks. Their number hangs by their crotch, naturally. Most of them are young, handsome, apparently unscathed by the damage one might expect from their occupation. I come to learn later that they do not work every night, are often students, have girlfriends and sometimes even live with their families, who pretend not to know where they get their pocket money. On the other hand, they all have cell phones and email so their most devoted clients can reach them anytime and anywhere, which leads one to suppose that the clubs' take is too big and that the boys always have to fend for themselves in order to get by. Some of them are older, and there's also a small contingent of seedy beefcake that clearly has its admirers. The latter are the loss leaders of the show; their presence highlights the youthful allure of all the others. Every three minutes, as the techno blasts relentlessly, two withdraw to the wings, two others take their place, and so on. When the entire troupe has had its turn in the spotlight, they all gather onstage for a Gloria Gaynor–style triumphant finale; the boys abandon their hieratic poise, whisper among themselves as they size up the clientele with facetious obscenities and solicit more openly; then the whole little show begins again, a little less stiff and disciplined as the night advances. At the hottest hour, when the room is packed to the rafters, the most reputable clubs put on what they call the "sexy show," a muddled pornographic pantomime that invariably ends with the buggering of a transvestite in a general uproar of merriment that is a little too exaggerated to be entirely genuine. The artists who perform this particular number work like the nude dancers on Place Pigalle; you see them in the street, drag queens in translucent chadors, hurrying from one club to the next to make their show. The boys, on the other hand, are committed to their club and stick with it. You can imagine the negotiations, underhanded deals, and danger involved in flouting the rules and what it must cost to lure a lover boy from the circuit. Cell phones and emails may make such transactions a little easier, but their expedience is only provisional; you can never get lost in this sprawling city, and don't bother applying for a visa to some distant haven until you've tied up all your loose ends back home.

Backstage is part of the spectacle. Behind the stage or in the wings, they are readily accessible to the eyes of curious members of the audience; these establishments aren't especially large, and effective marketing ensures that the audience has no time to grow pensive or bored. In any case, while they wait to return to the stage the boys keep an eye on the room as they pretend to be engaged in highly absorbing activities; they watch variety or sports shows on the TV, they do gymnastics exercises on complex machines, read the newspaper, or chat idly among themselves, boxers' towels draped around their necks. When a waiter comes to whisper that they've been selected, they put a checkmark in a little box on a blackboard before drifting over to the bar with an air of utter detachment, while the other boys politely turn a blind eye to the transaction under way. Management presumably takes note of the night's activities, as reflected on the blackboard, before closing time. Once a reservation has been confirmed, the boy hurriedly dresses backstage and returns; all that's left is to pay for the drinks, settle the client's commission to the club, and make your way through the throng of bowing, smirking puppets who serve as waiters and hail you shrilly in English: "Good night, sir, see you again." You can take two boys or more; there's no problem since the answer to everything is: *I want you happy.* Contrary to the common assumption, there are few Western sex fiends in the audience; most of the clientele is local, middle-aged, and quite presentable, traveling in groups mildly lit up on whiskey and Cokes. The handful of Caucasians who wash up at the Spartacus tend to stand out in the crowd, but it is also true that they are offered the best tables.

Obviously, I've read everything available on the traffic in boys here and seen a great many films and reports; despite my skepticism concerning the truthfulness of the media, I know that there is some truth to their tabloid investigations: the ignorance or bitterness of most of the families, the widespread poverty, the pimping community overrun by thugs and criminals, the mountains of cash to be earned while the kids themselves live on crumbs, the devastation and dependency of drugs, the diseases, all the sordid little details of the trade. I get by on a strong dose of everyday cowardice, I spend lavishly to ease my conscience, I turn it all into a novel in my head and splash it all with plenty of sentiment; I never stop thinking about it, but that doesn't stop me from coming back. All these beauty-pageant-cum-slave-market rituals are a real turn-on for me. The lighting is terrible, the music wears on my nerves, the shows are dreary, and you might think that such a spectacle, abhorrent from a moral point of view, would also be repellently vulgar. But I love it beyond reason. The profusion of very attractive and readily available boys puts me in a state of desire that I have no need to curb or conceal. Money and sex, I'm right at the heart of the system— a system that really works, since I know I won't be rejected. I can assess, fantasize, invent stories about each boy; that's what they're there for, and so am I. It all comes down to choice. I can have something I've never had—a choice. The only thing expected of me, in my own time and with no obligation of any kind, is that I choose. I can settle everything I owe with a fistful of bahts, and I am free—absolutely free—to play with my own desire and to choose. The Western morality, eternal guilt and shame to which I am chained, suddenly drop away—and the world be damned, as someone once said.

There are certainly establishments of this kind in places other than Thailand; Amsterdam or Hamburg, perhaps? But I've put in too much time and come from too far away to stop now, I need to forge ahead to get what I came for; I don't want to run the risk of meeting boys who remind me of others, of finding myself in a familiar situation, of hearing words I might understand. I need the unknown, terra incognita, a country without landmarks. In a place where no one will ever know anything about me, there is always the chance, tenuous though it might be, that I will find freedom and oblivion, that my shackles will melt away and my past dissolve. Choice.

Just as they say it is with hard drugs, I've never fully re-experienced the ineffable shock of the first time, but it's no matter because the wave I'm riding is far more powerful than the relative lessening of intensity that comes with habituation. I treat myself with alcohol, a gentle haze fuels the compulsion, and there is always another boy that I have yet to notice. I'm never really disappointed. They close at two and reopen the next day. I also know that this is nothing but a sinister farce I recite to myself. Resist as I might, the lie falls apart the minute I board the return flight; reality shoves my nose into my own shit as soon as I reach Paris. Remorse—driven mad by the fear of having lost all trace of me—climbs back in the saddle and rides me for all I'm worth.

MY BOY abruptly removes his T-shirt, just as he must do when he plays sports, with no real awareness of the virile grace of his movements, and he shakes his head to settle his hair, which has been ruffled by his collar. This vision paralyzes me even more completely as I watch him from the door; I am unable to approach, I can't loosen the vise around my neck or control the trembling that comes over me. It has been a long time since I've experienced such turbulent feelings. Oddly, he has a hard time removing his pants and boxers, he avoids my gaze from some innate sense of modesty, perhaps a hint of perplexity about my behavior, which must seem exaggerated and weird to him. These kids are largely used to men even though they don't especially like them, they're gratified by their desire but also openly and perpetually astonished by it; there's the occasional nut job or two, and a transitory Westerner who appears to be relatively young does not jibe with the usual clientele; at my age, in this city, you can find yourself a sweetheart for free when you enjoy the prestige and privileges reserved for foreigners; you can always buy him a Walkman before you leave. Some old queen in makeup would seem less threatening and more run-of-the-mill. Still, his hesitation is brief, he certainly doesn't want to put himself in the wrong; he carefully folds his things, puts them on the television console and finally looks me in the eye with a budding smile. Everything is just right, as well defined as the rest. Where does that myth about the diminutive size of their members come from? I can attest to the contrary, although I have no interest in indulging in the comparison of superlatives that monopolizes the conversations of some gay men.

I awake from my stupor, place a few crumpled bills on his clothes—considerably more than the appropriate sum quoted by the club manager, but he doesn't seem to notice. As strange as it may seem, prostitution is taboo in this country, so much so that there is no word for it in their language. The wad of money has no value at that moment, he's embarrassed by it and will only focus on it afterward, not as payment for an exchange, nor as a fee for a specific service, but rather by way of a friendly reward with no suggestion of reciprocal obligation. It would be distasteful, even insulting for me to insist that he take it. The money will vanish later when I'm not looking, as if by magic. But while I'm almost ashamed of having committed a breach of etiquette whose code I'm unfamiliar with, I realize that it's the same old fear of a difficult negotiation at the last moment, of being rejected, even, just as I'm about to reach a strongly desired goal. I have always paid right away to gain the upper hand and put my adversary off balance. Corruption is a blind man's sport; you are so uncertain of attaining your desire that you hold the money just beyond his reach and make him grope for it. I've got it wrong in this particular instance, but fortunately he doesn't hold it against me; he's blithely following his own rule, which is to make me happy, for he knows no other. With a little hand signal he indicates the bathroom, he walks past without touching me, uses his teeth to tear at the foil wrappers around the towels and washcloth, and steps into the shower, inviting me to join him with a toss of the head. What if I were the kind of man who refuses to wash? For these boys, who are rightly fanatical about cleanliness, a reluctance to bathe would be another warning sign, although it would be too late to back out at this point and rude to let one's repugnance show. I undress and join him in the shower; if he had any doubts about the effect he would have on me, they're all gone by now and he happily soaps me down, fully reassured. Everything is normal. In France, it can be a whole production to get most call boys hard, but we're definitely not in France now, and we use the washcloth, the soap, and the shower attachment to explore and measure ourselves against each other. He's almost as tall as I am and certainly a lot firmer, built like one of those kickboxers who can lay you out in a flash. But I have nothing to fear from him, it's all a delightful game, and I abandon myself to it with eyes closed, filled with joy and confidence. It's hard to tell which one of us is protecting the other.

We towel each other down very carefully; it wouldn't take much for my body to betray me and for it all to be over. Just like that. I don't know if the same thought has occurred to him, but he's perfectly willing for me to take my time and lets me take the lead. I haven't had the nerve to kiss him yet, but I caress and touch him and he reciprocates. We return to the room; they really have thought of everything, right down to a dimmer for the lights. Now that we are lying down, I try kissing the boy on the lips; I was wrong to hesitate, he kisses incredibly well, probably with the same skill he uses on his girlfriend; he goes at it as long as I want, his lips cool, tongue deep, the salty saliva of a young man with no trace of tobacco or alcohol. His skin is exquisitely soft, his supple body twists when I stroke and squeeze him, and I get the sense that he experiences pleasure wherever I touch him. The fact that we can't understand each other only heightens the intensity of what I'm feeling, and I would swear it's the same for him. That doesn't stop me from talking, from saying sweet nothings that he picks up and repeats nonsensically, laughing out loud. He licks me with fantastic delicacy, and I can see the back of his head, his back, his ass in the ceiling mirror, the bluish highlights in his thick hair when I lower my head to look at his face, which is attentive to my every reaction. I don't know where he gets the condoms from, but he slips them on us both in the wink of an eye and with the dexterity of a cat burglar. He's in charge now, and things start to get heavy; his body completely encompasses mine, his smile reveals a neat row of teeth, his eyes stare into mine; there is no hardness in them, only a glimmer of cunning mischief and joy, as if he's more surprised than anyone at what he's doing. There are some things I no longer take for granted since a bad experience I had thirty years ago with a Moroccan in a sauna. He was an immigrant worker, pretty good-looking, who thought only of his own pleasure and took his revenge for everything else, a tough guy who fought the class war with his dick buried to the hilt up the ass of the young bourgeoisie. He'd hurt me and infected me with a disease that took months of painful and secret suffering to cure. That was the end of that. But it's different here; it doesn't even hurt, I let him take

me where he will, so long as it's with him. He's become my man.
I catch glimpses of myself overhead, like an American starlet
in an old-time movie, ardent and maternal, a look of distant
melancholy on her face. Joan Crawford in Patpong. That really
would be a stretch, since maternity was hardly Joan Crawford's
forte, even if she was briefly married to that old queen Cary
Grant. I always trip myself up when I let my mind wander. But
my boy isn't in Hollywood, he's here where the boys remain
when desire has fled and they find themselves alone; I can feel
his heart beating wildly against mine, but he turns his head and
rolls on his side. Joan Crawford can stare at herself in the mirror as long as she likes, thinking that it might be best to dim the
lights even more. When he rises abruptly to leave, I'm stricken
by my habitual anxiety; that's why I usually come first, so I don't
have to witness their lassitude. Sometimes that's enough for me
and we end it there; sometimes I feel like continuing and so do
they; there's a little leeway when that happens. My boy is game
for anything to keep up his end of the bargain—when he says
I want you happy, he means it. He's come back beside me, his
expression a little veiled as if he were sorry to have gotten up
so fast and regretted his absence. We start over, but differently;
now I'm the one who makes the decisions and I want all the
pleasure to myself. I've never felt so blissful and so powerful.
He's closed his eyes, I don't know what to make of the traces of
moisture beneath his eyelids, the rings, a little sweat, perhaps,
in the hollow of his temples, or tears of exhaustion—is there
such a thing as tears of exhaustion? The side mirror reflects our
image—me as a madman, he as a corpse—and it staggers me.
I'm overcome by a deep feeling of compassion and tenderness
for him, at seeing him so passive and helpless, whereas earlier
he'd struck me as the freest and strongest of them all, the young
king of the nightclubs lying with another fucking duplicitous
foreigner, waiting for it all to pass. Like a child's sorrow my

shame drifts over his silence and his naked body, envelops his clothes folded neatly atop the television, and finds no words; he wouldn't understand them anyway. My desire evaporates as fast as the sky train that will bring him home to his festering suburb later tonight, a few bahts in his pocket to spend on useless trinkets. I can hear the taxi drivers and waiters hurling shrill abuse at each other outside; the exhaust fan pumps in the stench of gas and oil from the parking lot. Any hint of joy or emotion has fled this ersatz clinic of a room. Thirty years of bad sex have led to this? I withdraw benignly—come now, it was all a game, nothing serious, we never would have stood a chance; he rubs his eyes, opens them, smiles again as I turn to the side and plunge headlong into the mirror, as inert as a stone. Does he suspect that I truly loved him for a fleeting moment and that I was filled with pity for him, for myself, for this whole unsustainable charade, and for leaving him like this in such a state of abandon? And yet I can still feel him beside me, he drums his fingers up and down my back and twitters little scraps of French that begin to sound less and less like those he spoke earlier. Surely he suspects nothing of the kind, it's just another of the stories I tell myself, it's just that we've each returned to our own worlds.

Afterward we fall asleep. Something must have happened for us to be so exhausted. By the time we go our separate ways, the clubs are closed and the souvenir vendors are making an infernal racket as they stow their junk in steel containers. I want to get his email address but he only knows it in the Thai alphabet; he makes me understand that all I need do is to write care of the club, using his number, but I find it hard to imagine that any mail could reach such a tenuous destination; he also reminds me that his name is Bird, but I haven't forgotten; it's a pretty name, Bird, even if it surely does not mean the same thing in their language. Others are named Tom or Brad; they get them from the movies, and when you dig a little you find a real Thai name that sounds similar; there aren't many options, they often share the same name, which is why they insist on having numbers. As he leaves, he shoots me one last beautiful smile and points toward the alley of the club, surely suggesting we meet there again in the evenings to come, and then he promptly vanishes, leaving me to the night where I had found him. I leave for Paris a few hours later. I think of him often, I hope that no one has hurt him; every time I go with a boy his image flashes across my mind's eye, standing in front of me in that horrible bunker-like room, and I feel as if I am betraying him, so far away over there, my Patpong boy.

UP ON the monitor, all I see is a flat line. The young male nurse with the Tintin cowlick had asked me earlier if I had tickets for the Mylène Farmer concert. Now, he pushes the button on the machine and it goes blank. He turns to us and says, "It's over." His vaguely ironic half-smile irritates me; I'm sure I'm mistaken, you have to be armored when you do this kind of work. It's an expression that must come naturally to him and it probably means nothing; just one way among many of enduring repeated reversals. I don't know Mylène Farmer very well; she's a very secretive pop star who cultivates her own enigma—a marketing ploy no doubt, but she's hard to get to know. If I called her agent I might be able to get tickets and gratify Tintin in the white smock; I'd take the opportunity to ask him about his work, how he feels when he turns the EKG machine off several times a week. In any case, I'm sure he thinks that at eighty-seven nothing could be more natural and there's no need to make a big fuss about it. People always think like that, even if they don't dare say so to your face. Right now, it is an evening in December, and my father has just died.

My stepmother cries; they've been married for more than forty years, she has always loved him and cared for him with a devotion I could never have mustered; he has been very weak ever since his attack six years ago. Now comes the great sorrow for which one is never really prepared, the sudden revival of that old fear of having to live without him from now on, along with the exhaustion of having waged an extended fight together to put off the day of reckoning as long as possible. Her daughter cries too. My father was not her father, but it's all the same; I always felt—just a little and without acknowledging it—that he liked her better than his own children; the only girl among the boys, theirs was a relationship based on choice, more free and without the usual litany of obligations and grievances. I never held it against them.

My uncle, the last surviving brother, left right after Tintin pressed the button. He looked shattered, though you never can be sure about the feelings of men of that generation in a family where they rarely touched, never cried, and meticulously concealed their emotions. Upbeat and eloquent in intellectual exchange, ready with the charm in the outside world and in the absence of an emotional threat, they withdrew in cold, dry diffidence rather than reveal anything of themselves. He certainly had no interest in being trapped in a round of tears, futile words of comfort, expressions that change nothing and then evaporate into thin air. And yet he isn't the type to run away; I wouldn't presume to claim to know his thoughts, but his hasty departure suggests that they were all confused in his head with memories of the whole saga of the four brothers. He's out there on the street right now, walking with no thought of finding his car, just wanting to be alone yet crushed by the thought that he truly is now, since he has no one left to talk to; well, there's his wife, but she's exhausted, and his sisters too, whereas he, with his heavy winter coat, sharp features, gray eyes, and notorious likeness to his brother, still has that vigor that they all retain until the very end. This isn't really the moment for me to follow him out there to express the affection I'm feeling for him for the first time. He'd hate that.

Tintin has left; they eat dinner early at the Invalides. The retired gendarme and his wife—who had watched the screen while the machine was still running and said: "He has an amazing heart! See how he's holding on?"—have gone home to find the appropriate blue suit for him. From the hallway, two generals in full dress uniform peak in to offer their condolences. Military hospital, Legion of Honor, family ties—I always forget that we're deep in *nomenklatura* country, where they don't stint on the observance of proprieties. My stepmother and her daughter leave; through the half-open door, I hear the weak echo of their voices as they launch into tentative conversation. I am alone with my father. It's an experience known to just about everyone in the world: the flesh is soft and warm, he almost looks like he's moving, I watch for his chest to rise for a breath. Something incomprehensible and irreversible happened a few moments ago, but what was it exactly? No, his body is still, he's already moving away from me at the amazing speed of death. And soon he'll be so far out of reach that I may be visited by that relative calm that comes when one is face to face with the remains of a loved one, solid evidence of a life that is over, with its own beginning and end, an existence I can picture in its entirety and synchronize with my own memories. But I haven't reached that point yet; the room is gloomy, it's cold outside, the next few days are not going to be much fun, and suddenly my only desire, growing into a compulsive obsession, is to run away one last time to Patpong.

IT'S BEEN a good three years since I was last on this flight, scattered with gay couples staring aggressively at the singles. These queens are solidly in the modern domestic mold, traveling in pairs, and Bangkok is the honeymoon destination par excel-

lence for those recently united under the new domestic partner-
ship laws. Unattached holdouts are out of style; they're seen as
troublemakers by a community that thinks it has rights over
them. A movie with Matt Damon (not as handsome as Brad Pitt,
but sexier), Cesária Évora on the sound system, and turbulence
over Bulgaria; a friendly young humanitarian volunteer tells me
about his problems understanding the Thais and his vacations
in La Baule with his in-laws. To avoid complications, I explain
that I have just a brief stopover in Bangkok before going on
to Cambodia to scout movie locations; I am inexhaustible on
the subjects of Angkor Wat, Sihanouk, and the Khmer Rouge.
I'll fudge the issue with any story that comes to mind, but I'll
never have the nerve to admit I'm stopping in Thailand. Still, it
might be fun to describe my Siamese adventures to my neighbor and see how he reacts, the way Robert Hirsch and Jacques
Charon played kissy-kissy in gas stations and took playful swats
at the attendants' asses, just to see—the old game of baiting the
straights. But I never take a chance with that sort of thing; the
old anxieties have their claws too deep into me. For that matter, with all my mortal sins I only have to think about the plane
crashing and I start worrying about having to go to hell. For
someone who likes to consider himself a freethinker, I still have
some work ahead of me. Somewhere over Turkey, during my
seat neighbor's second friendly tennis tournament at the Hotel
des Pins—the one where he met his wife—I fall fast asleep.

As a matter of fact, I was not far from Thailand only a few
months earlier and had every intention of making a stop there.
I was on my way to Jakarta for a television broadcast and flying over the forests of Malaysia into which that closet queen
Jim Thompson, whose magnificent house in Bangkok I had once
visited, vanished forever; the spectacular descent into Singapore;
the tourist brochures in the airport, singing the praises of that
puritanical and moneyed Chinese island with the catchphrase

"No go-go bars here, try somewhere else"; the string of essentially desert islands beyond the Malacca Straits where the Thai pirates hide out after murderous, mercenary rampages during which they scuttle rusting hulks filled with destitute immigrants and the fine yachts of clueless Englishmen with equal-opportunity rapacity, sparing only the young women; the blanket of steaming humidity that envelops you on arrival, and that slightly fetid smell that permeates the polluted, dung-heap cities of Asia—everything reminded me of Bangkok and fed into my nostalgia for it.

Jakarta is of no interest to anyone outside the businessmen holed up in air-conditioned, Suharto-era luxury hotels, where they take the pulse of poor, sick Indonesia as they await the cure promised by a return to universal corruption and shady dealings. It's said to be dangerous, labyrinthine, a den of thieves and fanatics of every stripe. Tourists shun it; they only want Bali and the Sunda Islands; a few adventurous types consider it to be a lesser evil, a mandatory point of departure for treks across Java. They never stay there for long. And yet it's a stirring city, a relatively orderly amalgam of Batavian colonial utopia, triumphalist Third World pipe dreams, pompous high-rises waiting for the economic dragon to awaken, and shantytown villages where syrupy musical soap operas pour from TV screens even in the heart of the cesspit. It's easy and quite safe to find your way around, despite the pestilential canals that decimated the Dutch, done in by their nostalgia for Amsterdam, and the hallucinatory drone of choking traffic. A city of Muslim Javanese who believe in spirits and magic, of Chinese who renounce their ancestry and prudently convert to Catholicism, of outcasts from distant islands, a mosaic of Malays and seafaring peoples of Melanesian extraction. Often gracious and colorfully dressed, good-humored and industrious, practitioners of the indulgent cynicism of those who have seen it all and have to find a way to live together, they have little sympathy for the crazy bomb-throwers who thrive in the general anarchy and little interest in the official civic bombast that provides a smokescreen for a polished, unpredictable police force and military men in dark glasses eager to milk the cash cow. From time to time, a great wave of collective psychosis sweeps over all that humanity in a tide of arson and butchery; the Javanese are usually the ones seeking to settle a score, while the Chinese foot the bill for the bloodbath; afterward, the shadow puppeteers come to an arrangement, the marionettes put away their submachine guns and their rancor, peace and tranquility are restored. Back to silk batik and pretty music. The visiting Westerner, shaken but no worse for wear, finds it all rather fantastic and a little romantic.

HEIDI ATTACHES himself to me near the McDonald's. Heidi insists on the proper spelling of his name, and I picture some refugee from the Bernese Oberland in his past, driven mad by love and the heat. He works down the street at the Hotel Indonesia, the one from *The Year of Living Dangerously*, the Mel Gibson movie about the bloody overthrow of the Sukarno regime. Heidi gets by in broken English, the universal patois, he's seen the movie and knows the whole story; although somewhat incongruous in the circumstances of our first encounter, it provides us with a topic of conversation appropriate to our surroundings. Twenty-three years old, pleasant looking without actually being handsome, educated, nimble-minded, a very nice guy. He's waiting for one of those rattletrap buses manned by some teenage conductor who leaps out, calls off the names of the stations ahead, viciously scolds the passengers as he herds them into the crammed, hellish interior, then hops back on as the vehicle pulls away in a cloud of black smoke. We wander about the neighborhood, talk about our jobs, the distant precinct where he lives; the bus-line Lucifers give me a pretext to redirect the discussion toward traditional crafts, everyday life, tipping customs. I really work it but I feel like I'm getting it all wrong; he must be one of those young people who enjoys talking to foreigners just for the pleasure of friendly conversation. I don't know Jakarta well yet and in the end I'm ready to make do with the somewhat demoralizing vision of emaciated kids cruising the shadows of the park outside my hotel and the bug-eyed creeps high on glue who zeroed in on me at the dreadful, overcrowded fag club I had found the night before. Frightening scenes and unnecessary risks. On the other hand, the misunderstanding with Heidi fades pretty quickly. This is a Muslim country, there's no flashy soliciting here, a minimal sense of restraint is required and my improvised cicerone behaves accordingly. And yet, it doesn't take me long to figure out that the city is not short on dissipations of all sorts and that pretty much everyone is available whether they know the code or not. Heidi clearly senses that I'm drifting and that our conversation is dragging. He keeps it at that, for propriety's sake, and offers to accompany me to my hotel; he knows the security guys and they let boyfriends up into the rooms. He says "boyfriends," plural, and proceeds to introduce me to several friends of his who are also waiting for their bus. The sudden proposal of new companions leaves me no time to react or to decline. At this time of day, the offices are letting out and shifts changing at the vast Hyatt Hotel shopping center; there are hordes of young people on the streets and in the underground passages used to cross them. With the armies of model employees in white shirts and sunglasses, it feels like watching one of those clone ballets from *The Matrix Reloaded*, Asian remix, with me playing a somewhat rumpled Keanu Reeves. Heidi knows just what he's doing and goes about his infernal casting call as he watches me from the corner of his eye; it's fascinating to watch him work like a sparrowhawk diving upon its prey. Within a few moments we find ourselves at the head of an affable, smiling little gang. All I have to do is choose. The great affluence around us is on display; this Westerner, wrung out by the equatorial humidity and his long flight, surrounded by all these young men so fresh they seem to have stepped straight out of the shower, is just another page in the great saga of the Third World's rebirth. I must look like an American prisoner of the Viet Cong or one of those dumb backpackers you take for a ride before fleecing. In a word, I have no idea what's going on; I've gone straight from a high school debate for deserving students to the prospect of an orgy with a bunch of strangers. I smell a trap. The atmosphere has turned sour, while claimants and bystanders call out and laugh with each other in Javanese, no doubt assessing the value of the wan, rumpled, sweaty article on offer. Embarrassment and scandal loom, everything I'm afraid of. I throw sidelong glances at the cops speeding past on their Japanese motorcycles, sirens wailing; if they did stop, I'm sure they'd rather hold me for ransom than come to my assistance. A sweet little Chinese man, better than cute and particularly desirable, takes advantage of my paralysis to latch on to me and proclaim himself the official winner, the *primus inter pares* of the whole brotherhood. Heidi whispers in my ear that he is an intimate friend of his, what a stroke of luck for me that he just happened to be in the neighborhood. In a burst of energy of which I did not think myself capable, claiming jet lag and exhaustion, I suggest a general demobilization while leaving open the vague possibility of a resumption of negotiations on the following day. All I want to do is leave and be by myself. But it turns out I was wrong about them: they yield to my resistance and the trap is released with no sign of bitterness or disappointment; everyone goes his separate way with a smile on his face and the handsome Chinese slips me his calling card, cell number and email address included, in case I change my mind. More unnecessary precautions; talking with Heidi on the way to the hotel, I come to see that he'd only been trying to do me a favor. We had each held back as reasonably and politely as we could, I out of timidity and he out of courtesy; the idea of moving onto a second phase by involving one or more newcomers had evolved naturally, since he could now vouch for me as confidently as he could for them. I thought I detected in this the twofold influence of Islamic urbanity and the Japanese occupation—a long phase of deferential observation followed by a collective pounce on the target—all very sweetly done in the hope that everyone would be well pleased by the time it was all over. We have no problems with the security guards, who resolutely turn a blind eye as we pass, and having locked the door to my room behind us, I wonder what in God's name I'm going to do with this rather unattractive boy. I have been in this situation before; I am sometimes dragged into these adventures by my strange need to be civil and not to disappoint; with my back to the wall, all I want to do is to cut the chitchat and go to sleep as fast as possible.

Fortunately, Heidi is no wild lover boy; he claims to be as tired as I am and we stretch out in front of the television like a couple of senior citizens. I see why he was glad to have the young Chinese man around; I imagine he usually delegates those duties to him. On the other hand, I've already grown very attached to his company; he really is very intelligent, good-humored, and discreet. He is at ease and appreciates the comforts of the room, and I find it interesting to talk with him about the lives of boys in Jakarta, their dreams, their experiences. Soon we are sleeping together every night like two brothers. I find his apparent lack of interest touching, and he seems genuinely happy to see me at the end of the day when his shift at the Hotel Indonesia is over. Heidi knows the city like the back of his hand and the brothels hold no secrets for him; he is determined to take me to them, while I am becoming increasingly modest and chaste. We live more or less naked in our room; I get great pleasure from feeling his skin, soft and matte, against mine as we lie together, but as there is no desire between us I would be ashamed to share my sexual fantasies with him. I can't explain why I feel this way, but I am resolved to stick to it. It has something to do with pride in having foresworn such behavior, the desire to protect the serenity of our feelings, an almost loving elation in knowing that our relationship will inexorably come to an end in a few days. Although he is very perceptive, Heidi can't figure out my moods at all and doesn't give a damn about my scruples. He returns regularly to the charge; since I insist on rejecting his Chinese friend, I must come with him to see the "nice boys very clean" who are clearly just dying to meet me. Again, this obsession with delegating, and surely, too, the hope of receiving a little extra consideration from his friends, while perhaps making himself even more indispensable to me. Since he believes that "to play with boys, it's fun," the white man's confusion comes across as a sort of rejection, which upsets him and makes him sad. There's no time to waste, I'm leaving the next day; I give in so there's no cloud between us, and also because I'm curious all the same to see what this "very good place" he's chosen for me looks like.

It doesn't work anything like the way it does in Bangkok; the brothels are spread out all over the city, there's no sophisticated backdrop of any kind, and the place where Heidi brings me is a kind of garage for boys, largely open to the street, where the candidates sprawl on mattresses on the ground, distractedly watching the usual schmaltzy programs on TV and telling dirty jokes while they leaf through porn magazines filled with naked Chinese and Japanese girls with come-hither eyes and flesh-toned G-strings at their crotch. The boss, his wife, and their children bustle about with sodas and bowls of soup; the kids channel-surf, it's all one big happy family. On the walls hang pictures of sportsmen and movie stars, Sukarno and his daughter, very matronly in her glasses and chignon—the fifty-year-old-dyke look so popular among respectable ladies—as well as second-rate prints of scenes from the life of the Prophet. It's kind of dirty, there's a smell of feet, cheap perfume, and some slop simmering in the next room. It could be a neighborhood recreation center for young working men, fussed over by a couple of big-hearted administrators. A stairway at the far end leads to the rooms, from which I hear the sounds of laughter, songs played on a Walkman, and someone showering. The clients are family men on their way home from the office, strapping cops or army officers who have swapped their uniforms for fake Adidas track-suits, motorcyclists who just happened to be driving by and are barely older than the postulants. No foreigners, and you get the feeling that everybody knows each other. No one agonizes over their choice, the boys put up no objections, the price is known in advance, the boss or his wife smile broadly as they take your money, you go upstairs as if on a social visit.

Heidi senses that I'm a little hesitant and suggests we go to another establishment. But we've already spent half an hour in one of those motorcycle taxis that ooze grease and threaten to snap in two at every bump, and the heat has turned me into a wet rag. Everything's a long drive away in this town. A beneficent rain begins to fall; a monsoon storm soon makes the street one gigantic pothole as it drums louder and louder on the corrugated sheet-metal roof. When Heidi finally shoves me inside, the boys are intrigued by my presence; they briefly lift their heads from their magazines and ask about me. French? Oh sure, Zidane, Barthes, Karambeu—with sponsors like these I'm their buddy from the get-go. Then it's over, they go back to their little Asiatic hotties, the droning television, the hustle and bustle of customers. I sit on the floor in a corner, wanting nothing and no one. The boys are not very good-looking or very clean. The greenish light shed by the bulbs hanging from the ceiling—which threaten to short-circuit any minute with all the water trickling through the ill-fitting sheet-metal and down the wires—is not exactly flattering. All I see are pimples, scabs, rotten teeth, smears of grime. They're all wearing grubby sports shirts, frayed shorts to emphasize their muscles, flip-flops revealing fat toes misshapen by a lifetime of roadside tramping. These are poor kids dressed in hand-me-downs and already half consumed by hardship; I prefer not to think about the diseases you could catch in their embrace, and I calculate how long it will take to get out of here in one piece from the moment a spark sets the shack ablaze to when the monsoon, now in its full fury, puts it out. Let's be gracious and order a soda, let's wait for the hideous soap-opera witch to turn into a beautiful princess and be serenaded by the young leading man, and then let's extricate ourselves politely without demanding our due. Heidi is despondent. I won't have sex with him, I'm not interested in the pretty Chinaman, I stick my nose up at these boys, who may not look so healthy but are pretty solid just the same. What exactly is it that I want? I can't answer him, I myself don't know anymore. It's been this way for quite a while, no doubt, but I'm only seeing it clearly now for the first time. I don't move, Heidi endures his misfortune patiently, he sits down beside me, watches television, and says nothing further. The boys ignore me even as business hums along; despite the incredible roar of cascading water and the puddles rising steadily around the mattresses, there's a flow of traffic on the stairs. I'm still dry in my corner and it's as if everyone's forgotten about me; maybe they think I only came in to seek shelter.

A big guy emerges from the storm; he's wearing a yellow oil-skin gleaming wet, some kind of safety helmet under a headscarf that covers practically his entire face; he looks like a samurai demonstrator in an Asian street battle. Heidi elbows me in the side; thanks, I noticed; the sudden appearance also wakes up the audience, who welcome the survivor from the storm with

profuse greetings and hearty laughter; he's clearly the leader of
the gang. He dumps his paraphernalia, takes off his baseball
T-shirt and wrings it out in the doorway as he merrily heckles his
acolytes. Sopping wet, his torso bare and powerful, he exudes
vigor and vitality; darkish, olive skin; an initiate's tattoos on his
shoulders, deeply etched features and bulging muscles, a peasant
who has not been destroyed by the city, very rustic and proud
of it at a time when the fashion calls for singing dolls. That old
steely grip, which I had thought gone forever, suddenly grabs me
by the neck; my flaccid resolutions fall away, my lethargy evaporates; come to think of it, the rain shows no sign of letting up; in
The Rains of Ranchipur, Lana Turner watched it fall for hours
and it drove her mad. This place is all right after all, it's my last
night in Jakarta and tomorrow I'll be on the plane.

His name is Bogos—you can't make up things like that, and
it turns out it's a very popular moniker around here. Obviously,
the room is beyond squalid and the pallet of rusty iron a tetanus
trap. I wipe a damp, disgusting towel over the oilcloth that covers the decaying mattress. The perfect housewife in me wins out
in spite of everything, and the savage samurai watches me with
a mocking gleam in his eye. Given what he's got in store for me
there's not much point in playing little miss Western biddy; I put
aside all dreams of bleach and focus what little wisdom remains
to me on taking some elementary precautions. What comes next
is not bad at all—a kind of exotic cruise through the sidereal
dreamscape of our silence set against the insistent thrum of the
rain. But the soundtrack has a hell of a surprise for us—suddenly, out of nowhere, a muezzin launches into the call to prayer.
Some pious hand has turned the cassette tape up full blast. *Allah
Akbar* steamrolls over everything in its way and Mohammed
el-Rasoul takes center stage. As if he were sending his disciples
out once again against the world of sinners, he parts the celestial
waters, invests every last corner of our room, crashes like a flood

tide against the walls. Stunned, I look for him out the skylight, in the cupboard, under the bed. Omnipresent, insubstantial, the messenger of the Compassionate, the servant of the Merciful One will not budge. He swells with the muezzin's voice, he sucks all the air out of the room, I'm paralyzed by his incantation of the word and the violence of his onslaught. I sense his piercing gaze upon me and I can almost feel his breath on my face. And what if my personal helmsman, abruptly brought to his senses by this counterattack of faith, were to take it into his head to repudiate me viciously and cry sacrilege? *Haram, haram,* the john is nothing but a *rumi* who corrupts young believers, let us resist sin and beat back the degenerate infidel. I imagine that one does not joke about religion and the safeguarding of morality on the high plains of Java; bearded men with wild eyes and little girls in hijabs file past me, calling down the wrath of heaven to return the young stray to the path of righteousness and trample the impious like venomous beasts. But no, my Bogos is broad-minded and amused by all the hullabaloo; smiling, he bangs on the partition beside the bed to show me that the muezzin is singing on the other side, the local mosque is directly next door and the walls are as thin as paper. I don't find that very comforting; the faithful surely heard us, any closer and we'd have been at it in the minaret. He doubles over in laughter at my reaction; I make an effort to appear calm as I await the end of this new storm; he lies watching and laughing at me as I sit guardedly at the edge of the bed. Soon the recording wraps up with one last *Allah Akbar,* the call to prayer comes to an end, and the muezzin falls silent; the Prophet, the bearded guys, and the little girls file out of the room and return to the mosque; now it's their turn to be overcome by the smells of the boss-lady's cooking and the teenagers howling at their singing idols on Channel V Indonesia. The rain seems to be abating; I've had a fright, I feel alone, strangely melancholic, my heart is heavy from being so far from home; can the boy tell that something's up? He holds me in his arms, very gently, he hums Koranic surahs in my ear as if he were whispering words of love. In Arabic, and without knowing that it's practically my second language.

"Nice boy?" Heidi asks me in English, confident of my answer. I nod unambiguously to please him. The unusual charms of my adventure are already beginning to fade in my mind, and all I want now is to shower in my own air-conditioned room at the hotel and order up room service. The motorcycle taxi weaves between puddles in which half-naked children paddle deliriously; Jakarta is drying out, gleaming in the night whenever we pass lights that have not been knocked out by the monsoon. Try as I might, I still can't figure out Heidi's motives, his underlying reason for insisting on introducing me to boys. The vague explanations I've come up with don't really make sense; I can't see what he had to gain from our visit to the brothel; if there was a commission involved it must have been pretty skimpy; all the effort, the waiting around, my moodiness after he's put in a full day's work—it hardly seems worth the trouble. I'm exhausted, drained by the ubiquitous, oozing misery; the jolting vehicle, the stink of gas and motor oil nauseate me, the noise is staggering. I haven't the slightest idea where we are because I can't see any of the office buildings I know from the slums we're driving through. I'm the typically clueless foreigner letting himself be led into the cutthroat's lair. And yet I know I have nothing to worry about, Heidi is 100 percent trustworthy, he never takes advantage of my vacant moments, he accommodates my silences and absences without appearing to notice them. He's quite bizarre, this young guy who busies himself with my pleasure and asks for practically nothing in return. A pack of Marlboros, a CD of a favorite singer, really very little. We leave the cesspit behind and come to the neighborhood of broad avenues, tall buildings, and underground passages where I first met him. It was only a few

days ago, I know so little about him, but we're living together as
if we've known each other a long, long time.

And now we reach the moment when it's time to say good-
bye. I have to be at the airport very early; I'll have just enough
time to pack and grab a little sleep. Alone. I stop the motorcycle
taxi at the shopping center and buy him a cell phone; his is broken, and at least it will be a real keepsake of me. But Heidi wants
nothing to do with it, he's figured out that I want to get rid of
him for my last night and is resolved not to let it happen. It's an
odd scene: me arguing on the sidewalk as I try to stuff the phone
into his bag, he refusing as he plants himself obstinately in the
motorcycle taxi, the driver losing patience as he revs his hunk of
junk. Our first fight. I look like an idiot with my useless gift, a
gadget that I myself don't know how to use and he doesn't want.
Trucks hurtle by just beside us, the rain begins to fall again, but
it is shame and remorse that overwhelm me. I know I'm hurting
him, I have no right to end our relationship just like that, without
warning and for no good reason. I'm the Westerner, the rich guy
who thinks he gets to decide everything and who can afford to
be nice since he's not in love and offers nothing in return. That
at least is what I think he says; his broken English is falling apart
under emotional stress. Mostly I get the sense that he is wounded,
unhappy, not okay with us parting so abruptly and the faux pas
that I've just committed. I climb back into the motorcycle taxi,
we head off, he sulks a little but perks up cheerfully when we get
to the hotel. He doesn't want to ruin the little time we have left
together. Lying on the bed in a dressing gown, he watches me as
I pack my bags, then we talk a little about one thing or another,
nothing very important no doubt, I've forgotten. We exchange
addresses, he finally agrees to keep the cell phone and jots down
the number. I turn off the light. He asks me several times: "When
you come back?" I say next year, probably. Same time next year.
I sound sure of myself. We could write. He falls asleep quite fast,

I can hear his breath rise and fall in his sleep. I leave at the break of day, making no sound; he'd asked me to wake him but I let him sleep. I write him an affectionate little note on which I draw palm trees for Indonesia, firs for France, and a plane shuttling back and forth between them. I place it in a conspicuous place on the night table. When I think about it now, I believe that he loved me and tried to make me understand with the means at his disposal. A proclivity for Europeans doesn't fully explain it, and I don't know what to make of it. There must be something about me that I don't see.

I never have returned to Jakarta and I have never heard from Heidi again. I sometimes think that, if I really wanted to, I could reach him on his cell phone.

I WAKE up over Burma. My neighbor, a nice young fellow in every respect, must have finally figured something out. My exposé on Cambodia was ridiculously prolix; you can tie yourself up in knots trying to make too much of a point. He's less sociable now, absorbed in his computer; that suits me, we won't need to waste any time playing the let's-keep-in-touch game, walking around with addresses and numbers you'll never use, but occasionally may be tempted to when things are really bad. I look out the window, the coast, islands, the amazing beauty of the Indian Ocean in spite of the humid heat that dampens contrasts and the leaden light that is so different from that of the Mediterranean. On the horizon looms the great cloud of pollution that envelops Bangkok. I am truly looking forward to landing in that fog. I'm quite used to the shortness of breath and blurred vision. Formalities—I'm always a little scared of being unmasked, I put "business" on the customs form but in any case the police couldn't care less, Thailand has gone all out to hold on to its contingent of tourists ever since the series of catastrophes that struck Southeast Asia. Highways—it's like that scene from

Solaris when Tarkovsky's astronaut soars above the endless urban agglomeration—life teeming below, skyscrapers poking up in random disorder, outsized billboards of Gong Li's little sister winking with a cell phone at her ear, hanging from the steel skeletons of construction sites shut down by the crisis. I'm feeling better every minute, unknown to everyone, free for a few days with a wad of bahts exchanged at the airport, the elation of false pretenses. The hotel is a 1930s caravansary designed by an Italian futurist architect at a time when Thailand was flirting with fascism. The whole neighborhood is of the same era, but now it's drowning in a sea of itinerant peddlers, raucous with indefatigable Thai individualism, covered in gigantic portraits of the royal family framed in countless multicolored lights; the rates are modest, the rooms vast and dreary. The cosmopolitan clientele comes here to escape the organized tour groups, but it's not the five-star crowd; nobody pays the least attention to your comings and goings. The owner is an old polyglot dragon lady in glasses framed with rhinestones; she pretends to recognize me as if I were a regular, which, all things considered, I'm well on my way to becoming. The plane arrives in the late morning, I have some time left; I can still fudge a little by claiming a tourist's prerogative, taking the same lovely stroll along the muddy river I take on every visit. Temples, wooden houses on stilts, grand hotels and office buildings out of a science fiction movie, ancient trading posts overgrown with vegetation, gigantic bridges, a Champs-Élysées of waterborne traffic, as fabulous as anything in Venice or the Bosporus. I'd be extremely pleased if I were one of those young American straights backpacking with his girlfriend and smoking joints on a high-speed launch. Teak palaces out of *The King and I*, the successive Hollywood remakes of which have been a sore trial to the Thais; walks along the canals, with and without floating markets; royal barges, a stop at the Oriental with Somerset Maugham on the way back;

evenings watching Thai boxing, surrounded by screaming pik-
ers, or traditional dance in a storm of Japanese flashbulbs; and
later a little souvenir shopping, contraband Burmese Buddhas
or statuettes from Angkor, portraits of Rama VII, father of all
Siamese, and silks by Jim Thompson. Who says Bangkok isn't a
marvelous city? I champ at the bit in the mellow twilight, waiting
for the night and the lights to go up on a whole other Bangkok.
I return to my hotel to change; it was right here on the street,
some fifteen years ago, that rival factions of students killed each
other with machetes before the police fired into the throng of
survivors. Their swollen corpses were hung from the posts now
hanging with colored bulbs; blood flowed even in this lobby,
where Germans now compare the sunburns they caught pool-
side; kids were chased screaming down the hallways that led
to rooms barricaded with beds and furniture, and it was from
the balustrade of the monumental staircase, where people now
stand and gripe whenever the elevators break down, that the
slender decapitated corpses of assailants and besieged alike were
thrown—killed in a fratricidal riot that no foreigner can begin
to understand. It was the older brothers of the boys I'm on my
way see in Patpong who did all that fine work, and luck alone
separates the dead from the living, the victims from their tortur-
ers. In American caps, brand-name T-shirts and jeans sopping
with the sweat of the chase, broad smiles across their angelic
faces as they posed for photographers with their bloody cudgels
and machetes, proudly pointing to the human remains and dis-
embodied heads—lively, cordial, and coy for the cameras. Their
younger brothers resemble them in every respect, and there's no
reason to believe that the family spirit has dissipated. The violence endures even if it's harder to pinpoint; over 1,500 deaths
have been registered in the past few months. The authorities call
it revenge killings between criminal gangs, snitches murdered
by an underworld that has been on the defensive ever since the

authorities declared war on drug traffickers; mostly, though, the bodies fished out of the canals are those of kids, while their sponsors, known to all and sundry, continue to romp with the stars on the televised public-service variety shows they produce for the police. The minister of the interior is popular; he organizes bathhouse raids to seize hauls of amphetamines and publicly humiliate a bunch of terrified old white queens, who could surely use Viagra a lot more than any other stimulant. War between the gangs and the heroic cops, the criminal empire is tottering and the rule of law triumphant; the king writes a book about his faithful dog and it flies off the shelves. Has the whole charade made him so cynical that he rates the qualities of his family pet higher than the virtues boasted by his own government? Despite everything, AIDS seems to be under control in Patpong, where trade is booming like never before. Big business has no need of traffickers or sick people.

This time I want to see everything, explore everywhere. There are at least thirty clubs; if I pace myself just a little I won't miss a single one and may even find the boy whose memory continues to haunt me. My tuk-tuk, a high-powered cousin of Jakarta's motorcycle taxi, zips through the Chinese quarter. As the driver swerves back and forth, he tells me that the entertainment district is more extensive than ever; having assessed my preferences, he offers to be my guide. The Jupiter is still the height of chic, it's been completely remodeled, "Young students, good show, very modern," he bellows in English; the Blue Night is still in the running, "Thai boxers, lot of fun, not expensive;" on the other hand, the Shangri-La is "no good, big trouble with police." My driver must have had a run-in with the management over his touting commission. His favorite is the Apollo: "bodybuilders, Australians like very much." He turns around to see if I look like an Australian, but I'm covered in grit and slumped back against the leatherette banquette, and he can tell by my accent that I'm not Australian. I'm French, and his eyes light up—that changes everything, he has a new suggestion for me: "Young boys, no trouble, very safe." I can see how far we've come by the changing reputation of the French, from the Gallic Hollywood-lover type of the 1930s to the closet pedophile of the new millennium. I decline his services, but he has such a look of imprecation on his face in the pallid light of the last traffic signal before Patpong that I promise to hire him for the return trip at closing time, 2 a.m., and that is enough to restore his good humor. I love these tuk-tuk rides, the way the sputtering engine leaps forward with every green light; the incomprehensible jokes the drivers exchange about the tourists in back while idling at every stop; the hot air and heavy scents whipping at your face; the brisk starts and stops, the sharp turns, the feeling of taking the bit between your teeth and rushing headlong through the night. Why do they drive so fast? I'm not complaining—you don't come to Bangkok for quiet and serenity.

It's hard to tell from one evening to the next if the district is bigger than it used to be, but in any case it's worse than ever. With the New Year's festivities, each second counts as they milk every last cent out of the sex tourists during this holy week, and money exchanges hands at a furious pace. The neighborhood has come more and more to justify the filthy reputation it enjoys in TV reportage; fair-haired queers descend on Patpong en masse, refugees from disaster, and the cradle-snatchers that the neighborhood is famous for (but were actually quite rare until recently) now stagger openly from one manic nightclub doorman to the next. "Good night, sir, come here, best boys." An American in a wheelchair, still young but so emaciated as to seem to be at death's door, is the luminary of all those disarticulated marionettes, who bow and scrape at his approach as if he were the golden calf; a black giant deftly maneuvers the chair and does not hesitate to distribute a resounding smack to anyone nervy enough to attempt to assume command. They gesticulate and twist themselves into knots to win the bruiser's favor as he steers the skeleton on wheels in the direction of his chosen club, indicated by the extension of a trembling, bony finger. This hideous duo leave their mid-range hotel the minute the neon lights are switched on and don't return until, in a scene resembling a mass abduction, the tuk-tuks hustle the last fares away to their luxury resort hotels on the riverbank. For six methodical hours, the invalid rides his stroller from one dive to the next, fondling the steroid-swollen gymnasts who beam at him as if he were a supermodel, and handing out consolation tips to every runt unlucky enough not to have been mauled by his spidery paws. What is he suffering from? Is he in the final stages of AIDS, and if so, has he come to take revenge or to say goodbye, with all the energy of despair, to that for which he lived and is the cause of his misfortune? The bodyguard doesn't care for the curious, he has a sharp eye out for guys like me, and under his threatening gaze I avoid staring too openly. Some clubs are walk-ups and are sadly unable to accommodate the spectral chariot. Having seen me come and go from one club to the next, the managers have come to recognize me and we have developed a superficial bond. They tell me little secrets infused with the complicity of vice and the skepticism of commerce. They are interested in and intrigued by my good manners and solitary ways, and I feel free in return to question them about their own lives. One is a middle-aged Englishman, very stylish and polished, who welcomes customers as if he were a butler in a great house. He is nothing like the pathetic wretch, cooing the virtues of his little darlings, that you might expect to find in an establishment with such a clearly defined clientele. He strikes me as a military man, once married with children, gone native after an exotic posting; that or a former Anglican vicar who got into a bit of trouble during his ministry at an elite school for boys. Well built, quite at home among his half-naked fighters and obsequious waiters,

and looking perfectly satisfied with his lot. The Thai managers
are more unctuous and distrustful; it's all about the money with
them, and they inquire about you behind your back; they're
required to provide information to the police even as they're
giving them discount rates. My favorite is a mother-hen madam,
impeccably coiffed in a great old chignon, who tells me that it
will never again be as good as it was during the Vietnam War,
the belle époque of GIs on leave, looking for girls and finding
boys. She had a knack for distinguishing between the outraged
lugs threatening to smash the place to smithereens, whom she
sent to the go-go girls across the street; the swaggering jokers
who laughed at the honest mistake; and the guileless kid from
Wisconsin or Idaho for whom such an adventure would prove
disastrous. She's a real bitch, cynical, hard, and very funny,
who befriended me the way a cobra hypnotizes a rabbit and
offers me free drinks so I'll stay longer because, according to
her, my presence raises the tone of the clientele. It's flattering,
and I have no expectation of such compliments from the New
Zealander next door, a big-mouthed brawler who hustles his
stable of pretty boys at breakneck speed and hurls abuse at customers who dawdle in calling a number. The technique works
for him and the club is always packed, but he doesn't care for
me, he's suspicious of loners with European features, smelling
a muckraking journalist or a troublemaking humanitarian, and
far prefers gangs of soldiers out on a tear, seminarians from Singapore, the Hawaiian-shirted legions of interior decorators and
computer programmers just off the boat from Sydney, dipping
their bald pates to sniff the boys' bare feet. A multitude of managers compete ferociously to attract the highest-earning boys
and to win the loyalty of a transient clientele with free souvenir
photos and calling cards that will end up in the bottom of a
drawer somewhere. Every night I progress little by little along
the path of understanding; the young waitresses at the Chinese

cafeteria were very taken with me but have been sulky ever since they figured out that I wasn't looking for girly bars. It was surely the bearded Frenchman, head honcho at the Pretty Club, who squealed on me. Every time I pass by the open door of his bar, its counter lined with pretty little whores, he buttonholes me with stories about his childhood in the Nièvre and how he knew my uncle François, but since I always try to avoid him and appear to have no interest in hearing more, he is as irritated by me, the queer nephew, as if I'd personally betrayed him. The bad whiskey helps me stay the course; the moment when I'll have had my fill of boys—when I'll finally get fed up and wonder what the hell I'm doing in such a dump—is always some time later. I sway a little on the sidewalks lined with stalls, steaming food carts, tradesmen, and pharmacies displaying flagons of Chinese aphrodisiacs, unlabeled Viagra, and scented condoms like ice cream cones. I'm bounced around between groups of giggling tourists, families doing their shopping, urchins shouting "Body body, foot massage—beautiful girls very clean"; pickpockets and their cop pals, harassed by futile complaints of muggings; transvestites scurrying from one club to the next; kids herding a sad little elephant calf and selling ears of corn to feed him with; girls who come out into the street to see what's what, wriggle their rumps, berate the passersby, and know with one glance that I'm not for them; pimps who circle me convulsively like sharks; boys ending their shifts and going off to the disco with the girlfriends waiting for them at McDonald's, the events of the past few hours erased by their black Armani T-shirts and gold-plated wristwatches. I become a little drunker still on the tuk-tuk fumes, the din of the human throng, the untiring, insistent rhythm of techno-pop. Even so I'm mindful, you have to watch where you put your feet; there are fewer rats in the adjacent alleyways than there once were, but the ground is dangerously rutted and strewn with peelings and all sorts of garbage.

Once, I almost stepped right on a tiny little child sleeping on the sidewalk like a corpse, a bundle of pathetic rags to whom no one paid the least attention, and whose misery sobered me up in one fell swoop. I would have liked to take the child with me, pamper him at the hotel, take him to France on the first plane out of town, poor abandoned thing clinging so tenuously to life; I didn't even have the nerve to try and wake him up, for fear that it would be pointless because he was actually dead. I summoned a cop, whose face contorted in revulsion as he nudged the boy with the tip of his baton, as if he were a lifeless dog, then shrugged his shoulders and threw me a suspicious glance when the child began to stir. I only had to be on my way, but I waited for the cop to move off, then returned to the child whom he had threatened. He was woozy with sleep, but did not dare drag himself to the steps of the bank next door, where he would have been out of the flow of foot traffic. I gave him a large bill; it took some time to sink in, then he suddenly ran off, frightened but with the treasure securely hidden in his rags, scampering like a wild animal before a forest fire.

By day, Patpong is a pleasant neighborhood, clean and quiet, traveled by schoolchildren with satchels on their backs, where you can't even locate the doors of the clubs, their storefronts, their hoardings of racy photographs. There's a Christian mission dating back to the last century, a health club where irreproachable thirty-something bodybuilders work out in the front window, three-star hotels for sales reps. Housewives in curlers sweep the sidewalks. Girls go about their shopping with the look of busy stewardesses; old people read newspapers. The touts play cards in the middle of the street with crisp movements—dry, virile little men no longer surrounded by their hordes of grimacing automatons. No boys, though—they're still asleep in their own distant neighborhoods, two hours away by sky train.

I thought I'd found my dear boy of memory in the same club

where I'd first met him. "Number ten, the hands-down favorite,"
the boss whispered in my ear, and you didn't need to look long to
see why. And yet, I wasn't sure. Over there, it's a little like those
scenes in police movies where a suspect stands in a line-up behind
a two-way mirror with a bunch of cops who look just like him
and you can't tell if it's him or not. I'd seen this boy again and
again in my dreams, I thought I knew every inch of him, but time,
imagination, and perhaps the commingled recollections of other
boys had slowly and gently worked to blur his image. I remembered the feeling perfectly, emotions stirred up by regret; he was
still with me, but he had also become unreal, indistinct and distant, like the dead whom we do not forget and continue to love,
but whose picture we need to consult to remember their specific
traits. Plus, I was surprised to find that this life had inflicted so
little damage on Number Ten; he was as handsome and sparkling
as ever after three years of practicing his hellish trade, and boys
spoil quickly in Patpong. Beside me, a couple of old Scandinavian
leeches were eating him up with their eyes; they were growing
increasingly agitated, I had to act quickly. I practically shouted
Number Ten in the ear of one of the marionettes, who pulled him
from the group with a leer. He displayed no particular surprise
or emotion, his only thought was to follow the usual program;
sweet, friendly, maybe a little pleased after all to have escaped
the two leeches, who looked fit to murder me on the spot—he
threw them several surreptitious glances of scathing irony from
the stage. I stared—it was my boy, and it was not my boy. When I
finally made up my mind to call him by his name, Bird, he smiled
without answering and indicated a number of boys—other Birds,
no doubt. All the same, the smile had changed; something natural and spontaneous had been lost, it was more mechanical and
professional. What had he been doing all this time? Despite the
plethora of Australians looking for a sweetheart, he still didn't
speak any English—just the practical words.

I had made arrangements to take precisely the same route, rent the same room, say more or less exactly the same words in French, but my stratagems were truly pathetic and evoked no response in him. Everything went quite smoothly, I made no demands and allowed myself to be led; I approached his body and my illusions as if they were made of crystal; it was enormously pleasurable, but so delicate, so fragile, I was afraid that I'd made a mistake and that I was shielding a mirage. He was cheerful and very pleased with me, the good foreign customer who causes no problems and tips generously. When we each went our separate ways I felt liberated; the past remained intact and I could acknowledge that it certainly hadn't been him. I saw him again the next day, but I was too late on the draw; a pudgy transvestite—a super-sized Thai Joan Collins—beat me to him; he held the almost naked boy impudently against his gaudy outfit, thrown together with expensive fakes, from the bulging, very décolleté pseudo-Versace dress to the big fake Vuitton bag, overflowing with sheaves of bahts for the contortionist waitstaff. A local celebrity, I suppose, owner of some sequin-spangled cabaret in the business district and sponsor of a stable of boxers. He didn't seem like the sort who might consider sharing. The boy cozied up to him like a kid who'd just found his mother; it pained my heart a little to think that this creature might be one of his regular customers. But a last vestige of contrariness prompted me to give a little friendly wave to my companion of the previous evening. The boy threw me a look of appalled hatred that froze my blood—a gob of spit in the face of the fool who dared to look under rocks, a sharp bite, a dose of venom, sudden death, no hope of recovery. I'd broken a law that allows for no exceptions, especially not for transient strangers; when the meter runs out you pick up a new client, and regulars have priority. For me, the most astounding thing was realizing that this sudden violent rejection and desire to crush me totally was the exact inverse yet otherwise entirely faithful reflection of the gentleness and intimacy that I'd remembered so fondly for so long. There was no longer any doubt; I had not been mistaken— I had indeed found the beacon of my dreams, the consolation for my solitary nights, my darling Patpong lover. I focused my pensive attention on all the other numbers until the couple left.

I'M READY to go home to France, but I have a week left to kill. I might regret it later if I cut my trip short; the prospect of spending a repentant New Year's in Paris holds little attraction for me, and I may never return to this country, which after all does have many other things to see. I spend my days sightseeing in town with a taciturn old biker who picks me up at the hotel and drives at breakneck speed through the traffic jams and speed demons. Sitting behind this stranger, decked out in an ancient, dented, ill-fitting helmet, I don't hold out much hope of escaping with my life, but the biker's survival instincts are stronger and he spares me the ultimate romantic ending, to which I was not especially attached in any case. I'm finding it easier every day to get around in this Bangkok, unknown to transient foreigners but increasingly comfortable for me as I come to appreciate the subtle allure of the past lingering in this full-blown urban jungle and the savage energy of unremitting hyperactivity. I am on vacation in the heart of an indifferent anthill. My hotel is as hectic and lugubrious as ever, but I manage to share some interesting conversation in the breakfast lounge with Mr. Lee, a retired Chinese man from Hong Kong who has come to restore himself in certain Buddhist temples that are not listed in my travel guide. He is an adorable man and has taken a liking to me; in perfect French learned in the Christian schools that thrived at the time of the Kuomintang, he tells me that the road to wisdom is strewn with pitfalls. He gives me his card and tells me that I mustn't forget him, and I tell him all about Chang, Tintin's friend, whose story

I know by heart. I also go for tea at the Oriental once or twice with Corinne, a Frenchwoman I met on the river who is married to a Thai architect. She had rearranged her entire life for him; I imagine he must be a very remarkable man for her to talk about him with such trust and affection. She has all the qualities I look for in a woman: gentleness, generosity, and humor, all against a backdrop of slightly melancholic detachment. Thanks to her I become even better acquainted with the city and the country, which she knows and loves deeply. I think that her husband is a very lucky man. She reminds me of Selma, whom I met in Libya and think about all the time—the same intelligence, the same enthusiastic liberality with her friendship. Such encounters are my saving grace and continue to keep me whole, I'm convinced of it, despite the distance and the passage of time. I understand that she has to come a long way every time we meet; I walk her back to the sky train and we feed the elephant that waits, swaying from side to side, at the foot of the escalators—a relative, perhaps, of the little orphan of Patpong. No one knows about our impromptu liaison; the secrecy amuses us and brings us even closer together; actually, she has told her husband about me, and he must be wondering what kind of a person I could possibly be. At night, I disappear into the boys' clubs and the trigger still works.

I learn by experience—not all boys are as easy or as nice as I'd like to believe. Some comply only reluctantly, allowing their anger and resentment to show. One unmistakable sign is that they take longer than the others to change after having been chosen, and they keep their cell phones on in the room so they can make a faster getaway. But as I always pretend not to notice, and as I soon acquire a reputation for openhandedness, it is precisely these sulkers and rebels who do their utmost to prolong our tricks or to appear before me more often so I'll call their number. I sometimes take them to dinner at the Chinese cafeteria, in groups of two or three; beer helps to cheer them up, they collapse into wild laughter like children released from bondage. They tell me about their "duty" and how some clients are "real sheet"; they ask me questions about France and say what a shame it's so far away. Unfortunately, I don't entirely fit the bill of the ideal customer: some Australian, "old and kind," who sets up his boy in a studio, pays his expenses and buys him a Honda, and returns every other weekend laden with duty-free goods. Two inseparable friends attach themselves to me; I've told them where I live and they come to the hotel one morning to look me up. We go to the coast and take a room in the tropical resort where they filmed *The Killing Fields*. The receptionist is very beautiful and missing a front tooth. The expat families that make up most of the clientele stare at me in disgust and snigger as we go by; I quite enjoy rubbing their noses in it, and the boys are delighted to lounge by the pool surrounded by all these blond children and their inflatable ducks. They carry their sacrosanct cell phones in their bathing suits; it gives them an extra dick and does not make things any easier for me with the nasty little Europeans. In the evening, we go to the port to eat grilled fish and fall asleep together like brothers. I have no desire to make love, and neither do they, of course. One is a Buddhist and says his prayers every morning upon waking up; he looks after my things as if he were my houseboy of long standing, like in the movies. The other is a Muslim from the Malay border region; more energetic and cheeky, he wants me to bring him back to France, where he promises to be very well behaved. I can just see him two months from now, freezing his ass off at Porte Dauphine. I'm surprised by their good manners, their scrupulousness, the sense of decency they've picked up god knows where and which they maintain despite a desperate desire to make a brand-new start of it, the ongoing tension of never being able to waste a single opportunity. I'd like to stay an extra day, but the cell phones begin to ring and I don't feel like I have the right to deprive the boys of their New Year's Eve in Bangkok. And I'm a little fed up with the pretty girl with the missing tooth, who depresses me, and the twisted leers of the oil company engineers on vacation from their servitude on the offshore rigs of Burma, that whole pseudo-wealthy lifestyle while children are selling themselves just down the beach.

New Year's is just about as dumb as it is in France. The whole city is on the streets, wandering around with firecrackers and confetti. I've left the two boys to their own devices; drenching themselves in Alain Delon cologne, they borrowed my Hawaiian shirts and ran off to meet their girlfriends. Even I'm a little infected by all this idiotic euphoria; I feel like finding the prettiest boy in Patpong to ring in the midnight with. The clubs are mobbed and the little touts are bouncing all over the place like panicky bunnies, their shrill voices tearing through the techno-pop, which has been cranked up an extra notch or two. I go to see the Englishman, more affected than ever in blue blazer and matching ascot, where I ask for Number Twelve, a little older than the others, jet-black hair, broad shoulders, and a kindly smile. None of those russet, blow-dried, Japanese-style dye-jobs that are all the rage; no buzz cuts; and no mincing or simpering either. Give me the long muscles of a champion swimmer and a look of disarming sincerity. Under the ghastly neon lighting in our room, I notice the spots and nasty marks on his skin—around his neck, beneath his armpits, below his tummy; you can't see this sort of detail when they're on the stage. I don't know how I'll bring myself to touch him, and at the same time, for no good reason at all, I want to offend him, to wound his sense of conviction that he remains seductive and attractive. When they begin to age, just at the start, that's what they cling to—the sexual power they exercise over men. It's their last refuge before their lives take a permanent nosedive. But he senses

my embarrassment and stands before me, arms at his side, his
lovely body sapped from within, still; I avert my gaze so as not
to meet his, which only moments before I'd found so appeal-
ing. This sort of thing is tricky—you never know if it's serious
or nothing at all. Ending one year by falling sick, beginning the
next by coming home contagious—if you go looking for trouble,
one day or another you're going to find it. But I stick to my decision; let no one say that I jilted him on a holiday, Happy New
Year to you and let's party with the lights down low. I take every
precaution and avoid every danger, mostly; I make a great show
of being happy, and so does he; he's entirely reassured, and as
I find myself a little distracted all the same, he must think that
you have to be gentle with these Frenchmen, perhaps they're shy,
prudish folk who shouldn't be forced.

I have some trouble shaking him afterward. We stick it out
past midnight, but then he absolutely insists on taking me to the
roof garden of a fancy hotel to watch the fireworks. I invent an
urgent email and ask him to meet me at the Englishman's the
next day. He seems really sad to be leaving me. The town is jam-
packed and the tuk-tuks backfire as they idle; you just have to
wait until it's all over. For my New Year's wish for myself, I pray I
don't run into Number Ten and his transvestite. As for the American, his bodyguard, and the wheelchair, I needn't worry—there
are so many people on the streets they won't dare go out. I amble
over to the old madam's; the joint is overflowing with boys and
customers, out onto the front stairs and into the street, a whole
warren of spring-loaded Energizer bunnies screaming "Happy
New Year!" at the top of their lungs. She spots me in the crowd,
treats me like an honored guest at a royal cotillion, and gets me
drunk on some indeterminate liquor served in grimy glasses that
I don't bother trying to clean after a while. She urges me to go up
on stage, I'd be the unprecedented star of the love show; she must
have gathered that I, too, work in show business, but I still have

an ounce of my wits about me and manage to decline her tempting offer. You never can overstate what can be accomplished with a little courtesy. The clubs close, the techno goes on. Everybody's dancing in the streets—the whores, the transvestites, the shopkeepers, the tuk-tuk drivers, the waiters and the marionettes, the girls and boys who haven't been chosen. All these people trapped in the district, who don't know me and whom I will never know, twirling to the techno beat between the trash cans and the flickering neon. A little puppet who would certainly prefer not to end the night alone unleashes a rapid-fire series of Happy New Years in my direction. Yes indeed, Happy New Year. Hearing him beside me, watching them all around me, I experience a sensation of strange quietude, something serene and peaceful that could be mistaken for happiness.

By the morning I'm feeling very sick. I send the two inseparables on their way with a thick wad of bahts. I was an excellent customer, and they leave totally recharged for a new season in Patpong. I'm coughing my guts out, I have a high fever. The taciturn biker drops me at a crossroads, in the pouring rain, in the middle of nowhere. I can't take another step, I feel like I'm about to die, what will they do with my body? I have just enough strength to call Corinne, who miraculously finds me, doses me with medicine, takes care of me, and puts me on my plane.

childhood
childhood

childhood

W HEN THEY brought out the coffin, I was surprised that it was so small, and I recalled his body—that beautiful body, longer and stronger than mine, that had haunted me for years before I finally stopped thinking about it: his broad shoulders, well-defined muscles, skin, and all the rest. Neither before nor since have I known a body as fine as that, a body I used to desire so much that I would press against it every night just to continue feeling its presence in my sleep. Lost, missed, and then gradually buried in my memory just as it was about to be buried in the earth.

I imagined that he had not greatly changed despite his indolence and self-neglect and the ravages of alcohol. I remembered his face too, his expressions, even his tone of voice; the faces of youth and insouciance, chaos and suffering; expressions that

continued to come to me at random moments long after I'd
stopped thinking about him. His voice—I could have heard it
just by closing my eyes, except that I no longer had any intention
of closing my eyes, not even for an instant. Before, I'd supposed
that one must feel a great sense of loss when one has lived inti-
mately with the body of another, and now I realized that it was
not of much importance; the feeling of loss comes when you say
good-bye and go your separate ways, and it dissolves along with
the others in the photograph. I still have plenty of pictures of
him, but I hardly ever look at them. And yet, standing before the
gleaming box in which they'd enclosed him, I again wondered
if I shouldn't have tried to see him one last time as I had my
grandmother and my father, which had been of some comfort to
me. But when a neighbor had called the police after seeing his
light on for days on end, they'd taken him away immediately,
and no one had been willing to identify the corpse. The routine
postmortem ascribed his death to a heart attack. I'd found out
about it too late; I'd have had to jump through hoops and go
down to the morgue, and I decided to spare myself that horror
show. And then, too, it wasn't like with my grandmother and
my father—the coldness of the flesh, the false sleep that trans-
fixes and softens the features might have awakened feelings of
waste and bitterness in me.

I didn't think about it for very long; despite the solemnity of
the task at hand, the staff were pressed for time. They had come
a long way, driving all through the night, to arrive on time. I'm
not sure you can schedule regular stops on a trip like that—pulling over for a stretch, having a coffee in a service station; you've
got to stop for gas from time to time. Seeing their eyes baggy
with fatigue and their rumpled clothes, I couldn't help imagining some dark comedy in which thieves mistakenly steal a hearse
parked in a lot and set off on a whole series of gags and chases;
in their profession, they probably tell stories like that all the time

to ease the tension. I felt no pain, just a sort of vague stupor at
finding myself face to face with a defunct existence from which
I'd detached myself so long before.

There weren't many of us at the Mougins cemetery: his stepsister, his two nephews, three of their friends, whom I didn't
know and had no interest in talking to; there was also Maurice T., a faithful holdover from the movie years, and my friend
Francis, who is always reliable; his father is buried a few rows
down. Francis had once come to my rescue when I'd gone totally
overboard in a sort of love frenzy, which seemed even more
inexplicable now in this funereal setting bathed in spring light.
I had the child with me too; I'd bought him some Eminem cassettes, hoping he'd stay in the car, but he doesn't like me to leave
him by himself. He behaved very well, staring curiously at the
tombstones; in his country, there's just a slab in the ground. I
supposed the indefatigable partygoers of yesteryear had not read
the death announcements in *Le Monde* or *Le Figaro*. In any
case, it was far too early in the morning—"the morning after,"
so to speak, and they themselves might have been in similarly
dire straights. No priest, either; a mass was slated to be said
later, in Paris. To no point, since he had no religion.

His stepsister and nephews were sad. They had stuck with
him at a time when I'd stopped answering his letters; at the very
end I didn't even bother trying to decipher his spidery handwriting. I seem to remember that they read out some passage or
other, I was having a hard time concentrating; I'd have preferred
trying to remember him without them. Then they scattered flowers on the coffin, and a cemetery employee in blue overalls came
to seal the tomb with cement. He will lie at rest beside his father,
with whom he didn't get along; his mother, whom he loved in a
sick, savage way that I'd always found incomprehensible; and an
aunt who meant nothing to him and whom I had never met. His
brother, who had also destroyed himself, was buried at La Bas-

tide, near the house in upper Provence that they'd been unable to hold on to and that still haunts my rueful dreams. Just another disaster story, that house, which we'd fixed up together before I left, and where he could have quietly recovered his equanimity instead of moldering there with his nightmares, his parasites, and his legal imbroglios. The most beautiful thing in my life, swept away by calamity with all the rest.

The gravedigger was a local country boy with a pleasant physique. I watched the back of his neck as he worked, crouching beside the vault, and I thought that he was the kind of guy that he definitely would have hit on; I've seen many like him come and go. One has such pathetic thoughts when rituals drag on and on. The gravestone was cracked and the boy worked slowly and with great caution to prevent it from falling apart entirely. A sentimental adage, the kind you read all over cemeteries, was carved into it, but he was obliged to cement over it because the stone was so fragile. I had the spontaneous idea of learning it by heart before it disappeared, but I forgot it soon afterward. But I do think that it was less conventional than what you generally read on tombstones, and it smacked of his mother, who had been an interesting and cultured woman. It was odd, but I felt rather sorry for her—all the trouble she went to, and all for naught, for a son who should have outlasted her by many years but who was now already lying beside her. When the boy had finished and stood up they gave him a little money; he thanked them in a southern accent. It was the first time anyone had heard his voice, as he'd worked in silence. I stared at him for a minute; that accent and his handsome mug pulled me out of my torpor. Francis smiled—he knows me better than anyone.

Afterward, because despite everything we couldn't just all go our separate ways immediately, I was afraid that we'd get caught up in the mythology of our wonderful former lives, the adventure of the movie business and all those fabulous people we'd known, nights at the Palace that we'd never see again, the house at La Bastide, always coming back to the house, which he'd have made into a little paradise if those bastard owners hadn't evicted him unfairly, driving him to despair. But the young people's cell phones started ringing, and we all remembered other things we needed to be doing. I was expected for lunch with Francis, the child wanted to see *Shrek*, the stepsister had a train to catch, and Maurice T. was running late for a party he was organizing for a production company at a rented villa. I don't know what the others were ringing for, young peoples' business I suppose; it was the first day of the Cannes film festival. So we left him in his grave and headed down to La Croisette.

In the car, Francis and I talked about the coincidental timing of the funeral, which had been so poorly attended, and the opening of the festival, which nothing could have made him miss, the deserted cemetery and his own parties, which were as popular then as Maurice T.'s are now.

LITANY

18 *"... in third grade at the Janson school ..."* Lycée Janson de Sailly, founded in the 1880s, is located in the 16th arrondissement of Paris and generally considered to be one of the best *lycées* in France.

24 *"... to turn mean like Zamor ..."* A French revolutionary originally from Bengal, he was sold by slave-traders as a child to the Countess du Barry, who raised and educated him, but whom he later betrayed to the *Comité de salut public*. Du Barry was beheaded in 1793.

25 *"On summer vacation in Évian ..."* Évian-les-Bains, a French resort town on the south shore of Lake Geneva, home to one of the largest casinos in Europe, and source of Evian mineral water.

36 *"Sometimes we push on to the souk ..."* Commercial or market quarter in an Arab or Berber city.

37 *"... who takes a young French child to the medina ..."* Native or non-European quarter of a North African city.

37 "*...was massacred by the FLN.*" National Liberation Front, the main liberation party that led Algeria's war of independence against France from 1954 to 1962. The FLN remains an important political party in Algeria.

42 "*. . . about the fighting in Bizerte.*" A city on the northern coast of Tunisia, Bizerte was retained as a French naval base even after Tunisia gained independence in 1956. Blockaded by the Tunisian armed forces, it was attacked in 1961, leading to a French response that resulted in hundreds of casualties. The French ultimately abandoned Bizerte in 1963.

43 "*. . . for a movie starring Michèle Morgan and Bourvil.*" French film actress Michèle Morgan, born Simone Renée Roussel in 1920. Her American-born son, Mike Marshall, died in 2005. André Bourvil, born André Robert Raimbourg (1917–1970), French singer and comic actor, starred in over 50 films.

44 "*. . . to the studio in Saint-Maurice . . .*" A suburb of Paris, some four miles south-east of the city center, home of the Gaumont-St. Maurice film studios.

45 "*Bourvil's character's name is Fortunat . . .*" The film is *Fortunat* (1960), directed by Alex Joffe for Cinétel.

57 "*. . . he's been called back to Cinecittà . . .*" Large film studio outside Rome, founded by Benito Mussolini in 1937.

SUMMER 1947

62 "*. . . as we all saw at the Molière Awards.*" French national theater awards. Danielle Darrieux won for best actress in 2003 at the age of 86.

THE CRUEL AND THE KIND

66 *". . . a private preview of Nurse Ratched."* Sadistic antagonist in Ken Kesey's 1962 novel *One Flew Over the Cuckoo's Nest* and character, played by Louise Fletcher, in Miloš Forman's 1975 film of the same name.

72 *". . . in La Comtesse de Ségur's Les Vacances . . ."* Sophie Feodorovna Rostopchine (1799–1874), French writer of Russian birth, best known for her novel *Les Malheurs de Sophie* (1858), of which *Les Vacances* (1859) is a sequel.

75 *". . . she did not watch television . . ."* Frédéric Mitterrand is well known in France as the host of numerous television shows, including *Acteur Studio* and *Du côté de chez Fred*.

78 *". . . to look like La Rambla . . ."* Busy boulevard in central Barcelona.

86 *"I became her own Bébé Cadum . . ."* Ubiquitous trademarked mascot of Cadum soap since the early twentieth century.

92 *" . . . Simone lived in Sainte-Geneviève-des-Bois . . ."* A commune approximately 15 miles south of Paris, known for its Russian Orthodox cemetery, final resting place of, among many, filmmaker Andrei Tarkovsky and ballet dancer Rudolph Nureyev.

95 *". . . no talk of harkis . . ."* Muslim Algerians serving with the French during the war of independence. The term is roughly equivalent to "collaborator."

CARMEN

103 *". . . a Real Madrid match on TV."* The most prominent of Madrid's three principal soccer teams.

105 *". . . in the Maghreb just across the water . . ."* North Africa, and more precisely the coastal area between the Mediterranean Sea and the Atlas Mountains.

109 *". . . and Greece is under the Colonels."* The brutal right-wing junta that ruled Greece from 1967 to 1974.

109 *". . . wearing the Falangist insignia . . ."* The Falange was the original Fascist party in Spain, founded by José Antonio Primo de Rivera in 1933 and co-opted by Francisco Franco during and after the Spanish Civil War.

113 *". . . Oneiro Apatilo, let us dream . . ."* Written by Apostolos Kaldaras, *Oneiro Apatilo* ("Deceptive Dream") was a hit for singer Stamatis Kokotas in 1967.

119 *"a Greek version of the Dominici affair . . ."* In 1952, three British tourists were murdered in the Alpine foothills of Provence. Gaston Dominici, a local farmowner, was accused, tried, and convicted on circumstantial evidence, and subsequently released, though not pardoned, by Charles de Gaulle in 1960. The affair remains shrouded in mystery and controversy to this day.

122 *". . . by the evil German baron . . ."* Baron Wilhelm von Gloeden (1856–1931), known for his homoerotic photographs of Sicilian boys. Many of his pictures were destroyed as pornography by Mussolini's police in 1936.

124 *". . . Tito was very handsome himself . . ."* Josip Broz Tito (1892–1980), Communist Prime Minister (1945–63) and President (1953–80) of Yugoslavia.

128 *"The theory of a fascist plot . . ."* Although Pelosi confessed to Pasolini's 1975 murder, he later recanted, claiming that the director had been murdered by fascists because of his communist sympathies. Subsequent investigations have shown it unlikely that Pasolini was killed by a single assailant, and various theories have arisen since, including the suggestion that he wanted to die and arranged his own murder.

134 *". . . the ghosts of Raquel Meller and Alfonso XIII . . ."* Raquel Meller, born Francisca Marqués López (1888–1962), Spanish actress and singer, considered a great star of the French music hall but died in obscurity and poverty. Alfonso León Fernando María Jaime Isidro Pascual Antonio de Borbón y Austria-Lorena (1886–1941), King of Spain from 1886–1931. He built the Palace Hotel in 1912 to house his wedding guests, and fled Spain in 1931 following the proclamation of the Second Republic.

QUENTIN

160 *". . . on the terrace in Saint-Germain-en-Laye . . ."* Elegant suburban commune 12 miles from central Paris, founded in 1020 and the birthplace of several French kings, including Louis XIV.

161 *". . . she was living in Le Pecq . . ."* Small commune straddling both banks of the Seine, and adjacent to Saint-Germain-en-Laye.

167 *". . . we plunge into Alesia . . ."* Gaulish city thought to be near present-day Dijon, and site of Julius Caesar's decisive victory over Vercingetorix, bringing all Gaul under Roman dominion. Caesar's account of the Gallic War is standard reading for Latin students.

HOWARD BROOKNER

175–76 *". . . was home to the delightful Albert Cossery . . ."* French writer (1913–2008) of Egyptian origin. Cossery has died since Mitterrand wrote these words.

177 *". . . the film I'd made in Somalia . . ." Lettres d'amour en Somalie*, winner of the 1983 César award for best first film.

185 *"It's crazy how much I love you . . ."* "C'est fou ce que je peux t'aimer/ Ce que je peux t'aimer des fois/ Des fois, je voudrais crier/ Car je n'ai jamais aimé/ Jamais aimé comme ça/ Ça je peux te le jurer/ Si jamais tu partais/ Partais et me quittais/ Me quittais pour toujours/ C'est sûr que j'en mourrais/ Que j'en mourrais d'amour/ Mon amour, mon amour . . ."

187 *". . . at which Jack Lang . . ."* French politician, born 1939, Minister of Culture from 1981 to 1986 and 1988 to 1993.

184 *"Padam, padam, listen to all the racket it makes . . ."* "Écoutez le chahut qu'il me fait/ Comme si tout mon passé défilai."

TENEREZZA/TENDERNESS

193 The unidentified people in this chapter are the actress Catherine Deneuve, her sister Françoise Dorléac, her husband Marcello Mastroianni, their daughter Chiara, the French novelist Françoise Sagan, and the author's uncle, President François Mitterrand. The fashion house referred to is Yves Saint-Laurent.

194 *". . . in the events of May 1968 . . ."* Among others, a general strike that paralyzed the entire country and a series of student uprisings that almost brought down the de Gaulle government.

194 *". . . the collaborationist writer Drieu la Rochelle . . ."* Pierre Eugène Drieu La Rochelle (1893–1945), Parisian writer, fascist, and collaborator with the Nazi occupiers as director of the *Nouvelle revue française*. Forced into hiding after the war, he committed suicide in 1945.

206 "Aspetta, aspetta . . ." Italian: "Wait, wait."

224 *"Talitha Getty also knew you."* Born Talitha Pol (1940–1971), Dutch actress and model, married to John Paul Getty and an avatar of the Swinging Sixties. Died of a heroin overdose.

225 *". . . the ear of his grandson . . ."* John Paul Getty Sr. (1892–1976) famously refused to pay the $17 million ransom of his grandson John Paul III until the boy's ear was cut off and sent to an Italian newspaper.

225 "*. . . her* riad *in Marrakesh . . .*" A traditional Moroccan house with an interior garden. Patrick Litchfield's famous 1969 photo of Talitha Getty on her *riad* rooftop became the symbol of "hippie chic."

BIRD

257 *"Joan Crawford in Patpong."* A notorious red light district of Bangkok.

259 ". . . and my father has just died." Robert Mitterrand (1915–2002), engineer and brother of former French President François Mitterrand (1916–1996).

263 "*. . . a relatively orderly amalgam of Batavian colonial utopia . . .*" Batavia was the Dutch colonial name for Jakarta from 1619 to 1942.

268 "*. . .Sukarno and his daughter . . .*" Diah Permata Megawati Setiawati Sukarnoputri (born 1947), Indonesian politician and President of Indonesia from 2001 to 2004.

271 "*. . . Mohammed el-Rasoul . . .*" Mohammed the Messenger.

272 "Haram, haram, *the john is nothing but a* rumi . . ." *Haram,* "forbidden" in Arabic. *Roumi,* more or less, "European" in Arabic (from "Roman").

277 *". . . and silks by Jim Thompson."* American businessman
and designer (1906–1967?) who helped to revive the Thai silk
industry. Thompson disappeared mysteriously while out for a
walk in the Malaysian countryside. Jim Thompson House is a
popular tourist destination in Bangkok.

FRÉDÉRIC MITTERRAND, born in Paris in 1947, graduated from the Institut d'Études Politiques of Paris. In 1971, his passion for the cinema motivated him to create a chain of art house movie theaters (the Olympic and Entrepôt theaters). He has produced and hosted television programs including *Étoiles Étoiles; Du Côté de Chez Fred;* and *Les Amants du Siècle*. He directed several short films and two feature films, *Lettres d'Amour en Somalie* in 1981 and *Madame Butterfly* in 1995. He is the author of historical narratives (*Les Aigles Foudroyés* and *Mémoires d'Exil*) and biographies (*Destins d'Étoiles*) as well as another memoir, *Le Festival de Cannes* (2007), in which he shares more of his unique life experiences, with the famed Cannes Film Festival as his muse. *The Bad Life*, first published as *La Mauvaise Vie* by Éditions Robert Laffont in 2005, has sold well over 250,000 copies in France. In June 2009, Frédéric Mitterrand was appointed Minister of Culture by French President Nicolas Sarkozy.

JESSE BROWNER has translated works by Jean Cocteau, Rainer Maria Rilke, Paul Eluard and others. He is the author, most recently, of *The Uncertain Hour*, a novel.

Printed in the United States
by Baker & Taylor Publisher Services